WE ALL SCREAM

THE FALL OF THE GIFFORD'S ICE CREAM EMPIRE

T0096760

ANDREW GIFFORD

sfwp.com

Library of Congress Cataloging-in-Publication Data

Names: Gifford, Andrew, 1974- author.
Title: We all scream : the fall of the Gifford's Ice Cream empire / Andrew Gifford.
Description: Santa Fe, NM : SFWP, [2017]
Identifiers: LCCN 2017023684| ISBN 9781939650795 (pbk. : alk. paper) | ISBN
    9781939650801 (pdf) | ISBN 9781939650818 (epub) | ISBN 9781939650825 (mobi)
Subjects: LCSH: Gifford's Ice Cream & Candy Co. | Gifford, Andrew, 1974- |
    Businesspeople—United States—Biography. | Ice cream industry—United   States. |
    Ice cream parlors—Washington (D.C.) | Business failures—United States.
Classification: LCC HD9281.U54 G545 2017 | DDC 338.7/637409753—dc23
LC record available at https://lccn.loc.gov/2017023684

Published by SFWP
369 Montezuma Ave. #350
Santa Fe, NM 87501
(505) 428-9045
sfwp.com

Find the author at andrewgifford.com

TABLE OF CONTENTS

To Jim and Heather, who taught me about family

To Rose and Jimmy, who taught me about faith

To Genie, who taught me about love

And to Alan, who tried to teach me about patience

A NOTE ON NAMES, PLACES, AND ICE CREAM

For reasons of privacy, I have changed the names—and, in certain cases, locales or other identifying details—of some of the individuals, companies, and organizations within these pages. These changes include all of the people at my college and at my places of employment.

In addition, I've occasionally condensed or simplified timelines for the sake of narrative flow. This is especially true in the sections that detail my childhood and those that take place throughout the 1990s.

The Gifford's base mix recipe and technique detailed herein have been cobbled together from the remembrances of multiple employees, contract workers, and my maternal grandfather. If readers wish to re-create the ice cream, it's important to remember the larger context of the recipe's history, as revealed in this narrative. Most likely, very few of the people with whom I spoke actually made the mix themselves. Proceed at your own risk.

PRELUDE

AT THE LAKE, 1979

We were ice cream people.

We ran a multi-million-dollar empire that had thrived since 1938. For generations of Washingtonians, our name was on the tip of the tongue when they thought of ice cream and candy. Presidents lined up for a scoop next to office workers and laborers. At the scarred wooden tables in the various Gifford's parlors around the DC area, lovers held hands and children celebrated their birthdays, year after year. Come opening time, there was almost always a line at the door. On more than one occasion, when a first-shift worker failed to show and the store didn't open on time, small mobs broke in and served themselves. Almost everyone left payment on the counter.

In the Gifford's parlor, watching a waitress balance a tray of sundaes as she approached your table, everything must have seemed perfect. Beautiful, even. Maybe I seemed perfect, too, that boy under his mother's wing as she swanned past the tables toward the back of the store. What a dream to be the prince of ice cream!

Except it wasn't.

In 1979, I was five—too young to understand much about our family business, let alone what was about to happen to it and to us. Today, I'm still not sure I understand.

Gifford's Ice Cream and Candy Company was founded by my grandfather, John Nash Gifford. He died in 1976, leaving the business in turmoil. His wife, my grandmother Mary Frances, lay dying in a hospital bed. My father, Robert Nash Gifford, struggled for control of the empire against both his father's last surviving partner and my maternal grandfather, Allen Currey, who maneuvered to take over in my name. In the chaos, my mother, Barbara, signed on with my dad in an elaborate plan to siphon off profits and plunder the payroll and pension accounts.

As a child, I knew none of this. My paternal grandparents were strangers to me—their history hidden, muddled, erased. From my parents I learned only that I was an accident, easily ignored. What little I thought I knew about my family was a lie, and it would take me over three decades to figure that out. The fact was, long before the public end of Gifford's Ice Cream, my father had decided to kill it.

This is a story about what was lost. It's a story about the dead. It's a story about me. It begins at a lake in western Maryland.

My earliest memory.

The water in Deep Creek Lake was dark, calm, and chilly, even under the harshest summer sun. My mother called it "mountain water" with a strange, spooky reverence in her voice. Water without a bottom, she said. Deep Creek Lake, though tamed by man, seemed primordial. There were a few man-made beaches, maintained by the Wisp or Alpine Village, the two major resort hotels, but most of the shoreline was comprised of drowned trees, rocks, and sticky black mud.

As we approached in our Caprice station wagon, we passed a turnoff just before the Wisp that led to an abandoned quarry. Three great caves had been blasted through the side of the mountain, and ruined chain-link fences had been thrown up as ineffectual barriers. Around these gaping maws, rusting equipment lay forgotten. Slippery humps of rocks made dangerous trails back into the darkness, each surrounded by oily black water.

Mom was a rockhound. The first thing we did after we checked into our hotel, instead of going to the lake, was to cross the road and climb to the quarry site. On our trip in 1979, new fences had been installed to block access to the caves. But Mom had anticipated this and carried along a set of bolt cutters. She made a hole in one of the fences, grabbed my hand, and led me through, producing a cheap flashlight that cast a weak beam as we slowly moved into the caves.

A cold breeze blew from within the heart of the mountain. A barely audible hum, punctuated by sounds of dripping water and skittering rocks, summoned mental visions of ghosts and monsters. Mom stopped to chip rocks out of the walls while I nervously watched the crumbling ceiling. Occasionally she would shout in triumph and bend down to show me the fossils she'd been extracting—strange, ancient creatures trapped in stone. I carefully touched the outlines of their bodies, and Mom told me that, one day, we would become fossils, too.

Eventually, we went far enough for the daylight behind us to grow distant and then vanish, leaving us alone with the flickering beam of Mom's flashlight. In that darkness, she shouted: "I am here! I have come!"

I feared that this might be a summons and waited nervously for a response. I looked up at her, her face hidden in shadow. She stood unflinching, waiting.

"I have brought Andrew!" she added.

Her hand, hard on my shoulder, kept me pinned at her side. After a few tense, quiet moments, we turned and left. She seemed disappointed. I asked what was wrong as we emerged back into the warm summer day. She shook her head, now sullen and distant, and pushed me along the dirt road. She didn't speak for the rest of the evening.

First thing every morning for the entire vacation—for every vacation at Deep Creek, year after year, rain or shine—my parents would rouse me and we would go out on the lake in a rented boat and motor around without any sort of goal in mind. We spent entire days motoring the lake like this, my father making endless circuits of the erratic shoreline, pausing to float near the most desolate stretches, where the water disappeared behind the gnarled branches of sunken trees.

Between the two of them, they would empty a cooler of beer and bourbon. Mom would take each can out and tap the top with her fingers before cracking it open with a sigh. When the gas got low, Dad would pull into a dock and refuel, and then we'd start off again. As we drifted aimlessly, my father sat in the captain's chair, staring ahead, while my mother turned the number of flattened beer cans into a math quiz.

"How many cans now, Andrew?"

I'd dutifully count them, prouder and prouder of my ability as the number went up throughout the day.

Despite the lazy tours of the lake and the alcohol, neither of them relaxed. They always seemed on edge, living underneath a layer of fear. If a fellow boater hailed us or asked if we were in trouble, Dad would start the engine and speed away at full throttle as Mom looked back and shouted: "I think they're following!"

My mother told me that I shouldn't trust anyone. I wasn't to speak to strangers, or leave the hotel room, or get out of the boat. If anyone spoke to me, she said, I must not forget that they were "the enemy." She told me that everyone out there—"a world full of strangers"—wanted to "steal" me. Because we were famous, my father would chime in. Mom would nod and say that they would "brutally rape and torture" me.

I learned three rules: trust no one, speak to no one, and tell no one your name.

These warnings extended beyond our summer vacations at the lake. Every Halloween, at Gene's Costumes in Kensington, Maryland, both Mom and Dad would point to a policeman costume and whisper in my ear: "Don't trust police officers, because they are probably just evil men in disguise. You can buy a cop's outfit and ID right here. Anyone can. Always remember that."

At Deep Creek Lake, by six each evening, we'd tie up the boat and head back to our rented cottage on the grounds of the Alpine Village. My parents ordered room service, and then they would sit together to drink and argue steadily until I passed out in front of the TV, their harsh, hushed voices my troubled lullaby.

Part of our daily circuits around the lake brought us into the long, thin cove where the dam loomed on the horizon. We usually gave the dam a wide berth, but one day we came very close to it, and Dad cut the engine. For several minutes, the boat drifted slowly closer, and I watched, staring in awe at the large structure in front of us, the tips of trees just visible in the valley beyond. In my child's mind, I pictured the dam from its other side—a colossal wall with all that dark, dark water backed up behind it and our tiny boat floating on top. It made me feel so very small, so very fragile. We were maybe a few hundred yards away from the dam, the current gently pulling us towards it, when Mom leaned down and told me a story.

"There once was a family just like ours," she said. "Mommy, Daddy, and a little boy. They used to always visit this lake, just like we do. Then, one day, something terrible happened . . ."

She let the tension build, the boat drifting closer to the dam as my father watched me levelly, occasionally sipping from a Dixie cup of bourbon.

"They were lost," Mom continued. "They got sucked under the dam, and nobody knew what happened to them until, weeks later, they found their boat far down the river."

Her arm stretched toward the dam and beyond to the hard-scrabble woods of western Maryland, her face serious, her eyes hidden behind aviator sunglasses that reflected the summer sky and the dark water around us.

"All that was left were three skeletons," she said, pointing at her chest, at Dad, and then at me. "Mommy, Daddy and a little boy . . ."

We drifted closer and closer, and then Mom laughed good-naturedly and went to start the engine. She turned the key, but nothing happened. A look of alarm spread across her face as she tried again, then again. She rushed back to the motor and pulled the emergency ripcord. The engine choked and sputtered but didn't start. Her voice low, shaking, she called my dad over and he tried to start the engine. One, two, three pulls on the chain. The motor coughed but never came to life.

"It won't start! Oh my God!"

Mom turned to me, her face a mask of terror. She clung to my father, who grimly stared at the engine. It was the first time I had seen them frightened, and I started to cry and shake, tearing my eyes off of them to look fearfully at the dam as we drew ever closer.

The warning signals from the dam started to sound—to my child's mind they seemed like great, piercing klaxons that screamed through the air. I covered my ears. We were close enough to see people watching from the shore and an observation platform, close enough to see the water being sucked towards the dam, to feel the boat pick up speed. I pissed my swim trunks and screamed.

Then Mom started to laugh. She gave my dad a playful punch on the shoulder. Grinning and chuckling under his breath, he took his seat at the wheel and turned the key. The engine started up right away. The boat turned and sped away from the dam. The klaxons cut off and, with nothing but the roar of the boat's engine and my mom's laughter in my ears, I lapsed into a shuddering silence, sitting in a puddle of my piss, staring back at the dam. I couldn't stop crying. I couldn't feel anything.

My mother's laughter faded. She watched me for a moment, then sneered and said: "Pull yourself together. Boys don't cry!"

But I couldn't stop crying. I stared at her, gasping, sobbing, shaking. She set her jaw and turned to my father, screaming at him, saying that he had frightened me. She yelled at him all the way back to the hotel docks, then through the lobby, out the back, and all along our short walk to the cottage. Guests and staff stared at us. Mom dragged me by my hand, and I stumbled behind her, still numb. My dad never shouted back—he only nodded meekly and mumbled his familiar refrain, repeating: "Sorry, Barb . . . sorry, Barb . . ."

They fought into the night as I huddled in my bed, unable to sleep, the sound of the dam's sirens echoing in my head. I couldn't stop crying, sucking in dry, heaving breaths, sweating through the sheets and shivering. A hotel worker came by and knocked on the door. I heard him say that Dad had forgotten to tie up the boat and that it had drifted into the lake. Mom yelled at him, then slammed the front door of the cottage repeatedly—banging it shut, opening it up again, and smashing it closed again, all the while unleashing incoherent animal shrieks.

Finally, there was silence. I heard the door open again, slam shut, and then Mom burst into my room, throwing the door aside with enough force to drive the doorknob into the drywall.

"Your dad's gone," she said in calm, even tones. "He left us because you cried. Because you just had to ruin a perfect vacation."

She ordered me to take down my pajama bottoms and lie on my stomach. Then she turned her diamond rings around so the big, sharp stones were facing inward. She spanked me until blood started to flow freely onto the sheets, each blow punctuating her words: "Your . . . father . . . is . . . gone . . . because . . . of . . . you . . ."

Dad had run away. He'd rented a car and was driving home while Mom spanked me until I bled.

My childhood is defined by moments like those at Deep Creek Lake. It was our summer getaway, but for me, especially after that 1979 trip, it was an annual torture. At the lake, my parents were free of the family business, not to mention most of the family itself. They behaved like animals briefly escaped from their cages, drinking wildly and concocting pranks at my expense or at the expense of neighboring guests and hotel employees.

After that episode in 1979, my parents avoided the dam. I developed a lifelong phobia of water, and on future trips to the lake I huddled at the bottom of the boat and tried never to look at the water, tried to push the thought of it beneath me from my mind. I spent each outing on the lake in a near catatonic state, thinking only of that dam.

I still dream of that dam. In my dreams, we get sucked under and I have to fight my way awake through the impenetrable, inescapable blackness of that cold, rushing mountain water.

PART ONE

FAMILY OF STRANGERS

CHAPTER ONE

THE LAND WHERE
THE ICE CREAM GROWS

I

I always loved books.

We had a library in the family house in Kensington, Maryland, with a window that looked out at the treetops in the backyard. The shelves were so deep and strong that I could climb them and touch my head to the ceiling. Painted entirely white, the room was the most comfortable place in the house. I remember hugging the thick, snow-white shag carpet more than I remember hugging either of my parents. I lay on that carpet and worked my way through the books, even if I was too young to understand everything they were saying.

Every shelf overflowed—books sitting on top of books, packed two deep. From Robert Jordan to Conan Doyle to Marcus Aurelius. A complete collection of gold-bound first-print Dickens vied for space with *Tutor from Lesbos* and the collected short stories of Ray Bradbury. Julius Caesar lay atop Richard Matheson. J.G. Ballard formed a wall behind which lurked *Sisterhood is Powerful* and Ed Sanders' *The Family*.

I got swept up in Benchley's *Jaws*, the shark lunging up the first edition's stark black cover toward an unsuspecting swimmer. I worked my way through a dusty, seemingly ancient Sherlock Holmes omnibus. Dickens felt like a gateway to a secret world. As Mom and Dad argued, I taught myself the harder words with a 1974 *Merriam-Webster Dictionary* open at my elbow. It was in that library where I hid and tried to keep away from my parents. Their battles raged through the house—if I kept quiet and stayed in the library I could often avoid the worst of it.

But not always. One day in 1980, when I was six and lost in some book, I spilled a glass of fruit juice onto the carpet. Stealthily, I ran for towels and toilet paper to try to clean up my mess, but Mom noticed the commotion. As I worked at the stain, her voice boomed: "What the fuck have you done?"

I jerked to attention and found her at the door, watching me. Crab-walking backwards, I hit the reading chair that dominated a corner of the room. Mom stalked over to the stain, and then looked up at me. Twisting her rings around, she headed my way.

Several days later my father called in Howie the handyman— a semi-permanent fixture at our house when I was a young boy. Howie marched upstairs and looked at the juice stain with Mom. As further punishment, I was now told to "witness my crime." My mother brought in a stepstool from the kitchen and set it up beside the stain, where I would watch Howie replace that section of carpet.

Mom and Howie spoke among themselves, and Howie laughed, then glanced sideways at me. To so many people, my mom was always "Mrs. Gifford," but Howie addressed her like he was a member of our family. He called her Barb, and sometimes they'd hold hands or talk in very low voices in her room.

Sitting on my stool, I shifted to a more comfortable position after Mom left me alone with him. He wasted no time, getting on his knees and cutting out the juice stain. We kept rolls of replacement carpet and replacement paint in the basement. My mom told me that this was because everything in the house was old and irreplaceable. But of course that wasn't true. The stockpile contained many ordinary items. For my whole childhood at that big house on West Bexhill Drive, a basement bedroom held nothing but cans of paint, wallpaper, carpeting, furnace parts, tools, and even replacement sections of plumbing and electrical wiring. With this cache, anything could be replaced, from windows to pipe fixtures to roof slates. Everything was organized and preserved, awaiting the day when some very selective apocalypse wiped out all the home supply stores.

Howie cut away at the carpet, his shiny pate sweating. After a while, he glanced up at my unwavering stare and hissed: "You really did a number on my carpet, you little prick."

He waited for a reply. When none came, he grinned and said: "You're just like your dad. A pansy."

He told me that my father was "taken up the you-know-what" all during his youth.

"Old John locked Bob up when he wasn't using him," Howie said to me.

He got on his hands and knees to make a thrusting motion with his hips, stretching his head out, making soft grunting sounds as he added: "Maybe that's what we should do to you!"

Then he reached over and pinched my leg, his grin growing toothy and wide. I kept my seat and let him pinch. I knew that if I left my post for any reason, the punishment would be severe. Howie watched me for a moment—my stony silence and stare now fixed on him instead of the square of carpet—and then he shrugged and went back to work.

Howie's allegations were corroborated by Mom. The stories she sometimes told me, usually on nights Dad stayed late at the Silver Spring store, confused me, and often contradicted themselves. But one note was always there—that Dad had been brutally abused. By the time I was six, I had a clear and intimate idea of what rape and sexual abuse were like, thanks to my mother's natural ability to tell a story, weaving a complicated narrative while occasionally acting out key scenes.

The story—and the telling and retelling of it—trumped any need to protect my childhood innocence. Mom made sure that I understood the intricacies of my father's extreme sexual abuse, allegedly at the hands of John Gifford, my paternal grandfather. Later, however, when I was a teenager, the abuser became my paternal grandmother, Mary Frances, the gruesome anatomical details of Mom's story shifting to accommodate the change in characters. Where once she described my grandfather raping his son, now Mary Frances performed a slow seduction in the basement. Mom described the scene, and then explained the gritty details as Mary Frances pressed Dad to the ground and mounted him.

Before these tales began, I had never feared the basement. A maze of collected junk and home supplies, it was filled with enough secret entrances and hidey-holes to make it a place of adventure. A laundry chute fed down through the house, terminating in a tiny, pantry-sized closet in a lonely corner of the basement with a door that could be closed and latched. The latch no longer held anything shut, but sported an antique padlock, rusted closed. I was curious about that padlock. A mystery! What had been locked up in there? Why was such a formidable padlock needed on what amounted to a laundry basket? How would Holmes solve this one?

Inside this laundry closet was a tiny, dark space just comfortable enough for a child. It was an excellent hiding place, and I would often huddle in there while Mom and Dad fought far above me in the house, the sound of Mom's screams echoing down the chute. One day, I decided to see how far I could climb up the chute. I wedged myself into the square metal tube and was surprised to find that the inside had been painted as far as an adult arm could reach. That seemed odd, even to my child's mind. I levered myself up so that half my body was in the chute, with enough space all around me to turn and even push my elbows out like wings before they touched the walls.

In front of me, barely visible, I saw where someone had clawed at the paint, peeling it back from the metal. Another mystery. Carefully lowering myself down, I ran to find a flashlight, and then returned to inspect the claw marks. Below the marks were what looked to be letters. I traced them with my own fingers, but they weren't all legible. Six letters, one of them an 'L', and, then, below those, five letters, one of them a 'Y'.

At the time I didn't understand what these markings were. I'm still unsure. Was it a message? Had Dad been here long ago, as a child? Or someone else? That day, I didn't let myself think about them. I worried more about being blamed for them and the punishment that would follow, so I said nothing, and hoped they'd never be discovered by Mom. This is the first I've ever talked about them.

Eventually, Mom's lurid stories had their effect on me. In the same year that I discovered the scratches in the laundry chute, I became convinced that the basement was haunted and began to fear being down there alone. The steps—carpeted in pale blue and bending at a tight angle into darkness—frightened me, and I would quietly lock the deadbolt on the basement door whenever I was unobserved. Once, I did this while my dad was down there, and Mom pretended that she couldn't hear him knocking for nearly an hour, whispering that I should ignore him as well.

This was all certainly something I couldn't discuss with my father. He and I rarely spoke anyway. Every morning at six, he got up and packed his brown leather briefcase with paperwork, books, snack food, a couple quarts of whiskey, and a carton of Newports, and then he left without a word. Many of the books he packed were adventure novels—Ian Fleming, John D. MacDonald, and others. Some of the books were how-to guides from Loompanics Press, an indie catalogue that specialized in survivalist and anarchist fare, with a wide range of bizarre titles like *Close Shaves: The Complete Guide to Razor Fighting*, several guides to making lock-pick sets, and *How to Hide Things in Public Places*.

My mom devoured these books as well, and both of them put what they learned to use. They built their own lock-pick sets and practiced on doors around the house—no doubt one source of my own fascination with things unopened. I'm not sure if Dad knew, but Mom also hid money and other supplies—baggies of prescription drugs, for example—throughout the house. I can't help wondering today if the current occupants of our house are sitting on top of a portion of the Gifford's fortune, crammed beneath floorboards, in the walls, and in sealed compartments hidden throughout the basement.

Dad always came home well after my bedtime. Most weekends and holidays, he went to the store as if it were a normal workday. When he was around the house, he'd stay on the phone for hours, laughing and agreeing to whatever was being said, but rarely speaking. A hundred-foot coiled cord ran from the phone to the handset and he'd end up wrapped up in it, perched on the kitchen counter over the sink, smoking, drinking, and carrying on like a nervous, stuttering version of Sybil Fawlty: "Oh! I know . . . I know . . ."

When he and I did speak, I sometimes asked about my grandparents. But he would narrow his eyes and stare down at me to say: "We don't talk about them."

Yet my curiosity demanded that I know. I pressured both my parents, again and again, to tell me stories. So they told me the story on the back of the menu.

"Your grandfather founded Gifford's in 1938 . . . In the same year . . ."

II

Gifford's Ice Cream & Candy Co. was founded in 1938 by John Nash Gifford. In the same year, he opened the first Gifford's on Georgia Avenue in Silver Spring, Maryland, where he sold his six original ice cream flavors. In 1940, he opened a second location on Wisconsin Avenue in Bethesda, Maryland. Today, with five locations, Gifford's stands by its family traditions.

That's what was written on the back of the menu when I was a child. The menu was a simple, laminated four-page fold-out, pink and white with black lettering. The front featured the company logo—the peach-colored silhouette of a slim brunette woman in a pilgrim outfit, offering a white cup of ice cream balanced perfectly on the palm of her delicate hand. On the cup, my grandfather John's script spelled "Gifford's."

At the pilgrim woman's eye level (unnerving to my young mind, she didn't actually have eyes), a placard hung from a signpost also read "Gifford's" in John's script, and, below it, "Ice Cream and Candies."

When I was very young, Mom used the menus to teach me my letters. I remember snippets from those days, playing in the kitchen or sunning in the garden while Mom quizzed me on the descriptions of each dish.

"Jumbo Swiss Sundae?"

"An unforgettable treat," I recited, "that meets the high standards of even the most avid ice cream devotee. Four scoops of ice cream, Swiss syrup, chopped nuts, and a—"

"Maraschino," Mom said, anticipating my stutter.

"Cherry!" I finished.

The history on the back of the menu was all that I knew about my family. Whenever I asked about John Gifford, who had died when I was two, my mother would say: "He was a very bad man."

Grandfather had hurt my father and he would have hurt me, too, she promised, if he were still alive. When I pressed, she developed her story into the basement rape saga, which left me so fearful that I stopped asking questions.

This was what I knew of John Gifford, founder of Gifford's Ice Cream and the man who made the fortune upon which our lives sat so comfortably. I never heard a kind word about him, never an interesting anecdote, and never a true telling of his life, history, or motivations. Nor was there ever any concrete evidence for his crimes and afflictions.

It's human nature for a child to want to know about his family. As much as I feared the basement stories, I still felt compelled to wonder about my dad's parents. Dad seemed unable to even speak their names. Mom, however, seemed glad to expand her catalog of startling tales about John and Mary Frances Gifford. When I was nine, Mom told me that John had been a madman. She said that he took orders from tiny blue men about six inches high, who would run around on his desk and tell him to hurt my father and to destroy the company. (Three decades later, Allen, my maternal grandfather, would back up every one of Mom's stories, telling me his own strange tales about John's little blue men.)

"Your father saved the company!" my mother said proudly. "Otherwise the blue men would have destroyed everything our family worked so hard to build."

Mom liked to tell this story, and the saga of John and the little blue men grew with each telling. The little blue men got names, and a culture, and fully fleshed-out backgrounds. The more questions I asked—what were the blue men's motivations? Where did they come from?—the more complicated the story became. Soon, John was barely mentioned. By the time I was twelve, the story was almost always about the little blue men and their troubled, supernatural origins. It seemed to be a strange, twisted take on *The Smurfs* more than a description of genuine mental illness, but I couldn't be sure. With Allen backing her up, it was impossible to parse what was true and what was fabrication.

Allen told me that, as John's madness increased, he once marched naked down Georgia Avenue with a shotgun and demanded that people go to Gifford's. In recent years, I found no mention of such bizarre behavior in police records or the newspapers. When I challenged Allen with that fact, he replied: "John owned the police. He founded Silver Spring, so he controlled everything. He was like a mob boss. He could—and did—get away with murder."

Of course, John Gifford was not the founder of Silver Spring. Even as a child I knew that the town was much older than that. But I rarely felt the inclination to refute my other grandfather, since Allen was the only family member who seemed reliably on my side. Besides, any wild story about this family of strangers seemed believable to me.

In 1980, Mary Frances Gifford died of pneumonia. I was six. My parents hid her death from me, and I wouldn't learn the truth of her passing until I was forty. When I was a child, I saw her only three times, always in her hospital room. Crippled by a stroke in 1977, she couldn't speak, and, each time we visited, my mother pushed me to the edge of her bed and stood wordlessly behind me, holding me in place as Mary Frances ran her gnarled fingers through my hair, drooling and nodding, her eyes glittering. To me, this woman was worse than a stranger. She was a villain in the story of my father's abuse. No longer visiting her was a relief.

On the day of her funeral, I was just a clueless six-year-old, playing with my Legos. I watched as Mom and Dad flitted around the house, dressed in their Sunday best. Mom packed up her purse, came into my room, and told me that she had a movie ready for me downstairs and I should watch it, be quiet, and not answer the door or the phone until they got back. As she said this, she grabbed my arm and began pulling me towards the stairs until I started to follow along.

In the living room, on our Betamax, she had stuck in *The War of the Worlds*. Then they were gone, leaving me alone in the big house for the first time. It was also the first time I'd seen *The War of the Worlds*. I sat in front of the TV and let the sound of the Martian war machines overtake me at top volume—the pulsating, alien hum when they moved, the shriek of their death rays. I watched, rapt, the panicked citizens being vaporized as society and cities collapsed until, defeated by the common cold, the invasion ground to a halt and the Martians all died in mucus-coated horror.

I became utterly obsessed with the ominous opening monologue, and rewound the tape again and again to listen to Cedric Hardwicke set the tone over pictures of the planets in our solar system: "No one would have believed, in the middle of the twentieth century, that human affairs were being watched keenly and closely by intelligences greater than Man's . . ."

As my mind swam in the possibilities—were we being observed by aliens, and could they invade us?—I meandered back upstairs. Most of all, I was thinking about what the world would have been like after the film. Brought to the brink of destruction, our victory against the Martians was an empty one. The survivors would have to rebuild, but surely the loss of life had been staggering. The world as we knew it would have ended. And what if there was a second wave? What of the Martians back on Mars?

I had entrenched myself with my sprawling Lego town to begin plotting a reenactment of the invasion when I heard a boom, as if something had hit the house. I ran to the top of the stairs and listened. After a few heartbeats, I imagined that I could hear the pulsing of the Martian war machines from the first floor. The scene where the Martian soldier stalks our hero and scream-prone Ann Robinson in the farmhouse flashed through my mind. I backed away from the stairs and hid under my bed until my parents came home. As I lay frozen to the spot in terror of imaginary Martian soldiers, Mom's calls for me echoed through the house, growing more and more frantic until my father stepped into my room, knelt down to peer at me under the bed, and then said softly over his shoulder: "He's here, Barb."

Somehow Mom heard him over her screaming, and she burst into my room.

"You're hiding?" she hissed. "You're hiding *from me?*"

She reached under the bed and took hold of my arm, dragging me out. My head whipped against the bedframe, and I watched in a daze as she turned her rings around to spank me. Dad slowly stood and left the room. To this day I'm unsure what caused the boom that had frightened me. Perhaps the sound had existed only in my mind. A six-year-old frightened half to death by a scary movie.

Though I didn't then know the circumstances, our life had changed. With Mary Frances gone, Gifford's Ice Cream was now completely in my dad's hands.

My father was president of Gifford's Ice Cream for only thirty-eight months, and, in that time, he would become even more of a stranger, showing up late to the handful of family events each year, like Christmas, Thanksgiving, and my birthday. I saw him less and less. He now spent only a few days at Deep Creek Lake each summer, leaving Mom and me to the rest of our vacations alone. When he came home at night, usually after I had gone to bed, Mom forbade me to get up and say hello. She never explained why. I was too afraid to ask. And anyway it was fine by me. My world barely extended past my Legos, whatever was playing on the TV, and a steady, constant fear of crossing my parents in some way and provoking Mom's violent wrath.

With both my paternal grandparents gone, my parents talked a bit more freely about them. My big question—since I didn't know that she had died—was why we didn't visit Mary Frances anymore. I was afraid the visits would resume, so I wondered: Was she out of bed? Had she gotten better? When I asked Mom, she answered smoothly, telling me that John had gone to the hospital room and he had hurt Mary Frances so badly that I couldn't see her again. I had assumed John was dead, though no one had told me that outright, so now I was more puzzled than ever.

"She was sleeping," Mom said, "the most peaceful I'd ever seen her. And then John came and scared her and now she's very, very sick."

Once, as I ate breakfast, and without prompting, Mom elaborated on how Mary Frances had first ended up in the hospital. She walked over to the fridge and put her hands against it.

"It was right here . . ." she said. "Right here where Mary Frances was murdered." She paused for effect, watching me grimly. Murdered? But how did this happen when she'd been at the hospital for years? I'd have known if she had returned home. I was deeply confused, but kept silent. I knew not to speak when Mom was on the verge of telling a story.

Mom continued. "She was moving the fridge!" She yanked on the fridge, causing it to scrape against the floor and move a couple of millimeters out of its nest between the yellow-green cabinets. She pointed at the floor.

"There was water," she said. "A leak—perhaps from under the fridge or the sink. We don't know. Nobody knows. But the floor was wet, and the plug to the fridge had been frayed." She rubbed her fingers along her thumb and then she mimed a sweeping motion.

"Mary Frances started cleaning, standing in the water, when—ZAP!—she was electrocuted. But she didn't die. She lay right here"—Mom pointed to the floor in front of the fridge—"for two whole days while John sat upstairs and ignored her cries for help."

Mom cupped her hands to her mouth and weakly called to the ceiling, in a scratchy, shaky voice: "Heeeelp meeee . . ."

She saw the horror take hold of me, my hands shaking, my breakfast forgotten, and she laughed and shook her head. "Oh, come on. Get a grip."

As a child, these wild tales were all I knew of my family beyond my dad, my mom, and her parents. We had no family photographs. But we did have a family Bible with the family tree inside. The Bible was huge—dusty, leatherbound, and ancient-looking. The pages crinkled like gossamer—some torn, many passages annotated in handwriting I didn't recognize with phrases like "This is good!" and "Moses = Jewish? Trickster?"

Water damage marked the entire bottom half of the book, swelling the leather, browning the pages. The gold-embossed letters that read "Gifford" had begun to warp and flake away so that only the indentations remained. The family tree spanned across two pages at the front, folding out to the size of a coffee table book. My name was at the very bottom, in Mom's neat script, and then my parents, and, above them, John and Mary Frances. Above their names, six generations of branches stretched far into the past, but all had been blacked over with marker or scratched out.

"So who were my great-grandparents?" I asked my mother, pointing to the redacted names above John's.

She sighed. "They're dead. When you die, your name is removed from the Bible."

Some of the names on the tree had been scratched out so viciously with a pen that the page had been torn through, obliterating any hint of the censored family members.

"So are Grandpa and Grandma Gifford still around?" I continued.

She nodded. "Good point."

I watched then as she got a jar of correction fluid and carefully painted over their names. This was the only confirmation I would ever get that my grandparents were both dead. That left the three of us—Mom, Dad, and me—at the very bottom of two pages of excised names. There was no more space after me.

"Looks like the Gifford family ends right here," she muttered, pointing at my name.

III

Just as there was no sense of family in my childhood world, there was no sense that I would one day run a successful company. There was no feeling that I was part of a legacy. That I might one day inherit my father's company and position was never talked about. My mom would occasionally pay lip service to the idea. She would sometimes call me "the prince of ice cream," or "the once and future king," but these things never really made sense to me. Dad said nothing.

I now suspect he had decided, perhaps even before I was born, to kill off the business, and saw no need to prepare me for it. But because it then consumed so much of his time, our bonding moments were few and far between, and usually involved something on TV. Mom once went on a vacation to San Francisco, and Dad was left alone with me. It was the only time when I felt at ease around one of my parents, and involved probably the greatest number of words that my father and I ever exchanged.

We watched a Sunday night movie from Disney called *The Spaceman and King Arthur* that was part of *Disney's Wonderful World*— an anthology series that ran from the 1950s until 1992 and dominated my Sunday nights. There was the heist flick *The Omega Connection*, a bizarrely re-edited version of *The London Connection*. We got the light-hearted Apple Dumpling Gang series of films with Don Knotts, juxtaposed with the shockingly violent *Sky Trap* and the creepy and terrifying *Child of Glass*.

For the most part, I watched the Sunday night movies alone, often with Mom and Dad fighting in the background. But for that one week while Mom was away, I sat next to Dad and we quietly watched *The Spaceman and King Arthur* together. In the movie, the sole pilot of a space shuttle (back when the shuttle was the newly christened embodiment of science fiction-cum-reality), along with his wise-cracking robot companion, is caught in a time vortex and thrown back to Arthurian days, where he is swept up in a tremendously simplified version of *A Connecticut Yankee In King Arthur's Court*. It's a clumsy mash-up of the Twain story and Buck Rogers, and it contains just over one hundred percent of the RDA of lame comedy.

Dad didn't speak or move throughout the entire film. He just sat, watching the screen blankly, and when the credits rolled, he put a hand on my shoulder.

"That was good, eh?" he asked. I nodded. Then he told me it was bedtime.

When Mom returned, Dad went back to ignoring me. But at the time this was a powerful bonding moment. It was certainly the most peaceful Sunday evening of my youth. Even though sitting next to a mannequin might have provided more rewarding conversation, Dad chose to spend this time with me. He wasn't drinking and he didn't smoke for the whole movie, which was highly unusual.

I now assume that he was doggedly going through whatever weird motions fulfilled his sense of paternal duty. Though we shared no meals, and we hardly spoke to each other, he did come home earlier each workday and left later in the mornings. He'd watch me prepare eggs or oatmeal, nodding approvingly, though he never ate in front of me. In the evenings, he'd supervise as I heated up frozen food. When I think of my father today, I like to picture him during that week. Calm, sober, and willing to watch a movie with me. At the time, it was the first crack in the shell around me—things were different when Mom was gone. There was an Other Normal. Another condition in which we could exist without constant fear or anger.

Otherwise, I relied on the escapism provided by TV, fantasy books, and my vast cityscape of Legos. For the most part, the TV was mine. At night, my dreams echoed the adventures depicted on the original *Battlestar Galactica* or *Space: 1999*, and a whole world of one-season sci-fi flops that most people probably haven't heard of. I couldn't run away in real life, so I ran away internally.

Some of my most comforting childhood memories involve Commander Adama and his ragtag post-apocalyptic space fleet. The desperate journey of the Galactica's crew into the unknown seemed so brave and so very noble. Then there was the troubled command of Commander Koenig on the runaway moon in *Space: 1999*. Initially a hard-nosed bureaucrat sent to straighten up the mess at Moonbase Alpha, the atomic accident that sends the moon hurtling into the unknown strands Koenig with his fractious crew of three-hundred-some scientists and workers, many of them unhappy with his command style. It was my only instruction in making difficult moral decisions.

This mixture of far-flung adventure and soapbox preaching in 1970s sci-fi, intertwined with an overall sense of hopelessness, spoke volumes to me. The Galactica's crew would never reach Earth during their generation, and they knew that. Koenig's moon could never return to Earth. Despite the hopelessness of their situations, these people were heroes. They kept going against all odds.

Not all of the sci-fi in the house belonged to me, though. My mother loved *V*, in which aliens arrive in their iconic ships, casting saucer-shaped shadows over our great cities. Proclaiming that they come in peace, they are soon proven to be bloodthirsty reptiles in disguise, here to rape our planet and eat our people. A not-too-subtle and depressing analogue of the rise of Nazi Germany, it was a major TV mini-series event in 1980. I was allowed to stay awake well past my bedtime to fill my brain, and that night's dreams, with the alien Nazis who so easily took over a gullible world. In *V*, humanity's only hope rests on the broad shoulders of Mike Donovan and in the sweet face of Juliet Parrish, who together lead a fragile resistance movement.

Of course Mom rooted for the alien Visitors. She thought the evil scientist Diana—who was basically a sci-fi version of Joseph Mengele—was a sexy, powerful woman to be admired.

My maternal grandfather, Allen, loved *Battlestar Galactica*. I spent most weekends with my grandparents in Silver Spring, Maryland, during those early years, and I looked forward to hunkering down with Allen for the latest sci-fi adventure. But he loved the Cylons—the menacing killer robots stalking the last human survivors. He would issue their catchphrase in a robotic voice: "By your command."

Why did my family always root for the bad guys? I saw the Galactica's crew and *V*'s resistance fighters as heroic versions of myself—isolated, persecuted, facing the unknown, yet still clear-minded enough to try to discover themselves and seek freedom. If only I could be as strong and brave as Mike Donovan. If only Commander Adama could be my dad.

My great complaint about sci-fi as a child was that I hungered for longer, more involved stories. While the tantalizing intelligence of a larger, linked storyline always seemed to flutter just beneath the surface of some shows, it was never the focus. Each episode ended cleanly, and each new episode began as if something horrifically apocalyptic hadn't happened a few days ago. One Friday evening, the crew meets and murders God—the next Friday, they all seem fine and are winking at one another over a feckless conman.

Then, at age seven, on my own in front of the TV, I stumbled across *Doctor Who*. Here was a show whose episodic format had an excuse. The Doctor flits off and lands a million years and a billion light years from the last adventure. In 1981, the show was at the end of the Tom Baker era, probably the most iconic iteration of the Doctor in the show's original run. The twenty-five-minute serialized episodes were brutally spliced together by Channel 26, DC's local public television station, into movie-length adventures that were two or more hours long. It aired on Sunday afternoons, but was often pre-empted by pledge drives, so it was during those times that I would join Allen for what he called his "Tesla Experiment."

Allen was fascinated with Nikola Tesla, the legendary pioneer of electricity. My grandfather never tired of telling me Tesla's tale, though his telling was infused with sinister conspiracy theories. Tesla is indeed surrounded by mystery and conspiracy. His fascinating life and lonely death, and the way the government reacted to his death, provide more fodder for conspiracy nuts than the Zapruder film.

In addition to AC current, Allen said that Tesla had invented a way to harvest free energy from the air and the earth. Unfortunately, he made this discovery while he was working for Thomas Edison. Edison, according to Allen, was "crippled by greed and gluttony." Edison saw the future much as it is today—everyone pays for power and "all the profits go to Edison." Even modern-day phone and power companies, Allen told me, were run by a secret ruling elite nominated by Edison before he died. The positions were inherited from generation to generation, and this elite was hiding the greatest secret ever discovered—Tesla's free power.

Allen claimed to have Tesla's last, unpublished journal. He said that Tesla was a Mason and that the hand-written, spiral-bound collection of papers was part of the Masonic library at Allen's local lodge. He proudly told me he had "liberated it at the first opportunity." But Allen kept it out of my reach and hid it away whenever I came into the room. I rarely questioned his claims—if he said he had Tesla's journal, I was willing to accept his word as truth.

Tesla's journal supposedly detailed the secret to harvesting energy from the air. Following its instructions, Allen hammered nails into all of the trees along the perimeter of his one-acre lot. Around each nail, he wrapped metal wiring. These he would check every weekend to make sure they were still in place, telling me that it would take time before we saw results.

"The nails need to link with the trees," he said. "This could take years, even decades. But, eventually, a power net will form around the property."

I followed him on his rounds and helped him take notes on the status of each nail. Many of them were "almost there," but the network wouldn't activate until they were all ready. He and I had a long wait ahead of us.

My grandparents' house was in an area of Silver Spring that was still rural when I was a child. The neighbors kept horses in their yard. There was nowhere to go and nothing to do on rainy days, or on hot days, but sit in my grandparents' glassed-in "Florida room" and watch TV. I was introverted and had no interest in sports. Allen and my grandmother never seemed to really know what to do with me.

My grandmother was quiet, hailing from deep in the mountains of West Virginia. She once told me that she didn't learn about Pearl Harbor, or World War II, until late 1942. She also told me that, when she was a child, her family worshipped the "spirit of the mountain," which was embodied in a phantom white horse. For his part, Allen seemed preoccupied with trying to make me "not like my father," and would often comment how much I looked like Dad, a note of sadness hanging in his voice that confused me.

Mom battled with Allen constantly, though theirs was a different sort of struggle. She didn't yell and scream like she did with Dad—she just yanked me around to stand in front of her like a human shield, saying things like: "We can vanish any time. One day here, the next day we'll be gone, and you'll never see or hear from Andrew again."

I ignored as much as I could. I let the TV be my guide and savior. Soon addicted to *Doctor Who*, I was struck by the episode "Genesis of the Daleks," my introduction to the frightening, single-minded space-Nazi pepperpots.

The story runs for a grim two hours. Two dying civilizations—the Kaleds and the Thals—have been fighting a war for a thousand years. What started out with laser guns has now come down to mustard gas and muskets. Each society, reduced to its last city, is post-apocalyptic in every way. Each is bent on the destruction of the other, and each seems to have forgotten how the war even started. The Kaleds, with the aid of the crippled genius Davros, are building a *wunderwaffen*: the Daleks. Self-aware and perfectly evil, the Daleks are ready to destroy the future and, along the way, all that is good.

Between these rivals lies a wasteland populated by mutants, which the Doctor crisscrosses trying to broker a peace. But he is finally forced to lead a desperate final assault on the bunker where the Daleks are gathering. In the finale, the Doctor rigs the Dalek bunker to explode.

The Doctor stands with the two wires that will trigger the terminal explosion and end the Dalek menace forever. His companions scream for him to do it. The audience has invested hours in the storyline. And then the Doctor pauses. He asks himself, eyes on the wires an inch apart: "Just touch these two strands together and the Daleks are finished. Have I that right?"

His companions say that he must do it.

"But the final responsibility is mine, and mine alone," he says.

He raises the equivalent of a "would you kill Hitler as a child" argument, and then muses: "Do I have that right? Simply touch one wire against the other and that's it. The Daleks cease to exist. Hundreds of millions of people, thousands of generations can live without fear, in peace, and never even know the word Dalek. But if I kill, wipe out a whole intelligent life form, then I become like them."

So he spares them. After all he's been through, he spares them. The show had been on for twelve years, and different incarnations of the Doctor had battled the Daleks many times. The Doctor knew the future. He knew it clearly. But he spared his great enemy. That episode became my moral touchstone—the one TV-taught lesson that stood above the rest. I could see the evil around me, but I wasn't old enough to escape it, wasn't big enough to mount any real resistance to it. All I had to do was endure it and not let it change me. I would have to be true to my own values and beliefs no matter what I heard or what I was told to do.

But how? All I ever wanted was to simply vanish forever. To be one of those characters on TV. Literally. I wanted to morph into Commander Adama, or the Doctor, and live the same adventures I watched over and over. But I knew that was impossible.

When I got a little older and more grounded, I wanted to be a long distance trucker—because that seemed to be a solitary occupation, where men without names could vanish down a different, unknown road each morning. I saw truckers as nomads, living on the highways of America, homeless, rootless, slumbering in their little cabins as their trucks idled through the night at some forlorn pull-off in the dark shadows of inner America. How perfect. How lucky. They answered to no one.

I felt exhausted by life and I daydreamed about being old, and about my life coming to a swift, painless end. I remember suicidal thoughts, although there was a fantastical element to them—I would commit suicide but only after successfully becoming a ninja. Maybe I'd be taken away by aliens and would die fighting bad guys among the stars. Instead, I decided that it would probably be best to die at the Gifford's store in Silver Spring. I could vanish into a dark corner, hidden by all the junk and refuse. People would wonder what that funny smell was for weeks before they found me.

IV

Whenever I speak about the Silver Spring store, most listeners lapse into nostalgia. They suggest that a childhood spent wandering around the bowels of the store was akin to a scene from *Willy Wonka & the Chocolate Factory*.

But that picture couldn't be further from the truth.

The store in Silver Spring was huge in comparison to tiny modern ice cream shops. The building still stands today on Georgia Avenue—an L-shaped structure that now houses a day-care center. But even with modern glass blocks instead of the old front parlor windows, and childish art taped on the windows that do remain, it's still hauntingly familiar to me.

When the building housed Gifford's, the public saw only the front parlor. Wrapped in glass, the front of the building offered a full view of everyone inside as they slammed spoonfuls of ice cream into their mouths. The hundred-seat parlor, dominated by two-top and four-top square tables, was always brightly lit. It seemed very much unchanged from the 1940s, though the wear and tear of four decades was starting to show. Waitresses rushed from table to table with trays and menus, wearing uniforms devolved over the decades from freshly starched cotton blouses and skirts to sad one-piece frocks of pilling polyester. Gifford's offered full table service up until the final days, though the quality of that service did get very spotty at the end. Girls balanced trays of sundaes, banana splits, and the famous Big Top—a gigantic sundae that Allen would joke, decades later, was probably single-handedly responsible for America's diabetes epidemic.

Standing inside the front door, a long counter formed an L on one side of the room. Behind this first section stood the candy ladies, part of a mysterious cabal of older women who rotated downstairs from close quarters on the second floor where they labored amid cubby-holes full of chocolate and ingredients that stretched from the floor to the ceiling. My favorites from the candies and chocolates were the turtles, with walnuts or pecans, depending on the day, covered in Gifford's country caramel and chocolate. I've never tasted a turtle that compares. The secret was the caramel—the Gifford's caramel recipe calls for the base mix that went into all of the ice cream, resulting in a creamy, subtle flavor that just isn't found in caramel today. This also made every caramel a butterfat sugar bomb.

The candy section of the counter was fairly short, maybe ten feet long, and then the ice cream began. What I call the "popular" flavors stretched another fifteen feet or so, ending at a pass-through for the servers. The counter then took its L-turn to the right, a twelve-foot section that held the "experimental" ice cream—actually seasonal flavors swapped out as the calendar demanded. That end of the counter also housed the sorbets and ices, a subset of ice cream that I disliked and avoided. In the Jim Crow era, a window within the window next to the sorbet section had been used to serve African-Americans, who were forbidden from entering the parlor. By the time I was exploring the store, a black man was manager, but that reminder of a troubled era remained.

Whenever I was brought to the store, my parents would cut me loose immediately and leave me to wander alone. I was fascinated by the people and the hustle and bustle of the front parlor, and would start my wanderings there.

My visit always began with a milkshake—chocolate ice cream and chocolate syrup only. Sometimes the servers would start making it as soon as they saw Mom pull into the parking lot. But I complained when they did that. The nails-on-a-blackboard bzzt-bzzt each time the metal shaker jostled against the spinning mixing blade thrilled me like a jolt of electricity. I imagined some magical element flaking from the stainless steel, giving the shake that special twist that no other chocolate shake in the world could ever hope to achieve. The staff indulged me in such things, too. To them, I was the heir to Gifford's Ice Cream.

It was a generational company—some of the employees had been at their stations since 1940 and had labored under John Gifford and then Dad. Most of them treated me as if I were next in line for a shining, golden throne. Despite such royal treatment, I was never rude to the employees, though that was not a lesson learned from my parents. Mom didn't encourage me to thank them for their service, and Dad didn't even look at me when I was in the store. I made a point of stepping up for both of them, a pint-sized Miss Manners, and bashfully thanked everybody. Mom would tell me that I was very polite, and that was very nice, but there really was no need to thank the servers for "doing what they were born to do." I felt bad for them when she said this within earshot, but most of the servers kept silent and stoically handed my milkshake to me with a strange, sad reverence.

What I didn't know then was that John Gifford's reign was notoriously cruel, especially in his final days. I've spoken to employees who tell stories of John stalking through the store, singling out random employees and firing them on the spot, without explanation.

When Dad took over, he showed himself to be even more unpredictable. He fired every administrative worker on the second floor—the secretarial pool, middle managers, human resources department, and accountants, all gone by 1983. My memories of the depopulated second floor are of a post-apocalyptic tableau where half-full coffee cups crawled with mold, unfinished paperwork lay forever waiting to be filed, dust gathered inches thick across desks, and jackets and sweaters lay abandoned and askew on the backs of chairs. It felt as if all of the upstairs employees—perhaps fifteen or twenty total—had simply vanished into thin air, leaving a cavernous second-floor wing occupied solely by my wraith-like father, who darted from shadow to shadow and avoided all human contact.

Looking back, I can see that all around me was a shipwreck waiting to happen, and that everyone was ready to jump overboard the moment an alarm sounded. But I was still a kid. I dedicated myself to quietly exploring the building, soaking in every inch of the store, starting with the front parlor, where the colorful ice cream sat in giant tubs laid out in sub-zero compartments. The complicated, mechanical scoops rested in little troughs built along the counter, through which hot water constantly circulated with a soothing gurgle.

Behind the L-counter were the always-hideous customer bathrooms on one side, while on the opposite side a conveyor belt delivered an endless stream of dishes and glasses from a busboy area, feeding them into giant, roaring dishwashers that belched clouds of steam. The conveyor was rarely cleaned, usually covered in dried ice cream and stinking that sour milk smell that permeated most of the store, creeping deep into hair and clothes. I'm confounded when people speak glowingly to me today about the smell of Gifford's—a smell made of rot, mold, and old milk. It was made of bowls of half-eaten ice cream collecting cockroaches that looked like they could arm wrestle you. It was made of the traps with dead rats left to fester, ignored, until the odor finally overwhelmed someone with stomach enough to clean it up.

Behind a door, a set of steep stairs led precariously down from the bussing area to the crypt-like basement, where an inch or two of black water lay on the floor. Makeshift walkways of wooden pallets led into an impenetrable darkness, the lights in the farthest regions having long since burned out. Near the stairs, boxes of menus, advertisements, and everyday supplies squatted under a few bare bulbs. In the areas where the lights didn't work, living things would crash and splash away from my flashlight beam. Fungus-covered cardboard boxes gave way to ancient wooden crates, some not opened since the 1940s. Even amid black mold, shattered light bulbs, and unseen rodents, I was consumed by the need to explore. But to stray too far from the pale light cast by the few bare bulbs was asking too much. Sometimes those crashing, splashing things didn't run from my flashlight beam—instead, a pair of shining eyes would brazenly stare right back at me, daring me to step forward into the unknown.

Back up on the main floor, past the bussing and prep area, a small set of stairs led to the main loading area, the forklifts and dollies as poorly maintained as the lighting and sanitation. An iron-cage freight elevator—last serviced in 1965, almost two decades before my wanderings—rattled up to the second floor where the candy ladies huddled.

Also on the second floor was a room where caramel, chocolate, and other syrups bubbled in large vats tended by men who used the elevator without fear, the cage-like car shaking unsteadily and banging against the shaft, the men in it laughing whenever they were almost knocked off their feet. The screaming and creaking of its mechanisms fueled my nightmares. Even Mom refrained from taking advantage of this particular fear of mine with a prank, or a threat, or a forced ride in the great beast, though I expected all of that to happen. Instead she'd just shake her head and say the thing was a "deathtrap."

Outside the elevator shaft on the main floor was an unused manufacturing room. Once bustling, it had become instead a vast network of paths between rusting, useless hulks of long-abandoned equipment. Most were too ancient to allow me to figure out what purpose they had served. Giant mechanical arms loomed over rusted vats that may have once been ice cream machines. Stacks of crates looked more like they belonged in some long-lost military bunker than in an ice cream shop. Some held machine parts—Mom would simply tell me that the boxes were full of "widgets." Others held empty pint or half-gallon waxed containers for the ice cream, mostly waterlogged and forgotten. Cockroaches ran unchecked and would boldly skitter across my shoe. The waitresses called their uniform shoes "roach-killers," referring to the pointy toes that served as the only pest control in the building.

Opposite the elevator were two doors. One led to a disused office, and one led to another bathroom, also disused. Neither had seen the light of day—or any light—for a decade. Like many such lonely parts of that big building, they had simply been abandoned. My trusty flashlight shone over flooded floors, rotting clothes, and forgotten relics of the last occupants. It seemed as if they had left quickly, or under duress.

Moving through this frightening back end of the Gifford's Ice Cream operation, the musty sour milk scent grew stronger. This part of the building was the realm of my father. There was no joy here to match the ice cream and happy customers out front, no mementos of family or love. Out of the public eye, the back end of the building housed only the shattered remnants of a family business that had been in a state of decay since before I was born. The rats here didn't just stare, as in the dark womb of the basement. Instead they sat fearlessly atop the abandoned desks, even in bright sunlight. A shout or a threatening gesture couldn't budge them. I'd stamp my foot and scream, but the rats only tilted their furry heads a bit. Were it possible for them to smile, I'm sure they would have done so.

Back out in the loading area, the dead machines gave way eventually to a high traffic section. Here was the giant, gleaming metal door of the freezer on one side, opposite the aged iron gate of the service entrance to the back alley. A narrow set of steep stairs took the candy ladies to their second floor lair—they were all terrified of the elevator, too. A big set of doors swung into the factory proper. From them flowed a constant stream of workers, pushing carts of ice cream bound for the front parlor or for the waiting trucks that would take it to other Gifford's locations, none of which made their inventory on the premises. Per John Gifford's orders, and then my dad's, every Gifford's location was beholden to "the Plant" in Silver Spring.

Just a few feet from this main avenue of activity sat a giant block of dry ice, used to pack ice cream traveling to the other stores. When a shipment was ready, a worker would come out and turn on a saw. Gears squealed, smoke belched. The saw terrified me as it effortlessly sliced through the dry ice. Then the cut block was manhandled into the boxes of ice cream waiting to be wheeled away.

A worker taught me how to cut off small pieces with a hand-held saw, and I would make a point of carefully putting on a pair of gloves like they showed me. I had once touched the dry ice and burned myself. When the workers heard my screams, several of them ran out to nurse me, swearing me to secrecy. If my parents found out, I was told, they'd all get fired. So they pitched in and got me a set of child-sized gloves, which were kept in a secret spot among the abandoned loading equipment. Wearing these, I'd get a tiny block of dry ice and a pan of water, then scurry among the dead machines and create a mini-movie set in the shadowy corners. On my hands and knees atop the filthy floor, I'd breathe deeply as the white carbon dioxide mist wreathed my head. The "high" that I received was blissful, and, once, I passed out and lay there in the shadows for several minutes in a refreshingly dreamless catatonia.

I would also play, unsupervised, in the giant freezer, where mountains of ice cream containers created a strange, frosty moonscape. The freezer was so large that I could hide from anyone else who came inside. I would creep around pretending I was an Arctic explorer until I started to shiver uncontrollably and retreated back outside.

Behind the large doors swinging into the loading area beat the heart of the Plant—the active manufacturing floor. Around this giant open space raced laborers dressed in dirty chef whites and hairnets, measuring, timing, and tasting the product of six huge whirring ice cream machines. Every flavor poured out of the machines into fifty-gallon buckets, where it was flash frozen atop a conveyor belt that carried them through a plastic-curtained door in the wall and into the freezer on the opposite side. Flies and cockroaches would swarm, but the Gifford's rats stayed away from the manufacturing floor during business hours. The ice cream cooks had no fear of the rodents' bold stares, and the occasional fur-lined bloodstain would be left to feed the cockroaches and serve as an example to the others.

Ingredients were always lying around, exposed. When peach ice cream was in season, staff members would go and buy all of the nearly rotten produce from Butler's Orchard in upper Montgomery County, Maryland, leaving it in pails to rot a little more before going into the mix, bugs and all.

My favorite time was when rum raisin was made—row after row of shallow cookie sheets crowded with raisins soaking in an inch of cheap rum. They would lie out for days, getting fat and plump with liquor. I grabbed them by the handful and greedily gobbled them up, eventually spinning around the factory floor in loopy fits of half-drunken giggles.

In a back room, sealed off from the main manufacturing floor, the more sensitive sugary stuff was made. Trays of home-made peppermint slowly dried on tall stacks of shelves. When just slightly chewy, it would be added to vanilla ice cream to make the popular peppermint flavor.

Even in the simple matter of ice cream flavors, though, Gifford's history is complicated and confusing. In 1978, my father announced that he had sealed a deal with Nabisco to become the first official maker of Oreo ice cream. Wikipedia, not in agreement with Dad, gives this distinction to a Portland, Oregon, ice cream company that started producing it in 1978, and it seems that many other companies have made the same claim, dating back to 1972. I would edit that Wikipedia entry, except in 1980 Mom told me that Dad had not, in fact, made a deal with Nabisco. And thirty-four years later, Allen told me that Dad had bought Oreos in bulk and crushed them to make what he called Oreo ice cream—without legal permission. According to Allen, Nabisco took action and Dad promptly changed the name.

So Gifford's is, arguably, the creator of the "cookies 'n' cream" ice cream flavor. But all I remember is that Dad's brief dalliance with the Oreo name resulted in a knockdown battle at home with Mom. She screamed at Dad for what felt like hours, and then, in a breathless frenzy, she ran into the library and clutched wildly at me.

"Your father's a cheat and a liar and now we're done for!" she said. "Nabisco is going to take everything from us! Everything! The fucking Nabisco Nazi pigs will destroy us!"

I didn't respond, my mouth working, my eyes wide, and she threw me backwards with enough force that my head bounced off one of the bookshelves. Then she returned to her fight with Dad. He stood, head down, silent, as Mom's shouting ramped up, and, finally, she went so far as to pick up a stool and throw it against the wall with a shattering crash. When the fight was over,

Mom pulled me to our arts and crafts table and said: "You and I are going to get even with the Nabisco Nazi Pigs. They think they can end the beloved Gifford's Ice Cream."

For weeks, she had me write letters to Nabisco, condemning them for their actions and demanding retribution. She dictated, I wrote in my child's scrawl. I would then be sent to run down the block and stick the letters in a mailbox. At the Plant, though, the large barrels of crushed Oreos were simply more sweets for the prince of ice cream, and I would fill my pockets to fuel my expeditions.

The workers all ignored me as long as I wasn't burning myself, or about to get chewed up by a machine, or otherwise in their way. No one watched after me. A monotonous, robotic feeling permeated the staff. I learned quickly to stay well out of the way, skirting around the edges of activity and keeping as small and as quiet as possible.

Going up the stairs to the second floor, I would turn and wave to the security guard. He sat in a glass booth elevated above the stairs, what my mother called "the machine-gun nest." If anyone came up the stairs, the guard watched carefully but, at eighty-something, there was little chance he could extricate himself from his crow's nest and intercept anyone before they could vanish into the warren of the second floor. I talked to the old guy, though, and listened attentively to his stories of bygone eras. He died in 1981, and his post was never filled. All of his personal belongings remained in place as if he had just stepped out: his coffee mug, a lunchbox with a rotten apple in it, his jacket draped on the chair, and the issue of *Life* from the week he died, open to a cigarette ad.

Straight ahead, as seen from the top of the stairs, there was that creaking, horrible service elevator, and the area where sauces cooked. In this hellish nightmare of flames, smoke, and steam, copper pots large enough to hold a man boiled and bubbled with caramel and chocolate. Trays sat on pool-table-sized platforms where caramel and other confectionary cooled and hardened, to be sliced into manageable pieces before being sent on. The employees who tended the sauces were all black men, all giant and stern-looking. Mom warned me to "watch out for the darkies," and then she'd warn me that all they wanted, more than anything in the world, was to cook me in the caramel. They did it to other boys all the time, after all. She'd run a hand through my hair and ask: "How do you think caramel gets its color?"

Allen reinforced her comments, telling me that, after sunset on winter days, the black men in the sauce room would sneak around and steal from everyone.

"You can only see a black man at night when he smiles," Allen told me. "And then it's too late for you . . ."

I know now, of course, that those men were perfectly ordinary, and I am equally certain that I would've been just as safe around them as I was around the other workers. But back then I feared the sauce room more than anything, and I never explored it. I'd tiptoe past the doors and break into a run when they opened, always with a blast of heat-mangled air.

Entering the candy room, past the sauce area, the sour milk smell immediately disappeared, replaced by the soothing aroma of chocolate and sugar. Here it was as if the walls were made of chocolate, lined with cubbyholes the size of postboxes, where raw chocolate waited uncovered. The candy ladies taught me that raw chocolate was incredibly durable, and could sit for years before going bad. They also claimed that the one-hundred-percent "liquor"—as they incorrectly called the chunks of raw chocolate—was impervious to pests. The roaches and the rats stayed away, they said, due to the bitterness. They would give me small bites, and I would be repulsed by the bitter flavor, then watch in awe as they laughed and gobbled up huge chunks.

It was in that quiet room—with the old ladies in their aprons and hodge-podge remnants of old Gifford's uniforms from multiple eras—where the candies were made, sorted, boxed, and set aside for distribution. The ladies were the kindest of the employees, and I would watch them, fascinated.

A few of the ladies had been there for decades, and they knew only one thing: making candy for Gifford's. Their conversations rarely strayed from what their hands were deftly doing. The topic was always either the shifting popularity of certain candies or the almost mystical nature of chocolate and how it was the world's great healer. The Cult of Candy ruled their lives, and whenever a new person joined the team, she would learn the ropes by word of mouth. There were no guides, no instruction booklets, no checklists. New employees were indoctrinated slowly into the coven, first performing menial tasks while jealously glaring at their elders, then stepping up through the ranks until they earned a spot at the central wooden table where the confectionary witchcraft took place.

The old ladies would point me out to new employees as I stood in my corner, always silent and watchful. They called me the "Sunshine Boy," taking a moment to run their fingers through my blonde hair. "You'll be working for the Sunshine Boy one day," they said to one another. Though sometimes I would hear puzzling remarks like, "He's a better man already." It was because of these ladies that I eventually abandoned my plans to kill myself in the Plant. They were all so sweet, and they'd all be so upset if I were to die.

I don't remember any of their names, this lovely handful of people who were kind to me. I can picture the faces, but even then, there's a generic quality to them. Old ladies, grey-haired, all overweight to varying degrees, their uniforms mismatched. To a child, they all fell into the category of "friendly elders." Even the newcomers being trained, who may have been in their twenties and thirties, seemed impossibly grown-up to me. But these anonymous women placed chocolate on my tongue and hugged me close to their breasts, and the combination of sensations overwhelmed me.

Outside the candy room, past the security post again, a long, dim hallway led back to a glass door, the word "Office" stenciled on its frosted pane. Behind this door lay my dad's lair. In the main room, four abandoned desks waited under bright lights for secretaries who would never return. Just behind these sat a darkened manager's office, also abandoned. In one corner perched a coat rack, on which a forgotten suit jacket still hung. Atop the manager's metal desk, a pair of eyeglasses gathered a greasy film of dust, cobwebs tethering them to a rotary-dial phone. A large staff had once filled the second floor with life. But its rooms were now vacated and, like the other offices downstairs, they seemed to have been hastily abandoned. In a nearby locker room, the metal doors still protected personal belongings left inside—watches, glasses, briefcases, clothes. As if an evacuation signal had sent people running, naked, into the streets, only to be vaporized. My dad used the locker room in the mornings, standing there among the detritus of his former staff, showering in the dark, singing to himself.

Behind a heavy oaken door was my dad's wood-paneled office. Piles of papers covered the mahogany desk, and a small lamp provided a dim yellow glow. A cloud of blue-grey cigarette smoke hung in the air, drifting languidly in unfelt currents. A foul odor drifted through the closed door of a filthy bathroom, the interior sprayed with dark yellow-brown piss and diarrhea.

Dad rarely drank openly. The alcohol was usually hidden in a Dixie cup. If he had to drink to keep up appearances—at a dinner or a party—he'd sip slowly at the glass. At home, he'd go down to the basement utility room, squeeze between the giant heating-oil tank and the cold brick wall to drink steadily from a bottle until he filled a paint can with crushed cigarette butts.

At work, he would drink inside a narrow closet next to that horrible bathroom. I'd sit and poke at the papers and ledgers on his desk, all dated decades earlier, and watch as he'd suddenly stand up, get a quart of whiskey, and then move to the closet. Like the rest of the office, the closet was packed with papers and books and hung with coats and clothes that had belonged to my grandfather John. The only things in that office that belonged to Dad were his briefcase and his coat on the back of the chair. The closet was so crammed with John Gifford's junk that it was impossible to close the door, even when Dad wasn't trying to fit inside. So he'd stand halfway out into the office, lean back against the solid wall of coats and papers, and drink straight from the whiskey bottle, staring ahead, his body unmoving except for the motion of his arm and the bob of his large Adam's apple as he swallowed. He seemed to enter some sort of fugue state. He wouldn't react to noises, and sometimes he wouldn't even blink, simply staring into the shadow- and smoke-filled office, concentrating on nothing in particular. Sometimes he would hold this pose until he finished the entire bottle.

Then he'd simply snap out of it and return to his desk as if nothing had happened. In all of these cases, Dad never appeared drunk. His attitude wouldn't change. He wouldn't loosen up or act weird. He was always exactly the same man—meek, even-tempered, and quiet.

I'd sit for a while and watch him, but soon enough the smoke, the smell from the bathroom, and the overall oppressive atmosphere would drive me out and back on my explorations.

<h1 style="text-align:center">V</h1>

Eventually, though, I grew bored with exploring the Silver Spring store. By the time I was eight, whenever I was separated from the TV and forced to hang out at the store, I turned to comics and books. Walking out of the service entrance and through the parking garage behind Gifford's, it was only a few more blocks to a comic-book store called Geppi's.

I wandered freely around downtown Silver Spring. Back then, it was a very different town, filled with dive bars and warehouses and a bus station with several unsavory types in residence, offering none of the glamour and glitter found in today's gentrified version of the suburb. I wasn't afraid, though. Mom had been teaching me how to avoid people. She'd been warning me since I could remember that everyone was out to get me, that they would molest me if I let them. So getting to Geppi's became a game. I'd run, or choose daring paths along the stony drainage ditch outside the garage, or simply zigzag erratically, all to confound imaginary followers.

This unnamed, general threat against me became better focused when Mom and Dad both started talking about the family's "real enemies," those made by John Gifford. That summer, after the blockbuster release of *Star Trek II: The Wrath of Khan*, I finally learned something new about my dad's father. Surprisingly, the information came unbidden. Mom sat me down shortly after we saw the movie and told me: "It's time you learned about your grandfather."

Reiterating the history on the back of the Gifford's menu, Mom said that John Gifford had worked at a dairy farm in New Jersey throughout the 1930s. But then she revealed something the menu did not—how that farm family who had pioneered a unique style of ice cream used a secret recipe to make it creamier and tastier than any ice cream ever. This was the first time anyone talked to me about a secret recipe. It sounded exciting, and I was hooked.

John's job at the dairy farm changed with each telling. Sometimes he was a cattle hand, sometimes a salesperson, sometimes "the guy who cleaned shit." Either way, he was a small fry, just scraping by. From his lowly perch, he saw that the farm family was making a fortune selling ice cream at their roadside stand, and, Mom said, John "got bit by the greed bug." He saw a "gold mine" and he "stole the secret recipes and skipped town."

In that first telling of the story, young John Gifford was drinking himself stupid at the local bar, seething about his lot in life to anyone who would listen. He had few friends, and everyone looked down on him and made fun of him. He came from a family of paupers. They'd lived in New Jersey since the Revolutionary War, when they fought for England and had to "hide for a hundred years in the pine barrens like rabid dogs."

Here, Mom went off on a tangent, telling me how the Giffords, who had remained loyal to England for the hundred years they spent in hiding, became snipers and killed good, red-blooded Americans who came too close to the woods. She knelt down on one knee, took aim at my face with an imaginary rifle, and then shouted: "KA-POW!"

From such treasonous stock came John Gifford, this pathetic salesperson/cattle herder/shit-cleaner. He was being karmically punished for the crimes of his ancestors, Mom said, and, most dangerous of all, he knew it. He wanted to change his sad fate. Just like Adolf Hitler, Mom told me, who was also on the rise in the 1930s.

"It was the age of the Antichrist," she whispered.

She told me how John got drunk and "finally grew some balls." He bought a gun from a man at his local bar. Mom furtively mimed the transaction, eyes darting around the kitchen. Then, triumphantly, she made a pistol out of her hand and raised it in the air.

With his gun, she said, John marched back to the dairy farm, where the farmer and his family were sleeping. He knocked down the door—Mom roundhoused an imaginary door and leapt through it like Emma Peel, with her finger-gun raised. The farmer heard the commotion and threw on the lights, rushing down with a baseball bat, his lovely family cowering behind him. Still making a gun of her hand, Mom suddenly turned serious and stared at me levelly, saying: "But that poor bastard brought a stick to a gunfight."

John turned the gun on the farmer. Mom screamed, aiming her finger gun: "Get down on the floor!"

The farmer complied, huddling with his family in a corner of the living room, begging for his life. John sneered a half-smile, looking down on the boss-man. He hocked up some spit and let it fly in the farmer's face. Mom fake-spat into my hair and grinned. Then John stepped toward the farmer's daughter. Mom crouched down to meet my eyes with hers.

"She was young. Very young. Maybe your age. Blonde like you are. Beautiful," she said as she ran a hand through my hair. "John took her. Right there in front of the family. Do you know what I mean when I say he took her?"

I shook my head. She smiled sadly.

"He pulled her out of the huddle. They were all so scared. They didn't scream or fight. John had his gun."

She made a gun again with her hand and waved it in my face.

"She was wearing pajamas . . . kind of like these."

Mom plucked at my silky red pajama top.

"He ripped them off and then he made her get on all fours like a little piggy and did a dirty thing to her with his penis. His gaze held the farmer's eyes the entire time."

Mom stared hard into my wide eyes, narrowing her own. Then she stood up.

"When he was done, he demanded the combination to the safe. The farmer told him. He'd been broken. His daughter was dead now, by the way, because that's what happens when you have sex with a woman. Inside that safe was the secret recipe for the ice cream."

John laughed triumphantly, fluttering the ice cream recipe at the farmer and his family, and then he fled. He ran into the night, stole a car, and drove all the way to DC—as Mom said, "that's where the gas ran out." In Silver Spring he made a shady deal with an underworld kingpin, a character sadly lacking description in Mom's story, and never mentioned again in future versions of it. Using the recipes as collateral ("because they were going to change the way ice cream was made"), John got a ninety-nine year lease on 8101 Georgia Avenue, the building that would become the Silver Spring store.

"The rest is history," Mom said, waving an arm to take in our kitchen.

She continued with her tale of the New Jersey farmer and his innocent, hard-working family who believed in their employees, God, America, and all that was right. The day after the incident, with their daughter dead, and with the secret recipe stolen, it all started to unravel. They lost their dairy farm, they lost their ice cream business, and then they lost their house. They went from millionaires to paupers just like that. Mom snapped her fingers.

"They had owned the farm since Revolutionary times," she said. "This was their life, their legacy. And it had been stolen by a mean and cowardly man."

Most of the rest of the farmer's family then died. The mother killed herself, unable to live with the vision of her daughter's rape and death. She hanged herself in the basement.

"It took them weeks to find her body, and when they did, it was so rotted that the body had separated from the neck." Mom smiled, then hung her tongue out of the side of her mouth.

Another daughter got into drugs and ran away. They found her dead. She had put a shotgun in her mouth and blown her brains out.

The father vanished. One day, stricken by grief and anger, he walked into the forest and was never heard from again. Though Mom cautioned: "The people around that farm say you can still hear a man crying at night from somewhere deep in the woods . . ."

Perhaps I understood that all of this was a lie when I was a child, but I don't recall. There were so many details, and the story was told with such earnestness, that I felt numb, confused, and horrified. So I sat and listened, I kept silent, I never questioned her. It felt like a classic ghost story, a fiction, but that didn't stop me from being frightened. Which is probably why Mom added one more detail.

There was a son. A tall man, with brown hair. The last survivor of this family destroyed by John Gifford. This farmer's son was now hunting us. He was driven by a mad need for revenge— "just like Khan in the movie." All he lived for was to destroy John Gifford's family. This man was out there now, somewhere. He knew where we lived.

"We're the most famous people in DC," Mom said—though, she added, this was also why this man couldn't simply kill us.

"But he might snatch you," Mom said. "You're weak." She pinched my arm. "That's why you should never answer the door, or the phone, and always keep the curtains drawn in the house. That farmer's son, and his minions, are always out there, always looking for revenge.

"We all are paying," Mom continued, "for your grandfather's sins. You can't be a criminal and get off scot-free. God won't allow it."

The stories of New Jersey eventually ended, however, when a new enemy surfaced. This threat lived in the faraway state of Maine. Mom named them the Usurpers.

"They call themselves Gifford's Ice Cream, too," she said, "but they aren't Giffords. They've stolen our name. Next they'll steal our skin, and then we'll be dead and gone and they will rule in our image."

She told me that my father would stop them. She told me that he had set in motion plans to destroy these "skinwalkers." She described how the Giffords of Maine would be hunted down and murdered. I didn't ask—or want to know—the details. By that point I was so worn out with these threatening stories that I wanted only to play outside and not come home till dusk.

The Giffords of Maine, in reality, are an unrelated, coincidentally-named family who ran a dairy farm for decades and then graduated into making their own brand of high butterfat ice cream in the 1980s. For a very long time, they were isolated in Maine and New England and have only begun to branch out as of 2012. In the 1980s, compared to Gifford's of DC, they were hardly of consequence. They were like any other small ma and pop ice cream business, countless examples of which had started popping up with greater and greater frequency. But the name . . . they shared our name, and that made my mom crazy.

I don't ever remember my father expressing anger toward—or any emotion about, or even mentioning—the Giffords of Maine. I remember the fights, though. As always, they were one-sided— Mom screaming at meek and quiet Dad. She screamed about the skinwalkers, the Usurpers, the liars, the cheats, the danger to us all—the Giffords of Maine. I'd play with my Legos, or cup my ears to better hear the TV as the one-sided battles raged. My dad didn't even have to be present, it seemed.

"What are you going to do, Bob?" she hollered. "Nothing! Right? You coward! You . . . pussy! But you can do something, can't you? Yes! You will destroy them! That's right! You have to bring them down. You have to eliminate the threat!"

After several months, though, these arguments took a turn that piqued my interest. A plan was coming together, to which my dad agreed in soft tones. He would go to Maine and try the ice cream for himself. If it was bad, we would expose the Usurpers. If it was good, then we would put Mom's plans into action.

Dad was to hire men—"hard men, tough men"—to go up to Maine and disrupt the business. Mom laid out a campaign of terror against Gifford's of Maine. Our hired thugs would break into their manufacturing plant and put "mercury, glass, and semen" into the ice cream. Fights would be staged at all of their store outlets. A smear campaign would be conducted in the papers. And, finally, "after we got into their heads," she said, Dad's hired men would hunt down every Gifford's of Maine family member and, one by one, "in dark alleys, and when they least suspect it—BANG! BANG, BANG, BANG!"

In the breathless silence that followed this, Dad muttered: "Yes, Barb . . . yes, Barb . . ."

For several periods in 1983, Dad was absent. Maybe a few days here, a few weeks there. Nobody told me why he was gone or where he had gone. Appraising Mom's seething mood, and the steady increase in her drinking, I decided not to ask. Dad was the sort of man you never really missed, anyway.

On one occasion, after hanging up from a phone call that seemed like it must have been with Dad, Mom did drift into better spirits and cheerfully announced: "Your father is going to arrange an accident for the Usurpers."

I aped my dad's habit and only nodded, muttering an affirmative response.

VI

At Geppi's Comic World—when I finally got there, having survived the hoards of imaginary kidnappers on the Silver Spring streets—I upgraded my literary fare to the glossy, dystopian sci-fi stories in *Heavy Metal* and other various comics I now religiously followed. These were mostly tie-in comics from TV and movie series, like *G.I. Joe*, *Star Wars*, *Conan*, and *Transformers*. Geppi's had a small used book section, as well, which I plundered for cheap fantasy and sci-fi. The first fantasy book I remember reading was

Alan Garner's *Red Shift*. An ode to adolescent despair, it ends with a letter written in cipher that the reader has to decode from clues scattered throughout the book. The code is lifted almost intact from Lewis Carroll. I loved that touch.

For the most part, these early fantasy tastes rested in comfortable zones for an eight-year-old: dragons and sorcery. By then, my nose was always in a book. Books proved to be more reliable than TV. I had seen every rerun of my favorite sci-fi shows half a dozen times. With the exception of *Doctor Who*, my favorite shows had been short-lived and off the air for years. In the *Planet of the Apes* TV series, for example, the astronauts going through the same twelve adventures over and over wasn't providing escapism anymore. It was too repetitive. But books seemed infinite. Row after row of sci-fi and fantasy waited for me. At some point, it dawned on me that I would die before I ran out of reading material. In this, I found great comfort. There would always be a new book to explore.

The one book I always returned to, though, was one I carried around for years as something of a talisman. It sits prominently on my shelf today, the perfect book for the scion of Gifford's Ice Cream: *The Land Where the Ice Cream Grows*, a somewhat twisted children's book written by Anthony Burgess, of *A Clockwork Orange* fame, and illustrated by Fulvio Testa.

In it, three vaguely Victorian men are trying to enjoy dinner at a restaurant when an addled old man at the next table starts ranting at the waiter: "Ice cream! I don't want to see ice cream ever again!"

Curious, our three heroes lean over to ask the old man why he doesn't like ice cream. How is that possible? Everyone likes ice cream.

The man asks if they know where ice cream comes from. He then tells them about the Land Where the Ice Cream Grows. Our three heroes say they must journey to this land, and the old man warily tells them that they'll need a blimp if they want to see it for themselves. That's no problem at all. They happen to have a blimp.

The three explorers—bearded, in parkas, and wearing glacier glasses—set off in their airship. The book becomes a journal, spanning the course of seven days—Munchday, Chewsday, Wethersday, Thawsday, Fryday, Shatterday, and Sundae. During that week, the three journey through forests and mountains made of ice cream and cones and cross raging rivers of hot fudge. They battle beasts who feed on sorbet, barely survive a whipped-cream volcano, and finally race back to their blimp, battered and exhausted.

As they head back to civilization, they break into the last of their supplies and there's nothing but ice cream left. One of the men says: "I never want to see ice cream again as long as I live. A terrible thing, ice cream. The most terrible thing in the world."

On the last page, confusingly, we discover that the entire book is a story that three boys have been making up while they pig out on ice cream at an ice cream parlor, basing it on a map and a toy blimp behind the counter. It's a very flawed, abrupt ending, and even Burgess later said that the book was "just a fucking farrago."

I ignored the ending. It was the exploration and adventure in the middle that I read over and over again. And that single line—"A terrible thing, ice cream."

When Dad stopped coming home, I barely even noticed. Sometime around Christmas of 1983, without explanation, he started living at the Silver Spring store. I was nine. When I asked if he was coming home, Mom would shrug or tell me "I don't know." She camped out in front of the TV with cases of Co-ors, steadily drinking through them and chain-smoking New-ports, and if I asked too many questions about Dad, she started screaming at me about how disrespectful I was. So I kept quiet. Another month passed. Then, one night early in the new year, I was washing my Legos, piece by piece—a nervous habit I had picked up—and was preparing to rebuild a miniature city large enough to fill a pool table when Mom appeared and said: "Come with me."

We drove to the Silver Spring store. It was around ten o'clock, after it had closed. The parking lot and the building were dark.

Mom left me in the car and slipped through one of the side entrances, emerging half an hour later. On the drive home, she said: "I'm going to ask you to keep a secret. Your father is going to be staying at the Plant. He has lots of work to do. You and I are going to help him. But you can't tell anyone about what we're doing—never ever. If anyone finds out, I'll know it was you who blabbed. I'll know it was you who betrayed us."

I nodded.

"Swear it."

I swore.

"Swear it on Christ. If anyone finds out, the ghosts in the basement will get you."

Shivering at the thought of the dark basement at Bexhill Drive, I swore on Christ. Whatever lurked there was more threatening than his wrath, especially given that all I really understood of the Christian deity was that he and my mom seemed to be on familiar terms. But then Mom and Dad were also students of anarchists and nonconformists—Mom had a particular fascination with Charles Manson, once telling me that he was "some poor drugged-out boy set up by the government."

On the next day, a cold, wintry Saturday, we started an art project. Mom got several pieces of lined paper and large index cards, and then she put me to work. We brewed coffee, then soaked the cards and paper in it, and then distressed a small percentage with folds, tears, and creases. Next, the paper was placed in the oven to cook. When it came out, it looked very old, and we set everything out to dry on the dining room table.

I went back to the second book in Saberhagen's Book of Swords trilogy while Mom retreated to her room for half an hour or so. When she reemerged, craft day continued. Mom pulled out a legal pad covered in my father's lunatic scrawl and, using that as a reference, copied out recipes onto the aged cards. Her conspiracy-book library had grown, and she prided herself on her forgery techniques, doodling for hours in different scripts and showing me the results. For the cards, she was using a familiar script—John Gifford's handwriting.

I stood by and watched for what felt like hours. When she was done, she tossed all of the paper into a folder, slammed it shut, and said: "Next task!"

She led me into the basement, and I was worried for a moment that she might lock me up down there. I was surprised to find instead that an area near the staircase had been cleared, a low table and a chair set up and waiting. On the table sat a soup can with its label removed and, next to it, a tiny gem hammer. Mom sat on the steps, overlooking this strange workspace, lit a cigarette, and hefted a large brown paper bag.

"Dump it out." She pointed with her cigarette, and I upended the bag. Dozens of thermometers spilled out, skittering across the table. Mom said: "This is a game. Break the thermometers, carefully, into the cans. Try not to touch the stuff that comes out. That's called mercury."

I took each thermometer and held it against the inside of the can, supporting the outside of the can with the same hand, and used the gem hammer to lightly break them up. This would take forever. But I didn't complain. Mom was behind me, and I could feel her rage, her intense presence. I cut myself on the third thermometer, and Mom stalked upstairs and returned with a pair of child-sized gardening gloves.

I got a history lesson on mercury as I smashed thermometer after thermometer into the soup can. Mom told me how archeologists found mercury in ancient tombs, how alchemists used it to try and make gold. She presented these wild, rolling stories using the language from my fantasy novels, talking about emperors, ancient scientists, Atlantis, Lemuria, alien visitors, and the lost civilizations of pre-history.

When I had smashed every single thermometer, she clapped her hands and said, "All done!" and then snapped a piece of plastic wrap, secured by a rubber band, over the can.

Every night, a bag of thermometers, a soup can full of shattered glass. At the end of the week, we would take multiple soup cans to the Plant. She left me in the car when she went in to visit my father. Sometimes I'd see a light come on in one of the upstairs offices, but I only ever saw the red glow of one cigarette. When Mom returned, she'd be empty-handed.

One night she asked: "Remember how I told you about mercury? How dangerous it is?"

I nodded.

"Good, good. You must remember never to eat ice cream from our stores ever again."

Once again, she swore me to secrecy in the name of Jesus, and she told me that each week's delivery was going into the base mix, the core ingredient for all of the ice cream and most of the candy, including the caramel in my beloved turtles.

At home, if we wanted ice cream, Mom now bought Breyers.

When I was in the store during business hours, I would watch the people eating their sundaes, devouring the candy, cheerfully buying the wildly popular ice cream logs in the shape of whatever the season demanded—pumpkins, turkeys, Easter bunnies . . .

Mom had told me what mercury does. She said that it rotted out organs and made the brain die. I was very nervous and worried about the people eating the ice cream. I have no conclusive evidence that Mom ever tainted the ice cream. Perhaps this was just another of her many cruel pranks? Everyone was always so happy at Gifford's, and when, as a nine-year-old, I watched the children and their families, I wondered: why would my parents want to hurt these people?

Dad started missing holidays in 1984. He missed my birthday that year, except for a phone call. He missed Christmas. And for about a year, we kept up the weekly thermometer shipments.

VII

When the end came, it came quietly. May 10, 1985, a Friday. My eleventh birthday. We hadn't been to the store in Silver Spring since early February. In fact, Mom never talked about Gifford's. With Dad absent, I drifted through my routine. I went to school, glad only to be away from home. I played in Rock Creek Park.

At about ten that Friday night I was in bed. There had been no birthday party or any other sort of celebration. I had come home from school, played with my Legos, taken a bath, and climbed into bed. My mother came into my room and flipped on the lights, standing in my doorway a moment until I fully woke. I stared at her, always unsure of the direction my life would take when she appeared like this.

"Come with me," she said.

I changed out of my pajamas, got dressed, and meekly followed her orders. I assumed we were going to the Plant, though I no longer held any curiosity about the orbits of my parents. I had stopped asking about Dad and did what I was told, hoping that whatever happened would only be a small interruption to my daydream fantasies.

We drove slowly through the dark streets of Kensington. When we turned towards Wheaton, I frowned.

"Where are we going?" I asked.

My mom shushed me.

We pulled into the parking lot of Jhoon Rhee Karate, a big, blocky building next to a Roy Rogers on busy Connecticut Avenue, about a mile from our house. The lot was poorly lit, and had only a few cars in it at that time. We parked, facing the Roy Rogers next door. Mom sat, smoking, not acknowledging me, watching the rearview mirror. I kept silent, obeying my survival rules—stay small, don't make eye contact. Ask no questions. Make no complaints. React only when told to react to something.

Eyes focused on the dashboard, I waited with her. Something was going to happen—I knew that much—and my imagination conjured countless dark possibilities. Mom saw something in the rearview and stabbed out her cigarette in the overflowing ashtray, then turned to me and said: "Okay, let's go."

We got out of the car and stood together by the tailgate, her hand roughly clasping my shoulder, nails biting into the flesh. Across the lot, my father fluidly moved through the shadows. He was wearing a Jhoon Rhee outfit, white with a brown belt, and held a gym bag in his hand. He wore a blue and yellow baseball cap—his "captain's cap" from our trips to Deep Creek Lake. Here, though, the hat made it look like he was in some sort of quirky disguise. I didn't see his car. He stopped in the shadows and didn't approach us. Mom pushed me forward and I walked over to him.

Even as I got very close, he didn't move to meet me. He stayed between two cars, immersed in the shadows, glancing around the lot. I approached slowly, looking back once at Mom, who had turned away to watch the street, lighting another cigarette with a flare of her red Bic.

I walked up to him, stopping next to a car's bumper, and he quickly knelt down on one knee, his hand reaching out to support himself on my shoulder. Once down, he took his hand away as if I were on fire and looked into my eyes. He said, matter-of-factly: "I'm going on a little trip to Charlottesville. I'll be back next Monday."

Mom had mentioned something like this, months before. She told me, shortly after Christmas, that Dad was scouting locations in Charlottesville, Virginia, and we would soon move down there. Gifford's was going to become a wholesale business, she said—"that means we sell to supermarkets and not to the fucking customers!" The wholesale warehouse was going to be in Charlottesville, and Mom and I had even taken a couple of weekends off to go house hunting down there.

Though the nature of this meeting in the parking lot felt sinister, I allowed myself to think, briefly, that everything might be okay. Dad had just been busy planning the new face of Gifford's. Dad was always busy. And moving was a big deal. So it made sense. He was going to Charlottesville and we'd follow. If Gifford's no longer had to deal with those "fucking customers," then maybe Mom and Dad would calm down and get along.

A wash of headlights briefly illuminated Dad, his white outfit flaring. He crab-walked a few steps deeper into the darkness and I felt his eyes turn back to me, searching. I peered through the darkness at him.

"Do you understand?" he asked.

I nodded, saying nothing, and then he stood, turned, and walked around the side of the building into the deeper shadows. My mom had silently come up behind me and she patted my shoulder. "Come on," she barked, tilting her head back towards the car.

We drove home without speaking of the encounter. Once back, Mom went into her room and slammed the door, leaving me to change back into my pajamas and return to bed.

That was the last time anyone saw or heard from Robert Gifford for fifteen years, at least as far as I would know. After he vanished, he left no trail, no records of his activities, no tax documents, no sign that he rented or bought property, no use of credit cards, no friends, no one who knew him. He vanished as completely as if he had simply been a figment of my imagination.

Along with my father, an estimated $2 million in cash also vanished, harvested from petty cash at all the Gifford's locations, embezzled from the employee pension and payroll accounts, and removed from the corporate and family bank accounts.

But I didn't know any of this when I woke up the next morning. For two weeks, everything was normal. I learned about the closure of the stores—and the bankruptcy—from the evening news, not from my family.

Then the sheriff came for our house. I didn't hear what the sheriff said to my mom, but she screamed at him incoherently and slammed the door in his face. After that, we were "under siege," as Mom said. She drew all of the curtains, unplugged all of the phones, and we weren't allowed to turn the lights on at night. When people knocked at the door, Mom would leap up from her seat, grab me, and we would hide behind the couch or in the windowless ground floor bathroom for intolerable periods of time. When people came to the windows and knocked on them, Mom had the same reaction. If we heard people outside walking around the property, we tiptoed and whispered like we were submariners evading destroyers.

We rarely left the house, and I missed a lot of school. Mom

would only tell me that "the bad people had finally come," mutter about how "everything has gone wrong," and then warn that "the bad people want to take the house away from us."

Nobody told me what was happening. The house was going up for auction, along with all of the stores, and potential buyers and people fascinated by the strange saga of Gifford's were coming to stare through the windows and mail slot, day and night. For two weeks this went on, and it was terrifying. I remember, one night, turning to one of the windows that looked out into the deep dark of our backyard. The window had that blank emptiness that windows get at night. Then, suddenly, a white face materialized out of the darkness, pressing against the glass and peering in at me. A horror movie trope come to life, and I screamed and ran upstairs only to run into Mom, who threw me down and shouted: "Keep. The. Lights. Off!"

The weeks passed like a fevered dream as we ate the last of the food in the house, as the power and the water cut off. Then Allen came. When he let himself through the front door, the first thing he said, shouting, was: "I saved your bacon . . . again!"

Without comment, Mom hauled two pre-packed suitcases out to his car. Allen took me by the hand and led me out, as well, locking the house behind him. And, like that, we had moved out.

CHAPTER TWO

INDIAN ROCK

I

Shortly before he'd left to live at the store, my father had done something that surprised me. Mom had been haranguing him for an hour, screaming behind the closed doors of the master bedroom on the second floor. I was downstairs turning up the TV volume by degrees, trying to drown her out as I worked my way through my Sunday morning sci-fi repeats.

Halfway through my umpteenth viewing of "Space Princess"—combining two completely unrelated episodes of *Space: 1999* from season two—Mom finished lashing Dad and he came slowly down the steps. I heard the bedroom door slam, and then Mom put on her Christian rock at top volume and began stomping on the floor. Almost time for me to leave the house, I thought.

We had the best backyard at Bexhill Drive. Well, it wasn't ours, but it was a public space big enough to feel like it belonged to us. Rock Creek Park stretches through DC and Maryland to cover some two thousand acres. One can walk from deep in the heart of DC out to the far suburbs and never leave the forest. For a boy who wanted to escape the smoke-filled confines of the Gifford house, it was the ultimate playground. This was where I planned to go that Sunday morning.

From the corner of my eye, I saw Dad standing at the base of the stairs, looking into the living room as I perched in front of the TV. Looking at me. I turned slowly and stared back at him.

"Where do you go?" he asked.

I wasn't sure how much to tell him. The park was wonderful, but it was also filthy and dangerous. Sewage polluted the creek, and people dumped their trash beyond the tree line. A transient subculture called the woods home. Right next to affluent Kensington, the trees sheltered semi-permanent structures and even full-on settlements. I ran through the woods and occasionally stumbled upon a driftwood-and-plastic cottage complete with chimney and welcome mat, or I found clearings that had been tilled and sown with crops. I always steered clear of these homeless settlements. There had been more than one rough encounter in the woods where, despite the roaring Beltway within sight through the trees and the rows of high priced homes only a few dozen feet away, I was in danger of becoming another face on a milk carton.

But the dangers didn't lessen my need to explore. I vanished into the woods as often as possible, year-round, rain or shine, lost in daydreams. The tangled woods were the only place where I could sink into fantasy without a TV or a book in front of me. Those woods were my Terabithia, my Narnia. In the winter, I would crunch through the snow and pretend I was at the Battle of the Bulge, or pursued by the White Witch, or just stand as the trees creaked and breathed around me.

In the summer, the dense underbrush could hide me, and I'd watch cars speed past on the Beltway, or deer pick their way carefully past me, or the occasional bum in a sheltered area cook lunch over a small fire, seemingly content with the pocket of rural life he'd discovered in the middle of a major metropolitan area.

About ten minutes into the woods from Kensington Parkway, there was a marsh where someone had laid planks between the dry islands to create a precarious walkway. The walkway was not obvious, and not intended to aid random passersby. Full of dead ends and hidden turns, I spent weeks teaching myself the best path from one end of the marsh to the other. It was a secret I shared only with whatever mysterious park-dweller had built it. In the middle of the marsh was the rusted, brown roof of a car. The first time I found it, I stepped onto it and balanced uncertainly, wondering if there were bodies entombed beneath my feet. Had this car careened off the Beltway one lonely night? Was this marsh, my playground, some drunk driver's tomb? Did his family miss him? Maybe they were happy he was gone, out of their lives. Forever forgotten in that narrow band of woods.

I never told anyone about the car. Even the mysterious plank-layer may not have known about it. The roof, barely visible, lay at the waterline. To get to it meant leaving the makeshift path and hopping along soggy tufts of grass. It meant getting wet, sinking into the mire. It was a little crazy, leaping over open water deep enough to swallow most of a car.

I loved the woods, and I loved the loneliness there. The homeless with their camouflaged lean-tos had the right idea. In the right spot, they could build a fire where no one from the Beltway or the nearby neighborhoods could see it. There was high ground when the creek flooded, and hidden verdant glades for those who grew subsistence crops. The homeless hunted and ate possum, raccoon, and deer. I found a small canoe and fishing equipment once, and the filthy, sewage-infested creek held a number of mid-sized catfish in the deeper pools. There were even ruins to explore. Old bridges, old wells, and old foundations. I found old stone houses that didn't need much more than a roof and a door to become habitable again. All of this in an area that was never much more than half a mile wide, bordered by the Beltway on one side and the suburbs on the other.

The lowlands of Kensington ended at the bottom of a steep hill that led up towards Forest Glen, about a mile or two from our house. In my pre-teen years, that was the natural boundary for my woodland wandering. There the weather had been quietly eating away at the rocks, leaving a crumbling cliff about thirty or forty feet high, with a treacherous path leading up its face.

On these "cliffs," I could sit above everyone. An anonymous shape in the tree line, I could look down on Jones Mill Road and watch the cars go by, or at the yuppies jogging on the bike path. Just beyond the trees, the Beltway roared, a shimmering monster eight lanes wide. I would watch for hours, counting cars, or laughing at people stuck in a traffic jam, or just staring into the sky and studying the clouds and the contrails.

"Where do you go?" my father repeated.

I blinked, shocked that he was addressing me directly. I almost turned around to see if there was someone else in the room.

"What?"

"Do you have a favorite place?"

"The cliffs!" I said.

"Cliffs?"

"By the Beltway. I climb up and like to look at the road."

"Across from the Beltway, right?"

I nodded.

He leaned against the wall. He looked very tired, and very sad. "The cliffs . . . wow."

I nodded again, not sure what direction the conversation was about to take. Part of me kept track of Mom's stomping as the music played. Mentally, I followed her progress through the room, counting down the minutes until the record ended. That part of me that constantly monitored her movements said it was time to get away. I also worried about Dad. What if she came down and found us talking like this? This was all very unusual.

Dad took a deep breath and sighed. "That's where Indian Rock used to be."

That got my attention. I asked him what Indian Rock was. He smiled sadly at me.

"It was a big rock, covered in petroglyphs—you know what those are?"

I did, thanks to Mom's amateur archeology bug. Dad continued: "I was the only one who knew what those petroglyphs said."

"What did they say?"

He replied with a brief history of the Indians who used to live here—the Chatterie. They were a noble tribe and, one day, they simply vanished. On Indian Rock, they'd left a final message, which said there was a cave somewhere around Rock Creek where they had left all of their treasures.

"You had to look carefully," he continued. "I searched and searched, but found nothing. I thought maybe there were other clues I was missing. I would spend days back there in the woods."

"Days?"

He nodded. "In the summer, I'd just camp out there for days and days."

There was nothing at the cliffs that matched his description of Indian Rock. I asked him where, exactly, the rock was. A pained look flashed across his face. He glanced at the ceiling and exhaled.

"They destroyed it. They blew it up in '56 when they made the Beltway."

Then he turned and stalked toward the basement, closing the door behind him, bound for a dark corner with his whiskey and cigarettes. Upstairs, the music ended. Within seconds, I had my shoes on and was out the door.

In the course of writing this book, I tracked down local historians who provided me with pictures of Indian Rock—a large wedge sitting beside Jones Mill Road that was, indeed, blasted clear in the 1950s to make room for the Beltway. It earned its name because it resembled the feathered Indian head on old coins. But it did not sport any petroglyphs. The Indian tribe Dad mentioned—the Chatterie—never existed.

II

Everything I knew as a child about the downfall of Robert Gifford and Gifford's Ice Cream I learned from the six o'clock news.

All Mom said was that we had been "exiled" to my grandfather Allen's house. She took over one of the guest bedrooms and I took over the other. We were separated by only a thin wall, yet I felt further away from her than ever. She closed and locked her door and spent all day in her room, using the back window as her entry and exit. She came out for dinner only occasionally and made a point of ignoring Allen.

We all watched the TV news, though. We watched the reporters stand in front of the Silver Spring store and talk about our lives. My grandmother sat in her favorite rocking chair, and my grandfather draped himself across the couch. I sat on the floor, and Mom sat ramrod straight in a chair at the back of the room, motionless, wearing reflective aviator sunglasses. She insisted that we videotape every single segment.

When the stories appeared on the TV, nobody reacted. I'd crane my head around hoping for an explanation, but every face was impassive. Mom would wait till the end of the segment and then call the studio and bark brutally at whoever answered: "If you want the real story, you'd better fucking talk to me!"

At this, my grandmother tutted and my grandfather blew a raspberry, but neither of them said anything else. Despite Mom's phone calls, no one talked to her. They talked to the last manager, Cal Headley, and to employees and customers. In one interview, Cal turned to the camera and said that he'd been "left holding the bag."

My grandfather nodded. "Poor Cal."

My mother laughed. "He's a traitor! Don't say 'poor Cal'!"

The news gave me a chance to ask questions. Is Dad really gone? What happened? Mom and my grandmother ignored me, and Allen would say only that we'd talk about it later. Within a few days, Gifford's was out of the TV news cycle anyway. Whatever happened was over.

But the news still fascinated me. So I would sneak the newspaper from the kitchen table and read about the ignoble fall of Gifford's Ice Cream. They said that Dad had vanished without a trace. They said that the stores had been sealed off by the police and that everything would be auctioned to pay my father's debts.

Both on TV and in the papers, there were shots of the crowded store at Bailey's Crossroads in Virginia, which looked like an apocalyptic free-for-all as people mobbed the counter for their last scoop of Gifford's Ice Cream. Man-on-the-street interviewees proudly waved menus and other nostalgia that they had snatched from the tables or ripped from the walls, looting the place while the last beleaguered employees scooped their way to the bottoms of the ice cream barrels. Someone ripped the "Gifford's" letters off of the outside wall of the store.

We lived with my grandparents through the rest of the spring and summer after my father disappeared. I kept busy in the yard with my grandparents' giant Newfoundland dogs. I didn't understand why we weren't going home. Nobody told me what was happening, and I still hadn't quite come to the realization that Dad was gone for good. Weeks and months of silence from him were nothing new, so I expected him to come swanning in at some point.

I spent a lot of time re-watching George Pal's 1960 adaptation of *The Time Machine*. From the safety of his machine, the misanthropic time traveller observes the changing world of his street, passively watching generations flit by, making snarky comments about the inhumanity of man as he does so. As I sat and watched the strange goings-on all around me, I could relate to that Victorian time traveler.

One night, several days after I last saw Dad, Mom told me to come with her for a drive. We went straight to the Silver Spring store and parked in the garage near the loading dock. After a few minutes, Allen's car pulled up next to us. He'd been following. In the back alley, by the loading area, an unmarked white truck was parked. The back doors to the store were wide open and two men stood waiting.

Mom grabbed a fully loaded grocery bag and told me to "stand guard." She skirted through the shadows and into the darkened womb of the store. Allen walked up, exchanged a few words with the men, and then the three of them also went inside.

In the car, I watched for a while, then started to doze off. It was early morning when I was woken by a bang. The men had started to move huge pieces of equipment out from the darkness and onto the truck. Freezers, mixers, display counters. Mom emerged with a hand truck that had three boxes on it, which she loaded into the back of our car along with the hand truck itself, before climbing into the driver's seat.

"All done!" she said, smiling.

The next morning, at my grandparent's house, I was surprised to see the cars out of the garage. When I went out to investigate, I found what looked like a makeshift ice cream store. The garage was large—large enough for two cars and my grandfather's workspace. The equipment from Gifford's lined all of the walls and formed a double-sided column down the middle, with just enough space on either end to walk through, completely blocking one of the two garage doors. Some of the equipment was piled on top of the rest, almost to the ceiling. Lighter, empty counters had been placed on top of heavy-duty freezers.

For months after this, Allen met with strangers in our driveway, shaking their hands, and accepting wads of money as, piece by piece, the equipment was hauled away. It was a cash-only bazaar. He stopped when he had only a few display cases and one freezer left. Shortly after that, Mom told me it was time to go back to Bexhill Drive.

Allen rarely let a moment pass without talking about the huge sacrifice he had made to pay off enough of Dad's debt to get us back into the Bexhill Drive house. He'd draw me aside and say: "We've done all this for you. Remember that."

Try as I might, though, I couldn't feel grateful. At my grandparent's house, Mom didn't rant or yell so much. She didn't spank me. She rarely even acknowledged me. I ate three home-cooked meals a day. My grandmother would laugh her happy laugh, always cherubic. The dogs let me hug them for hours. And the house was clean and free of smoke. Trading all of this for the hell of Bexhill Drive seemed like a punishment. But I never said anything. I cried instead. Now I want to go back in time and scream at my grandfather: "You're enabling the continuation of my nightmare!"

Bexhill Drive had been sealed up for months. As soon as we arrived, though, Mom stalked upstairs to her room, slammed the door, and I didn't see her for two days. The house was hot, stuffy, and smelled of stale nicotine and mildew. The fridge was full of rotting food. The freezer held gallon containers of melted, moldy Gifford's Ice Cream, which may have been contaminated with mercury, for all I knew. Without the meals my grandmother sent along, I would have gone hungry.

I turned on the TV and fiddled with the antenna. It was a Sunday afternoon and *Doctor Who* was on. A gothic episode, filmed in claustrophobic caves and tunnels, with nothing but dim lighting and dark backdrops dripping water. It seemed the perfect welcome back to Bexhill Drive.

But then everything changed, again. Mom took a secretarial position at the National Naval Medical Center in Bethesda, and her daily schedule soon mirrored Dad's old schedule. With my mother out of the house for ten or more hours each day, I became—gratefully, wonderfully—a latchkey kid. A quiet hour every morning after she left and before school, another few every evening after school and before she got home.

Once a week, my grandparents would come by to drop off bags of groceries, and my grandmother would show me how to cook and clean. Soon I was largely self-sufficient. Mom would rarely cook and, if she did, the meals were fraught with fighting and sniping. If our fights escalated, any dinner she was cooking might end up in the trash or hurtled across the room, aimed at my head. I quickly learned to cook and eat my dinner before she got home.

So I entered the sixth grade at my parochial school, St. Catherine Laboure, with one hell of a summer story—exile, a house almost lost, a father vanished. I shared none of it, though. I barely associated with my classmates, and I can't recall any of my teachers. Every day went by like this: I woke up, cooked breakfast, went to school, came home, cooked dinner, and hid from Mom until she passed out. It was a simple routine, designed simply to avoid as much harm as possible.

I signed up to be an altar boy on weekends because it gave me another way to escape Mom. I volunteered for every gig throughout the week, too, working six or seven morning masses. Mom said that I "had been called by God" and would become a priest. She was in love with the idea and seemed very happy with me for it. But just as quickly, she'd forget this happiness and say I was just like my dad, that I made the world so much harder for her to live in.

Becoming a priest sounded fine to me, though. I didn't have to believe the fables in the Bible to preach them. Becoming a priest would be all about embracing the anonymity of "Father

Andrew." My family name was still occasionally in the news, and people would still ask me: "Gifford . . . like Gifford's Ice Cream?"

But Father Andrew would have no last name. Father Andrew could travel anywhere on the church's dime. I could work in some rural village, or leave the country, and I would have no family but Jesus Christ, Mother Mary, and God. And in the modern era they generally kept their temper in check.

Hiding behind piety was easy. I let Mom take me to seminaries to talk about my new career choice, which thrilled her. In school, it was a natural excuse for my shyness. Indeed, I figured everything would be fine when I turned eighteen. I could go to seminary and never be Andrew Gifford again.

As time passed, only the occasional person asked about my last name. It seemed, just eighteen months after closing, that Gifford's Ice Cream was ancient history, even forgotten. And that was a good thing, as far as I was concerned. Without Dad as Mom's foil, though, life at home became more complicated. Nearing twelve, puberty weighed on me, and because I was then Mom's only target, I found my old survival techniques weren't working as well as they once had. More and more, Mom and I started to collide. Lacking my father's Zen temperament, and perhaps taking too much after her, my temper would flare, too.

The arguments themselves were strange, tangential rants. I began to understand why Dad had never responded to her. Mom's anger over a bad grade, or a broken bowl, would fluctuate dramatically as her rage ramped up. It often seemed like my presence wasn't even necessary. She'd switch topics in mid-scream, referring to things that hadn't happened, acting as if I had offered up replies or counter-arguments I had not.

Most of her rants ended with the accusation that I was in cahoots with my father and that we were both plotting against her. I looked so much like him, she said, that it was impossible we weren't the same person, here to destroy her.

She'd often scream about Allen, too—a battle that had raged since she was old enough to talk, no doubt. Mom had become convinced that her own father was the devil. The actual biblical devil. His soul, she told me, had been possessed and he was now an agent of evil. She would tell me the awful things he had done when she was a child—he beat her, he ruined her life, and now he was trying to steal me away. She told me that he was behind the fall of Gifford's, that he had driven Dad away. Allen, she said, had tried to steal Gifford's and usurp my legacy.

"The only way Bob could save Gifford's is by doing what he did!" she insisted, apparently forgetting that "Bob" had been "your fucking father" minutes before. "Bob saved the company for you, because Dad would have screwed all of us!"

But Mom's battle against Allen was also a distraction I welcomed. After she called him and screamed over the phone, she would seal herself in her room. Or she would share elaborate plans with me to exorcise the devil from him. She showed me prayers that she had written for this future rite, telling me that she would kidnap Allen and hold him somewhere where I could work my priestly magic on him.

"When you become a priest," she told me, "you can purify Dad. You can save him."

Then one day she drew me aside and told me that a bird had come to her. In a bizarre take on the sermon of St. Francis of Assisi, she said that this bird had preached to her. In fact, she said, this bird was Jesus Christ reborn.

"He never said he'd come back as a man," she reminded me. "He came back, though, and just to me. I will speak for him."

Each morning, she would go to the window in her study and call out "Jesu! Jesu!" and a bird would often come to the tree a couple of feet from the window ledge. She had me witness this, and I pretended to be awed by her ability to control the birds. But she was using seeds and suet to attract them. The sleight of hand was obvious.

She would pretend to have conversations with the bird, nodding and talking as if in answer to questions only she could hear. She'd then relay the news to me. Sometimes Jesu would have mundane messages—we should go on a pilgrimage to holy sites in Thurmont, Maryland, where the soon-to-be first American saint, Elizabeth Seton, had lived and died. Or maybe Jesu would simply praise my efforts in school—"Jesu is very proud of your A in Bible Studies."

Jesu had an ominous message every now and then. As puberty firmly took hold, Jesu told Mom to inform me that masturbation was evil. If I masturbated, I would become like Dad. Jesu told her to tell me that all sex with women, no matter the situation, was rape.

"It's a good thing you're becoming a priest," Mom said, "because otherwise you would be a rapist who would hurt every woman in your life."

She became increasingly fixated on St. Francis of Assisi, devouring history books and visiting all of the Franciscan monasteries within driving distance. Her obsession eventually focused on the singer John Michael Talbot who, like her, had converted from a Protestant faith to Catholicism, and who had, even better, become a Franciscan monk.

For hours every night, she would play his records and spin wildly in tight circles like a dervish. As her religious fervor grew, I felt the chasm between us widen even further. But I had no complaint. After discovering John Michael Talbot, she didn't yell and scream as much, and I was often left alone as she wrapped herself in a wall of music and dizzy dancing.

In the spring of 1986, I turned twelve—a big year for me. It was the year people started asking me what I wanted to be when I grew up. I stood by the claim that I wanted to be a priest. I lacked commitment to religion, though. I couldn't embrace the faith. Religion was for crazy people like Mom.

I started to write stories where God was exposed as secretly evil. Stories in which it was actually Satan who came to Earth in the guise of Jesus Christ. For a few short years he played the part, slowly building up the myth that is worshiped today. Mankind's misdirected faith, prayers, and devotion then gave Satan all the power he needed to take over. Where once we were an enlightened civilization, the world after this false Christ was one where libraries burned, where wars lay waste to the globe, where fathers left and mothers turned their rings around before spanking their children mercilessly.

It was probably not the sort of writing that would go over well in seminary school. But at that point, I planned still to toe the line. I'd say whatever I had to say if there was an easy escape. And the priesthood was both an escape and easy. The coordinator of altar boys, Father Kevin, drove a Mercedes. The priesthood was good to him. I wouldn't really have to work and yet I could still drive a luxury vehicle.

I have no doubt that I could have drifted through Catholic school and gone on to the priesthood. I was a quiet kid, a respectful kid, and there wasn't an ounce of overt rebellion in my body. Even when I wrote heretical stories, I kept them to myself. My teen years might have been perfect, I've often thought, if I could have stayed in Catholic school—and as long as John Michael Talbot pumped out a new record for Mom every year. It all started to become clear—Gifford's was dead, I would become a priest, and the world would forever ignore my family's past.

But then our school principal, Sister Anne, decided to excommunicate me.

III

On the very last day of sixth grade, our class took a field trip to Wheaton Regional Park—a sprawling collection of slides, jungle gyms, and other play areas, a nature trail along a man-made lake, and a very large and popular botanical garden area. We were given orders by my teacher not to go to the botanical gardens.

Most of the kids played on the playground equipment, and a few took the little kiddie train ride around the park with one of the chaperones. I sat moodily on the sidelines, watching my peers, idly flipping through a fantasy book, not really paying attention to the story. Occasionally I'd look up past the main play area to the deep woods and the path that I knew led down to the lake and the botanical gardens. People streamed up and down the path, laughing, enjoying a perfect early June day. I was falling prey to my greatest vice.

I wanted to explore.

I stood up and looked over at my assigned chaperone. She had her nose down in a romance novel and seemed unaware of the world, so I slipped away. I walked down the trail and explored the edges of the scummy lake. Not enough. The real treasure in my explorer's heart was the botanical gardens. On an earlier visit, I had been enthralled by the architecture, the greenhouses, and the exotic plants. So I followed the trail to the gardens and attached myself to a tour group.

The guide described the trees and flowers, the insects and animals, their relationships, and the life cycle of our world. These were things not taught to me in school. Or if they were taught, every lesson began or ended with the rider that God had created these things and only His grace allowed them to continue to exist. Flowers bloomed because Jesus had saved us. That's why they bloomed in the spring, around the time He was resurrected. He was behind every blossom. Animals were our servants, put here for us. All flora and fauna had been put here on Earth, by God, specifically for us. Everything had descended from the plants and creatures of Eden.

Mom backed all this up. The more manic she became about religion, the more she ignored her rockhound hobby. Her pale blue archaeologist's toolkit sat forgotten in the basement and became a home to spiders. Her tales of the Earth's dynamic past faded away into talk about St. Francis and Elizabeth Seton and biblical heroes.

Part of me was sad for her, especially at times like that day at Wheaton Regional as I stood rapt by the guide's talk. Mom had turned her back on her obvious passions and hobbies for what, in my mind, was clearly hokum cooked up by madmen. Even as a shut-in, sheltered child, I could clearly see that the Bible was hardly better than a Hardy Boys adventure, and barely made sense if you read more than a paragraph. I'd seen lousy z-grade sci-fi on Sunday mornings that had clearer continuity and character motivations.

The guide at the botanical gardens lived in another world, one with a much more logical cycle, one that didn't really need us. His world wasn't created by Monty Python's version of God floating around on a cloud. We were at a fallen tree, and the guide was pointing out moss and fungus on the gnarled trunk when he suddenly fell silent, his eyes focusing on something over my shoulder. I spun around just as two Park Police officers closed in on me. One grabbed me by the arm while the other crouched down and looked into my face.

"Are you Andrew Gifford?"

Oh my God, I thought. The farmer's son from New Jersey had finally come for me! It was happening. Mom and Dad had been right all along about John Gifford's long-ago transgressions and his brutal rape and torture of that ruined ice-cream family. I panicked and started screaming and fighting against the iron hands holding my upper arms. The cop picked me up and threw me over his shoulder like a sack, turning back towards the path. I looked up at the tour group staring after me and pleaded for help.

"They're not cops!" I screamed. "They're kidnapping me! They're going to rape me!"

The crowd and the guide watched with wide eyes until we were out of sight. I imagined that it was all over for me as the cop carried me past the lake, up along the trail. I was going to be raped and murdered by the enemies of our family. I'd never be seen again, and nobody was stepping up to save me, no matter how loudly I screamed for help at everyone we passed. The cop cursed a few times and his partner rapped me lightly on the head.

"Shut it," he growled.

They brought me back to a cluster of teachers and nuns, all anxiously talking to other cops. My handler set me down and pushed me roughly toward my teacher. She caught me by the arms, her nails digging in.

"Where were you?" she hissed. "We've been searching for hours!"

Maybe I'd been gone for one. But back at St. Catherine's, I sat across from the principal, the feared Sister Anne, eyes down. Sister Anne was a diminutive woman in her late forties. She had a reputation for harshness, though it was rare that our paths crossed. Despite my otherwise clean record, my punishment for "disobeying orders" was extreme and delivered immediately after dressing me down for my actions at Wheaton Regional. Mom had not been called, so alone I sat and accepted my punishment. The following day was the first day of summer vacation.

"But," Sister Anne said, "you are staying in school."

For the first two weeks of summer vacation, I was to show up as if it were a normal school day. But instead of classes, I'd spend each day cleaning the walls of the school with a toothbrush. Sister Anne wrote down the details of my crime and punishment and sent me home.

When Mom read the note, she agreed with it whole-heartedly, and broke her own protocol with a phone call to my grandparents—the devil and his slave. Allen apparently picked up the phone because she screamed: "Mom! Give me Mom!"

He must have complied without comment, handing the phone over, and I listened to Mom's staccato, emotionless review of the incident: "Andrew's been bad. Real bad. Big problem at school. They punished him, and he has to go to two weeks of extra classes." She paused over this lie. "Yes, I know. Like summer school."

Another pause, then Mom ramped up instantly from robotic to angry, shouting that she was my mother, she was in charge, and my grandmother would do as she was told. Then she slammed the phone down.

I had to be escorted to "summer school," and that didn't work with Mom's schedule, so it was up to my grandparents to get me there and home again. My grandmother apparently relented to Mom, because she picked me up and drove me to school that first day, largely keeping her silence. She had packed a lunch for me. As I had been told to do by Mom, I brought all of my schoolbooks and wore my uniform.

Sister Anne was waiting for me at the doors to the school. She waved to my grandmother with one hand while roughly pushing me inside with the other, and then she waited and watched as my grandmother's car cruised out of the parking lot. Spinning around, she pointed towards the wall by the bathrooms, where a large bucket full of soapy water sat.

"Pick that up."

I needed both hands to do so. Then she put a toothbrush in my uniform shirt pocket.

"Start in C wing," she said, turning and stomping away.

From 7:50 a.m. to 2:00 p.m., with only a half hour for lunch and no other breaks, I scrubbed the walls with the toothbrush. When I needed to go to the bathroom, I had to ask permission and Sister Anne would stand behind me and watch as I urinated, escorting me back to the soapy bucket. I started on the walls at floor level and, with the help of precariously balanced chairs and tables, got up to the ceiling. Sister Anne would stomp down the hall every forty-five minutes or so, inspect my work, point out missed spots, and tell me to keep working. At two in the afternoon, she told me to clean up and sit in a classroom with my books out. My grandmother would arrive at around two-fifteen, and Sister Anne made me wave at her through the windows before sending me out to the car.

The next day was the same. On the third day, though, my grandmother showed up an hour early. Her intention, she told me later, was to tell Sister Anne that enough was enough. Three days of summer vacation lost was enough punishment for any young boy, and two weeks was excessive.

I was scrubbing away, coming to the junction of the main hallway, which stretched far down to the language rooms and all the way back up past Sister Anne's office. If the little offshoot had taken three days, I dreaded to think of the time it would take to scrub the walls of the main hallway. Already, my toothbrush was splayed and brown.

I heard heavy footsteps. They came to an abrupt stop at the mouth of the hallway, and I looked up, expecting to see the sister. Instead, it was my grandmother, staring at me in open-mouthed horror.

I was on all fours, scrubbing at the grouting where the floor met the wall, the bucket beside me. My grandmother blinked, stunned. I stared back forlornly. Then she hauled me to my feet. I started shaking, meeting her wide eyes. Her mouth was working, but no sound came out. I thought she was having some sort of heart attack. The long moment of silence between us was horrifying.

Finally, she said: "You do not do work like this."

She pulled me into the main hall and pushed me towards the doors to the schoolyard.

"Go wait in the car," she said.

She was angry, and this was something I had never seen in her—and would never see again—in my life. I marched out to her car and climbed in, afraid to look back. The June sun was beating down, cooking me slowly. The electric windows had me trapped, but the rear passenger window was cracked, about three fingers wide, so I crawled into the back and sat beneath the thin breeze that crept in through the slit.

Twenty minutes passed with no sign of my grandmother. Finally, I saw the blue-and-white polyester swirl of Sister Anne, stomping through the doors, her habit flowing out dramatically behind her. She stormed up to the car and tried to open the door, but I locked it just in time. She pounded her fist against the glass, glaring at me, and then she crammed her mouth to the window, causing me to recoil across the seat and hug myself.

"You will never come back to this school," she said, her lips pressed through the crack. "You will never be allowed in another school in this county. You will never go to church here again. You are excommunicated!"

She stepped back, staring at me with hard eyes, and then she slammed her open palm against the window with as much force as she could muster before spinning around and stomping back into the school. A couple of minutes later my grandmother came out. She opened the driver-side door and looked inside at me curiously.

"Did she come out here and yell at you?" she asked.

I nodded. My grandmother's eyes narrowed, and she looked up toward the school. I saw her hand tense, white-knuckled, on the door. She closed her eyes, exhaled, apparently thought better of whatever was brewing in her mind, and got into the car. As we left the school parking lot, she said: "It's going to be okay now."

Sister Anne was true to her word. I was barred from parochial school in Montgomery County, and Allen hastily pulled some strings to make sure I was clear to begin seventh grade in public school, at Westland Junior High. Mom seemed strangely unmoved by all of this, accepting it with a shrug. She was upset, however, that my altar boy boss, Father Kevin, effectively fired me, calling Mom to deliver the news that I was barred from mass.

The following Sunday, defiantly, we went to mass as usual. When we approached the main doors, though, the ushers stopped us. They apologized profusely, and looked pained, but they said I could not enter the church.

"It's impossible for you to stop him from worshipping," Mom shouted. "This is America, and we have freedom of religion!"

I was allowed, she said, to walk into any church in the country, "by the laws of God and Man!" The ushers stepped back, but didn't budge. They repeated their orders. Mom protested half-heartedly for another few minutes, and then she shrugged and told me to sit on the curb and wait for her.

The ushers watched me carefully, and, after mass had begun, one was posted outside the door to keep an eye on me for the entire hour. When I got up to walk around the church, he followed a few paces behind, never losing sight of me. I made a game of it, trying to lead him away from the church, but that didn't work. As soon as I was a few yards from the curb he'd stop and watch.

As I sat and stared back at that usher, I had my first truly focused, unclouded feelings towards the world: I was angry. I watched the usher and wished that I could burn him through with my eyes. I imagined him mangled in a car crash, or falling in the shower and cracking his head open, brains leaking out, undiscovered for days. For the next four Sundays, Mom tried to defy the "excommunication," bringing me to mass and going through the same routine. Each time, I remained barred and spent the hour sitting under a tree, staring hatefully at the usher.

At one point, as I sat outside the church, Father Kevin came and sat down next to me. He asked why I had stopped being an altar boy and, confused, I told him that I thought he had called Mom and "fired" me. He seemed confused as well, and he asked me for the whole story, which I told him in a blurting, stammering rush. He fell into silence, scrunching his face up, and then he patted me on the shoulder. Later, I saw him in an animated conversation with Mom. I couldn't hear them, but my status didn't change.

Soon enough I was left to my own devices at home on Sundays as Mom went to mass. After several months, Mom told me: "Grandmommie really let Sister Anne have it. Anne said that she was afraid for her life."

Mom took a long draw on her Newport and went silent for a bit.

"You know what's happened to Grandmommie, right?" she said.

I shook my head. Mom shook her head, too, and said sadly: "It's Satan. He's in her heart now. He's taken her. I tried so hard to save her but she's gone now. She's dead. Replaced by a changeling."

In 2014, days before he died, Allen told me that he had been paying for my tuition at St. Catherine's. But early in my final semester, he told Mom he was going to stop paying, and insisted I be sent to public school. His version of the events clearly implied that much of the "excommunication" was staged. Yes, I broke the rules. Yes, there was a conflict between Anne and my grandmother about the punishment. And yes, Anne overstepped when she stormed out and yelled at me. But she didn't actually have the power to block me from going to church. In fact, Allen said, the church had no idea. There was probably nobody on the other end of that alleged call from Father Kevin. He told me how Mom had announced her plan to my grandmother: if I was being bounced to public school, then "it would happen in style."

Had she forced the ushers to persist in this charade? Why would they go along with such a crazy plan? I still find it mystifying.

I spent the summer of 1986 enjoying my freedom while Mom was away at work. Those long, peaceful days were lost to exploration in Rock Creek Park and to playing with my Lego sets. I can describe in detail the various sets that I made, spread across the Town, Space, and Castle systems. Soaring spaceships, imposing castles, and all of the buildings and storefronts needed to assemble a replica of Main Street, USA (or Denmark, I suppose)—an airport rising in the distance, the bus station at the other end of town, and streets full of cars and trucks. I began writing a Lego-based novel—*Where the Sun Shines Cold*—which ended the summer as a 450-page space opera.

Today, I could more easily draw you a map of the Lego town I made than I could tell you what my father's voice sounded like or what my mother's face looked like.

On the finer days, I would race around in the woods, playing out live-action versions of Lego battles, chattering to myself, and scribbling down notes as ideas for the novel occurred to me. I always seemed to end up at the cliffs across from the Beltway, where Indian Rock used to be—a spot that had now comforted two generations of Gifford boys.

In the woods, sorting through whatever trash I found, I collected wallets discarded by thieves and pretended I was the people in the driver's license photos. I found my first pornography—a cache of *Hustler* magazines. I hoarded them in the shelter of an old bridge, poring over the unfamiliar shapes of the naked women. I lost the magazines to a flood and was heartbroken. My first girlfriends had been claimed by the arbitrary waters of Rock Creek.

I found money. My biggest haul was a handful of grubby twenty-dollar bills that I carefully washed and used to buy food. Mom seemed to be living solely on beer and cigarettes, and while my grandparents still brought a weekly grocery supply, there was no allowance. So any money on the side was welcome. Then summer came to an end, and I set out for a very different first day of school.

IV

From the very beginning of my first day of seventh grade—from the politics of the bus stop to the sophisticated stratification of cliques—everything about public school was alien. Without stalking nuns as police, the school seemed like a zoo where the animals had taken over. I was overwhelmed, jostled from all sides in the teeming hallways, and stumbled blindly from class to class, afraid to even ask for directions or help.

Math class was a shock. The teacher began writing in what appeared to be an alien language, the blackboard filling with strange figures. At St. Catherine's, I had never seen decimals, had never been told something like algebra even existed. Sixth grade, at St. Catherine's, had never advanced beyond multiplication tables. I was below remedial. A stranger fallen from the sky, meekly asking for help from a teacher who simply couldn't believe that I had never been taught fractions.

Science class was equally eye-opening. The concept of evolution was laid out in front of me for the first time, a picture of ape progressing into man. Chemistry and the other sciences were well beyond me, as alien as the never-before-seen algebra. I had learned nothing in Catholic school that could be applied to the real world, and so junior high became a monumental struggle.

I received very little help at home. Mom returned from work to drink case after case of Coors, camped out in her room or in front of the TV, and discussions with her usually ended in arguments. Allen and my grandmother were not welcome. I had no other family close by. My aunt and my uncle—my mother's siblings—were on the other side of the country and had only visited us a couple of times when I was a child. My innate wanderlust demanded that we travel, but when I asked Mom if there were plans to visit distant family, she shook her head. My aunt, she said, was "a ditz and a slut." My uncle was "a pussy" or a "pompous, arrogant asshole." He had published a book to massive critical acclaim, and would send us clippings and letters talking about his literary adventures. Mom read each one to me in a mocking voice, providing commentary on what a terrible, annoying person he was.

Allen's clandestine grocery deliveries usually included some minor tutoring in math and science to help me through junior high. With their gifts of food, surreptitious emotional support, and help with my schooling, my grandparents deserve the credit for the fact that I pulled through seventh grade. Allen insisted that I would never be held back a year—a real threat issued by the school administration. That's for "retards," he said.

"You're not retarded," he assured me. "Just uneducated."

Mom seemed not to care. "You probably are a little retarded." She shrugged. "After all, your father was."

But I squeaked through. Fall of 1987 saw me move on to eighth grade. I still hadn't mastered math and science, but public school forced some socialization on me. I had made friends. I had established myself. I eked by on the coursework with a C average, learning just about everything—including many aspects of English and history—for the first time.

At school, we had a free period and lunch, and I was exempt from gym due to an injury back in seventh grade, when I'd shattered my elbow while goofing around on a trampoline. With all this extra time, I averaged two hours a day in the school library educating myself. I started to fall in love with history. Perhaps I embraced it as another sort of escapism.

I read Herodotus's history of the Greco-Persian wars and Suetonius's biographies of early Roman rulers. I read about Caesar sweeping across Gaul and then crossing the Rubicon and facing his vengeful and murderous peers. It was gripping stuff.

For a woman who lived in a house full of books, Mom's reaction to my new studiousness was bizarre. Whenever she caught me reading, she would rip the book away and hide it somewhere. She'd take the books to her room or into the basement, and I would have to ferret them out during my latchkey hours. She told some of her friends that I never read, that I was barely literate. She played up my academic problems to my grandparents. Though it was clear that she was sabotaging me, I couldn't figure out why.

I'm still not sure. But trying to stand up to her then would have been suicidal.

She went so far as to hire a tutor for reading and writing. The tutor was surprised when I read flawlessly, with only a hint of my childhood stutter. We talked happily about the novels I'd written featuring my Lego fantasyland, and I shared a first chapter with her.

The tutor tried to tell my mom that there was no problem, but Mom insisted that she come once a week and sit with me at the dining room table. So she'd set her remedial reading books aside, and we would talk about ancient Rome and my Legos and *Doctor Who* and the final season of *Magnum PI*. I don't remember my tutor's name, but I remember how fun it was to have an adult sit and listen to me for an hour, even if she was being paid to do so. Listening is pretty much all she did when I veered into pop culture, though she had some instructional notes about ancient Rome that piqued my interest.

Without the common bond of Catholicism, Mom and I grew more distant than ever. I figured if the Catholic Church didn't want me, then I didn't want it. So when she wasn't dancing to John Michael Talbot albums in her room, Mom sought me out and screamed about how I was as evil as my father. She told me that when Dad had lived at the store, he'd been sleeping with whores.

"Every night," she said, "he was fucking three, four different women. Using his penis—like all men—to hurt them!"

She told me graphic tales of his rendezvous, painting grim pictures of Silver Spring alleyways, all apparently full of 1880s-style London prostitutes. She said that he had killed several hookers and hidden the bodies in the basement of the store. Dad stalked through Silver Spring and preyed upon these poor girls. I recognized in her description elements of the murder scenes in the movie *Time After Time*, where David Warner delivers an intimate and compelling performance as Dr. Stevenson—a.k.a. Jack the Ripper. Mom watched the movie several times every weekend. If Dad wasn't killing the hookers, she said, then he would bring them back to the store and, Mom told me: "They would help him collect his semen throughout the night—every night—and he would mix it into the ice cream."

Such a scenario actually seemed less horrific to me than mercury and crushed glass. I still felt guilty about my part in whatever had happened, and I imagined that people were sick, or had their lives shortened, because of me. I barely reacted when Mom told me about the semen, and she took this to be a sign of sickness in me. Another chance to say I was just like my father: "Unemotional, impassive . . . like a fucking killer rapist monster."

But despite her never-ending ravings, Mom was flagging, losing the sharp edge of rage, becoming unfocused. Sometimes she'd seem heavily sedated and dreamy, sometimes she'd chatter to herself and have entire conversations with unseen people. So far in this narrative, I've tried to present her as she appeared to me: inexplicable, unknowable, a force of nature without explanation. But of course no one acts like my mother did without cause. I now believe that she had a serious drug problem. Throughout the day, she consumed two full bottles of Excedrin, and constantly popped pills from little baggies.

I've spoken with other individuals who have alleged that Mom was involved in a mini drug cartel that stemmed out of her work at the Bethesda Naval Hospital, but there's no other evidence to back this up. I didn't care—and I don't care now—because the upshot of her alleged drug use was that my life was easier. Her bouts of rage quickly petered out, as if she'd finally exhausted herself.

Meanwhile, I struggled with my own blossoming rage. The only time I've ever thrown a punch occurred towards the end of eighth grade. I was in the library at school and a seventh grader was picking on me, getting in my face and making fun of my stutter. When I snapped, my reaction was swift and unforgiving. Years and years of being bullied by Mom built up in my right hand. I didn't knock him down, but his nose exploded in a wash of blood.

For a few long heartbeats, everyone in the library froze. With a casual calm I watched the bully bleed, until security came and dragged me down the hallway to the principal's office.

An hour later, the seventh grader had been cleaned up with no real damage done, and Mom had arrived along with his parents.

She seemed cool and collected. There was no wild screaming or yelling. She and I sat at one end of a long conference table, while the principal, the vice principal, the security guard, the seventh grader, two witnesses, and the seventh grader's parents all clustered at the opposite end. Mom wore her reflective aviator sunglasses throughout the meeting.

The seventh grader told his side of the story, weeping, sobbing, his tiny voice barely audible. He painted me as the bully. I told my side of the story, saying that he was picking on me. But I was bigger, older, and more intimidating. I lost.

The principal said that I would be suspended for two weeks unless I apologized. Mom, who had remained quiet and impassive the whole time, finally spoke. In a cold, hard voice, she said: "He's not fucking apologizing."

We all looked at her blankly. She shrugged.

"Boys will be boys. This one"—she tilted her head down the table towards the seventh grader—"has just been taught an important lesson. This one"—she tilted her head to me—"has helped correct him. It won't happen again."

Then she smiled, her lips smacking as they parted. Suddenly, the shuddering anger returned to her voice, and she leaned forward, her sunglasses reflecting the appalled faces at the other end of the table as she said: "There will be no fucking apology, and there will be no fucking suspension."

After a few moments, her eyebrows shot up and she raised her hands, palms up.

"Have I been clear?"

The principal stumbled over her reply—a stammered "yes, ma'am"—while the seventh grader's parents simply looked as if they'd gazed into the open pit to hell.

For me, it felt like sweet, clean vengeance against Sister Anne and my expulsion from St. Catherine's. Mom laughed as we drove home, aping the reactions of the other side, and she even hugged me before I went to bed and told me I'd done a good job. She said: "You should fucking murder anyone who picks on you again. This is what I want to see from you."

But I knew that I would never throw a punch in anger again. I would find other outlets for my rage.

Life at Bexhill Drive returned to a manageable routine, perhaps because Mom began to self-medicate a bit more aggressively. Allen asked me to spy on her and report her habits, and to steal samples of the pills she was taking for analysis.

I don't know what he found out, but whatever she was taking, it was helping. Mom spent all of her spare time locked in her room, John Michael Talbot at full volume, drinking and popping pills. I kept up my self-tutoring so that I could keep up in school and, when the weather was nice, wandered around the woods. My grandparents delivered groceries and fell into fights picked by Mom.

Allen was paying the property taxes, and the limits of his schoolteacher salary became obvious as the big house in Kensington began to fall into disrepair. When the gutters collapsed, they weren't replaced. A fallen tree lay across the yard for a month. Windows cracked and broke and went unrepaired, with Ziploc bags or moldy cardboard taking the place of the missing panes. Mom's toilet backed up, so she simply abandoned the master bathroom and used mine instead. The filth festered in her toilet until the stink filled the entire second floor.

Many people I've talked to say that children don't know any better than the lives they're given, and abused children assume the madness is normal. I feel fortunate that this never happened to me. Though our old life when Dad was around was nothing to write home about, it still served as a measure of what life *could* be. I looked back to that life and knew that things could—and probably should—be better. Where once we had cleaners, now we had stacks of hoarded trash filling the house. Where once we had fresh air and open windows, now we sat behind drawn curtains, nicotine caking the walls, a thin yellow film forming on the windowpanes. Where once we had a garden, we now had an untamed meadow for a back yard, the swing set rotting into a pile of termite-riddled debris. The railings on the sundeck gave way. Water filled the basement unchecked and soaked through boxes full of books, papers, clothes, and God-knows-what. Bexhill Drive was the physical embodiment of angry, broken people.

I concentrated on escaping. Thirteen was a key year for me. "Teen" was a powerful word. At twelve, my eventual escape had seemed far away. But once I got into my teens, eighteen felt very close. I would be free at eighteen. I would be able to get away from Mom and everything related to Gifford's. It was only a matter of counting down. All of my attention was now focused forward, on May 10, 1992, my eighteenth birthday.

I made it through junior high and, in the fall of 1988, headed to Bethesda-Chevy Chase High School. The size of a small college, B-CC left me shaken trying to find my way between classes. But my small network of friends from junior high journeyed along with me, so the landing at this new school was much easier. The world around me was starting to make more sense.

V

B-CC was close to home. I could walk to and from school along an abandoned railway spur, alone with the overgrown brush and weeds. Always seeking quiet, and always up for an adventure, I walked this path home as often as the weather allowed. I scrambled down from the bustle of East-West Highway, the world growing quiet as the overgrown tracks embraced me. In one direction, deeper into Bethesda, the tracks vanished into a tunnel. I struck out in the opposite direction to get home, the tracks curving into the distance.

The tracks were a lonely stretch of urban decay, and I could sometimes walk miles without seeing another human being, except where the railway bisected a golf course whose members were notoriously sadistic. Once, while walking through, a golf ball struck my backpack with enough force to swing me around. I stared, dumbfounded, at a golfer who had turned his back on the green. Seeing me, he pointed his driver at me, then teed up and hit another ball in my direction. I broke into a run, and his incomprehensible shouts of delight followed me. Another time, a golf ball screamed past my head close enough to shift my hair. I stumbled off the tracks. Another man pointed and yelled at me, and this time, I ran onto the course itself to get away from him. The golf balls followed me, thudding into the ground, as I skidded to a stop near an ornamental bridge leading to one of the greens. I cowered under the bridge as the club member stood on the train tracks, knocking ball after ball in my direction. The explosive bursts as the balls hit the bridge pounded in my ears for nearly half an hour. I was afraid to move until the golfer drove his cart down towards the bridge and shouted: "You're free to go now, asshole!"

Even with Mom at work, I hated going home because she would soon enough join me there. I feared the weekends and holidays. A snow day was a curse. The last bell every school day, and every step on the three-mile track to Kensington, brought me closer and closer to another claustrophobic evening haunted by Mom. For the most part, though, Mom's weird pill- and alcohol-filled equilibrium held. I enjoyed a relatively strife-free year. Until everything fell apart.

In 1989, without any warning, Gifford's Ice Cream was revived by a woman named Dolly Hunt. To much fanfare, she opened her store on Woodmont Avenue, a few blocks from B-CC.

Gifford's Ice Cream and Candy Company was back.

The first I heard about it was in *The Tattler*, the B-CC school newspaper. A spread on page two featured Dolly Hunt and her son, James, standing behind the counter and grinning. The title—"Gifford's Tradition Returns!"—struck me like a blow to the chest. I opened to the page, saw my name, and began to sweat and shiver at the same time. In the lunchroom, surrounded by my peers, I felt on the verge of hysteria.

I skipped class and for an hour I huddled under the East-West Highway bridge, in the cool embrace of the abandoned rail tracks, and sobbed. Gifford's Ice Cream, the monster that had terrorized all of us, had returned. Back it came in a blaze of glory, hailed by every generation of Washingtonians, including my peers. Peers who, once again, started to take notice of my last name.

For the first time since stories of Gifford's had faded out of the news two years before, I started to get the big question again. First day of a class, during roll call, the teacher would pause on my name and ask, "Any relation to Gifford's Ice Cream?" Each time, the question left me short of breath with my hands clenched at my sides.

I didn't know what I could do, or what I could change, but I wanted to challenge Dolly Hunt. I wanted to tell her that bringing back Gifford's was killing me.

The revived Gifford's was a very small space, much like most modern ice cream shops, so it didn't have the same imposing presence as the old stores. Still, the bank of sub-zero counter-freezers, full of vats of multi-colored ice cream, looked hauntingly familiar. Hunt was a collector, and she had dedicated a portion of her store to memorabilia—old menus and other trappings from the original Gifford's. Copies of the menus from which I'd learned to read more than a decade earlier sat on display, along with notes and receipts that featured John Gifford's handwriting, and Allen's, and my dad's. Our family was enshrined in a stranger's museum.

Hunt proved to be a kind-hearted, joyful woman. A true fan of Gifford's. From the moment I shook her hand, this was obvious, but I told myself not to be fooled. Gifford's was evil, however jovial its face.

She had bought the trademark and a set of recipes for $1,500, she told me. I was stunned. Allen still went on and on about how much debt he was in, and how much it cost to maintain our lifestyle at Bexhill Drive. Yet he could have bought and owned everything Gifford's for half of what the yearly property tax cost. He wasn't willing to divert such a small amount to regain possession of Gifford's Ice Cream? Our family was fixated on money, and yet seemed to be wholly incapable of earning it, keeping it, or investing it. The missed opportunity of repurchasing Gifford's Ice Cream for a paltry $1,500 filled me with the old familiar anger that had driven my fist into a seventh grader's face, and I judged Dolly Hunt through the lens of that anger. I'm saddened by my reaction, but I don't think it would have been possible then for me to react any differently.

Hunt gave me a tour of her little store, showed me where the ice cream was made, flashed typed-out copies of her recipes, and asked me to help her identify some memorabilia on the wall. Whose handwriting was this? What was this receipt for? I moved in a daze. I don't remember what I said, or any firm details of that meeting. I felt numb. When I left and headed home, it took me hours to walk down the train tracks to Kensington. I lost track of where I was and where I was going, my mind wiped clean by the horror of it all.

I couldn't believe that anyone would want to pick up where my father left off. I didn't understand it. Gifford's was filthy. I looked back and remembered rats, bugs, rotting ice cream, and my father standing in the closet drinking whiskey. As far as I knew, he and Mom had been poisoning the ice cream, murdering people, and pulling me into the middle of it. He had vanished, with all of our money. He had left me with a madwoman. And now Dolly Hunt had resurrected him and was making money off of my name. It didn't seem right that one man could take everything from me, only to allow some stranger to cash in on my legacy.

Now I had more to escape from than just Mom and Bexhill Drive. The legacy of Gifford's, I realized, would forever permeate DC. I crossed off the days on my calendar with bolder, thicker lines.

Mom didn't handle the return of Gifford's well. Dolly Hunt stirred every demon in our house. The moment news of the revival hit the major media circuits, my mom began to talk about how she would destroy the Hunts. She plotted acts of vandalism against the store and, once, she excitedly told me how she planned to poison the ice cream. She drew up an intricate plan that involved breaking into the store at night and injecting HIV-positive blood into the ice cream.

"I'll kill everyone with the gay disease!" she announced.

I retreated as far into my shell as I could, letting Mom rant and rave at the walls and the ceiling. Still she tried to involve me in her increasingly zany plans to destroy the Hunts. She made me write an op-ed to my school newspaper, standing behind me to edit as I wrote, chain-smoking, slurping down can after can of beer. I spent an entire weekend, with little rest, crafting a lengthy op-ed condemning Dolly Hunt and the new Gifford's. I was, as Mom had me write in the piece, "the last Gifford and true heir to Gifford's Ice Cream."

The op-ed read like a mad child had written it, of course. It blathered on about the authenticity and proud tradition of Gifford's, aping the language on the menu, and painted Hunt as a shyster. A variation on Mom's now familiar theme of "usurpers" and "skinwalkers." And of course all the op-ed did was make more people ask—was I really part of the Gifford's Ice Cream family?

My grandparents went to the new store and moodily tried the ice cream. My grandfather then broke their truce to visit Mom—to talk about the results. After years of a familial Cold War, it was bizarre to see them back in one room and talking rationally. Allen assumed his usual paternal pose—his large frame leaning back in the kitchen chair, staring down hard at his troublesome daughter, an air of barely contained strength around him.

"She's a shyster," he told Mom, speaking of Dolly Hunt. "They're cheating on everything. Worst ice cream I've ever tasted!"

My mom talked about suing the Hunts, but Allen replied that it wasn't worth it.

"They'll crash and burn," he said. "They don't know what they're doing. Amateur hour there."

"And these recipes she says she has?" Mom asked.

My ears perked up. Dolly had shown me her recipes—printed copies she said she'd bought along with the name and trademark. She seemed very proud of them, as if they were sacred. At home, the myth of the secret family recipes was always strong. We were supposed to have them at home, locked away for safekeeping, but I hadn't seen them. When Dolly had shown me her binder of recipes, my first response was confusion. Were these copied from those forgeries Mom had crafted years before? Or had Dolly Hunt somehow gotten her hands on the real thing?

My grandfather laughed at Mom's question. "Nope! You know what she has. We got her there, Barb."

After the Hunts resurrected Gifford's, the reboot occupied Mom and Allen. Dolly Hunt had, in fact, done me a great service by waking up our demons. Mom became hyper-focused on this new enemy and, like when Dad was still around, I became anonymous, drifting from the TV to my bedroom without being noticed.

A few weeks after the apparent thaw in the battle between Mom and her parents, I was having dinner at their house when Allen said, apropos of nothing: "Whew boy, we sure got Benny Fischer."

This was a name I hadn't heard before. I asked who Benny Fischer was, and my grandfather said: "He's just some kike. Don't worry about it. Your legacy is safe. Your pops and I got his tail."

I had a million questions, but didn't know where to begin. I just worked my jaw. Now we were talking about Gifford's? Or were we? It seemed like half the things Allen said were non sequiturs more than anything else.

After dinner, he took me to the basement and he opened a box that was crammed with pictures and papers. He pulled out a clear plastic bag and showed it to me. Inside were stained, yellowing index cards, each one with barely legible handwriting scrawled in blue or black ink.

"These are the secret recipes," he told me. "These are yours."

I reached out for the bag, but he turned and replaced it in the box, flipping its lid up from the grimy basement floor and slamming it back in place.

"For when you grow up," he said.

This was the first time I saw the "secret family recipes." They weren't the cards that Mom had forged several years before. These looked different—older, dirtier.

"Does Dolly Hunt have these, too?" I asked.

He shook his head and blew a raspberry.

"No! I told you. We got old Benny Fischer by the tail on that one."

"Who's Benny Fischer?" I asked again, my voice wheedling up as the confusion and frustration mounted.

My grandfather just winked and said: "A sucker."

I wouldn't hear Benny Fischer's name again for a long time, but that night, as I lay in bed listening to the sounds of my grandparent's house, I did overhear Allen tell my grandmother that Dolly Hunt was using "Barb's recipes," and because of that, she was "doomed."

Fine, whatever, I thought. As long as Mom and my grandparents were occupied with this nonsense, my life was happier. So I kept counting down the days and went back to my routine.

Hunt's operation was a small, humble one. Once the initial fanfare of her revival left the news cycle, I hoped I could again ignore Gifford's Ice Cream. But the prickling reality was always there. No matter how much I tried to tune it out, I heard Gifford's mentioned more frequently. Friends went on dates to Gifford's, and parents and teachers talked fondly of it. So I lived more than ever for my escape. Soon, I would leave DC. No one in Paris would talk about Gifford's. Or in Montreal, or California, or Mexico City. There was a whole world out there not talking about Gifford's fucking Ice Cream. I would join it.

By 1990, I felt like I could see the light at the end of the tunnel. I was almost out of tenth grade. Two more years. But for Mom, perhaps, the pressure of the Gifford's revival was too much. Her last links to reality broke, and I watched it happen, powerless to help or get away from the fallout.

VI

When the dreams started, Mom's mood shifted yet again. She seemed to grow more exhausted, to age more quickly. Her black hair started to sport grey streaks. Her evenings were spent with beer, pills, and loud music. And what once had been a white-hot rage now morphed into something coldly violent and frighteningly calm.

Her dreams began with prophetic visions from St. Francis of Assisi, who took her on walks along forest paths. Eventually, he led her to a grotto where she met Jesus Christ. They would speak at length, but she rarely shared any details of these conversations, except to tell me that she had received orders for "the next step in our lives."

The frank way she talked about this fantasy, despite the peace it seemed to bring her, set off alarms. Were these delusions a sign of a psychotic break? I thought of Jim Jones and his deadly Kool-Aid, which had filled the news a few years earlier, and I worried that the "next steps" she spoke of might involve something just as drastic. She made me nervous when I was alone with her. After Mom started to visit my room in the early morning hours to share small snippets of her dreams, I began tying little bells to the doorknob.

Her conversations with St. Francis and Jesus became more involved, the orders more clear. As summer approached, Mom said that St. Francis had told her that James Hickey was going to visit us at Bexhill Drive. He was the archbishop of the Washington Diocese, recently appointed a cardinal. St. Francis told her that she must clean the entire house for Cardinal Hickey.

We began on the second floor, cleaning every inch of her filthy bathroom—the overflowing, broken toilet, the mold creeping up the walls and along the floor. We scrubbed the carpet, yellow-brown nicotine soiling the water as I ran a sponge back and forth across every inch of floor. We washed the grimy, dusty windows, and it was strange to suddenly have such a clear view outside. Mom laundered all the curtains and, perhaps as a backhanded homage to Sister Anne's long-ago punishment, I found myself working at the molding with a toothbrush.

We moved downstairs, where Mom spent an entire week on her hands and knees scrubbing the hardwood floors with a small brush. The house was soon the cleanest I had ever seen it. Then I was forbidden to behave normally. I had to take off my shoes and socks and wear little booties that Mom took from her job at the naval hospital. We weren't allowed to eat in the house and instead went out, usually to the Hong Kong Restaurant in Kensington, where they came to know us by name. But no leftovers. Grocery deliveries from my grandparents were also suspended. I had to sleep on top of my covers so that we wouldn't have to make the bed.

Every day, for four months, she would continue cleaning in the evenings, repeatedly working over floors, polishing walls and the banister, even scrubbing the front door and the outside of the house with soap and water.

Of course, the cardinal never came. If St. Francis and Jesus were still talking about his visit, Mom didn't say. Everything seemed to go back to normal. I knew better than to test her with questions.

Then, toward the end of the summer, she began to receive nocturnal visitations from my maternal great-grandfather, Everett Earl Currey, who had died in 1961. Once a week, for many months, Everett appeared to her. I would wake in the mornings to find her sitting at the foot of my bed, smoking. She would tell me about the dreams, marveling at each vivid detail.

At first, she said, Everett appeared silently in a chair near her bed. She would wake up, saying that she "smelled him." Afraid to move, she would lie there and watch as Everett, sitting in the shadows, smoked a rolled cigarette, saying nothing.

"He's just watching me sleep," she murmured. "Watching over me, because he knows"—she reached out and grabbed my hand—"that we will soon be with him."

"I was his favorite," she told me, crying. "He loved me more than the others. He just tolerated them. I was special."

Soon enough, Everett started to talk to her. She would relate these conversations in two different voices. When playing herself, she spoke in a high, girlish voice, scrunching up her face into a grimace. When she was Everett, she lowered her voice to a growl. At first, though, all Everett could say was her name, over and over: "Barbara . . . Barbara . . ."

Then she would shrug, sucking on her Newport.

"Like he was trying to push through from beyond . . ."

This scared the pants off me. She'd once told me how the ghost of John Gifford haunted the basement. "You're fine as long as you aren't down there alone," she told me, "because then he'll take over your soul and use your skin." She said Mary Frances haunted the garage because "that's where she was brutally murdered by John—clubbed to death." By 1990, I had heard a dozen stories about the demise of Mary Frances, all of them different. Now, the ghost of the great-grandfather I'd never known was coming for us.

Weeks later, Everett finally made it through from the other side. Mom shook me awake at three in the morning.

"Everett's here . . ." she whispered, glancing over her shoulder at the open closet in my bedroom.

She left me alone to ponder this. I lay awake, staring at the closet, too afraid to move until the sun came up. The next morning, as I sat exhausted at the kitchen table and listlessly pushed my spoon around a bowl of instant oatmeal, Mom told me about the latest dream. Everett had appeared in the chair by her bed.

"He was mad this time," she said in a hollow voice, her eyes dull and far away. "I could feel his anger. He leaned forward and he said, 'What have you done with my gold bricks?'"

She barked each word, emphasizing them with a stab of her cigarette. Then a rare thing happened. So rare that it shocked me. She began to cry. Great, heaving sobs, and she hid her face behind her hands. I'd rarely seen her cry before, and never with such force or heartbreak.

"The gold bricks," she sobbed. "They were my responsibility! Mine! And I've lost them." Her sobs turned in an instant to rage. She slammed a fist on the table and she screamed: "It was your fucking father! He lost them!"

She stormed off to her room and, as usual, slammed her door so hard that it bounced back open. So she slammed it again, and then again, leaving me to wonder what she was talking about. The gold bricks were not something I'd heard of before. Before I went to bed that evening, though, I got the story of the bricks.

"I was six years old," she told me.

The family was visiting Everett Earl in Parkersburg, West Virginia. Everett was a literary man and a carpenter—"Just like Jesus," Mom said. Across from his Ann Street row house, the old Parkersburg post office was being torn down. Everett sat with my mother on his front porch and they watched. Mom, ever the tomboy, was fascinated by the demolition process. She described Everett to me as if she were still six, her voice small, her hands miming her description.

"He had no hair, and glasses, and he drank quietly from his special bottle."

She described the demolition, marveling at how the men would put hooks in the crumbling brick walls and pull away, narrowly missing being crushed to death. How the big machines plowed through ceilings, walls, and foundations. She sniffed the air, her eyes closed, and said: "Dust was everywhere, the whole street smelled like the inside of an old, dry building."

At day's end, when the workmen left, Everett got up and walked across the street, standing in the wreckage and poking at the debris with his cane. Finally, he turned to Mom and beckoned her to join him. She paused the story to look down at me, her face splitting into a grin.

"He loved me so much," she said.

Resuming her tale, she recalled how she bounded off of the porch and ran over to him, stumbling on bricks and pieces of metal to stand next to him. He hugged her close and waved a hand over the wreckage.

"Pick out two bricks," he said.

She looked around, squatted down, and began methodically picking through the shattered bricks. If Everett wanted two bricks, they had better be perfect. She eventually found two whole bricks, hauling them out one by one and handing them over to Everett. He nodded and smiled.

"Good picks," he said, and took the bricks home to his work shed.

The next time my mom visited him, the post office was long gone, and in its place had risen a new hospital. She and Everett again sat on his porch, and he told her all about the future. How America was about progress, and when there was no more progress to have, America would decay and die. She looked sad for a moment, then smiled again.

"That's when he handed me a heavy package."

Wrapped clumsily in dirty newspaper, the package was almost too heavy for her to hold. She clunked it onto the metal table between their chairs and tore the wrapping away to reveal the two bricks she had selected from the demolition site. They had been painted a bright, shining gold.

Everett smiled. "Those are yours. Gold bricks. Keep them safe."

"And now they're lost . . ." she said, gazing out the window into our overgrown backyard, "and now Everett is angry and cannot rest."

I didn't see her for nearly a day after that. She sat behind closed doors, music blaring, and didn't come out for food or water or to go to work. Then another dream came and she burst into my room, again at three in the morning, and shook me awake, excitedly chattering.

"They aren't lost! They aren't lost!" She hauled me out of bed. "Everett says if you help me we can find them!"

In those dark, lonely hours, we began searching the house. Room by room, we looked in every cupboard, every drawer, under every stick of furniture. It was nine in the morning before we got to the basement. We rifled through everything—clothes that fell apart when touched and boxes sealed since the 1950s. She made me climb into dark recesses in the walls and under the stairs, where spiderwebs coated my skin and many decades' worth of desiccated bugs crunched under my hands.

By midday, the search took us to the garage. An attic room above was accessible only by a narrow flight of stairs, and Mom dramatically ripped open the door that led to them. She gasped, hand flying to her mouth, and stepped back, leaning onto me as if she were about to collapse.

I looked from her to the attic stairs. There, in the middle of a wooden tread, sat the two gold bricks, one atop the other. Since I frequented the attic room as one of my many hiding places, I immediately had my doubts.

"I was just up there yesterday. I would have noticed those."

She nodded and replied without hesitation, "Everett put them there this morning." Then she got down on one knee and turned me around so I was facing her. "He did it because you helped me."

That was the last time Everett Earl visited. Mom said that since we'd found the bricks, he was finally at rest. At peace. All thanks to me.

VII

B-CC had an open campus policy for lunch, which I took advantage of on nice days to wander the streets of Bethesda, enjoying what was then a sleepy suburban town. Our subway station had opened in late 1984, six months before Dad vanished, and the slow, glacial gentrification that came along with it was barely noticeable six years later. There were only three or four tall buildings in Bethesda, and old houses still hugged streets where today there are glittering condo towers. Most of the shops and restaurants nestled in low, two-story strips.

Olsson's was my favorite local book and record store. I drifted through the stacks and flipped through the records, though I rarely had the extra cash to buy anything. The store competed bitterly with Crown Books, which was closer to B-CC. A Hot Shoppes sat on the corner of the main intersection, always good for refills of Coke. The Tastee Diner was the all-night hangout for the cool kids. There were a few head shops along Wisconsin Avenue, and I loved checking them out and looking at all the weird stuff: colorful glass pipes, T-shirts with rude messages, old toys from some forgotten decade before my birth, and crazy sunglasses and hats.

At the front counter of one such shop in the Connor Building, in the same complex that housed Dolly Hunt's Gifford's parlor, I found my first zines, homemade collections of writing that ranged from politics to literature to fan-fiction. In the head shop, an entire shelf below the clerk's counter was given over to the cluttered, Xeroxed screeds. The clerk sat high above everyone, the counter taller than normal, the zines piled so clumsily I had to get on my knees to rifle through them.

Most of the zines were free, and those that charged rarely asked for more than a dollar. The clerk would let me page through them for a few minutes before telling me to "pay up or get out" and I always found myself buying a few in addition to taking a copy of all of the free ones. The content didn't matter. It was in this inhospitable, dusty head shop that I was introduced to the power of zine culture.

I was drawn at first to the bizarre art. Almost every zine cover featured hand-drawn images or collage-style clip-art, nutty and surreal. The illustrations highlighted the writing inside, which I devoured. Some rambled on about politics. Others were pornographic, violent, and alarming. Some were so funny—improbable stories about family madness and social anarchy—that I laughed out loud as I paged through them. A few were bizarre, internalized rants that felt like they weren't meant for public consumption—cries in the night from severely damaged people. And some were literary zines in humble packaging that featured extraordinary poetry and prose from authors around the world. I read all of them, and they taught me a valuable lesson: I wasn't alone.

1990 was the tail end of zine culture. Back then, zines were our Facebook, our Twitter, our ranty blogs. People could put one together, say whatever they wanted, and others could follow them either through mail order or at a local record shop.

The repressed emotion that made me hit that seventh grader in the face—festering for years as I silently endured my family's insanity—seemed to boil over as I encountered the lives of these zine authors. I had written novels about my Lego fantasies, always scribbling away, but never with a purpose or goal in mind. I wrote because I felt compelled to do so. When I describe this compulsion today, I reference Alice Flaherty's book about the "neural basis of creativity," titled *The Midnight Disease*. In it she talks about "hypergraphia"—the overwhelming urge to write. We write because we can't control it. It's a flaw, a quirk, a squiggle in the brain.

Zines showed me that maybe my writing—my squiggle in the brain—could become an outlet for my own particular distress. I began to write with that purpose, and immediately, my writing

changed. No longer was I simply journaling my escapist fantasies—I was writing to air my angst. The tell-all attitude of the
zine authors inspired me to be a bit of an exhibitionist. I started
to show my experimental short stories to friends and teachers
without shame. And in ninth grade, I began a protest project in
the margins of my escapist fantasy journaling. I wrote the first
few pages of "The Most Holy Boble," in which the creator of the
world was a rather silly man called God Bob.

I was ignorant of the Church of the Subgenius, which had
started as a joke in the 1970s and centered on the all-seeing, all-
knowing everyman Bob Dobbs. Sadly, and perhaps predictably
for me, my understanding of God Bob came from a series of TV
car commercials. In them, the driver was a whitebread Everyman
named Bob who was treated like he was king of the world. "Oh
. . . it's you, Bob!" says a cop, in awe, after Bob drives his fancy
new car up on the sidewalk and parks in a spot marked, in big,
white letters, "BOB."

My God Bob was a more passive version of the teen-anarchy
trope embodied in works ranging from *Catcher in the Rye* to *The
Breakfast Club*. *The Boble* was a direct parody of the Bible, and my
margins eventually featured the entire book of Genesis, as told
from the viewpoint of an exhausted, fed-up God Bob and his
various creations. Every page was graphic, rude, obscene, and
sacrilegious. I was very proud.

In tenth grade, I turned the whole thing into a major personal writing project, and by the middle of eleventh grade, I had
completed a hundred pages of "The Old Testicle." I cheerfully
showed my work to my friends and *The Boble* became a shared
joke, complete with a church to which I appointed my friends as
popes and bishops, who performed various ridiculous rituals. I
assumed my first pseudonym—the not-very-clever-at-all "Werdna
Droffig"—and I presided over marriages and baptisms, the rites
for which I wrote from scratch. A marriage involved sharing each
other's gum during a kiss, in classic rom-com style. A baptism
involved being locked in the trunk of a car while someone drove
at breakneck speed around an abandoned industrial lot. Newly

baptized members of the church would stumble out of the trunk, bruised, occasionally vomiting, as I solemnly pronounced them to be "one with Bob."

God Bob was cool, but he was also a bit of an idiot and unable to connect with anyone. Bob was falsely confident, with no idea what he was doing, what was happening, or what he would do next. Bob was a sex god, but his relationships always landed him in hot water—one mistress, his chief angel Binaca, was at odds with his other mistress, mankind's former creator goddess, the ousted pagan "Blood Mistress" Kraal. Everything Bob did was just slightly wrong—as, in my opinion, everything God does in the Bible doesn't quite work out as planned.

Within the pages of *The Boble*, I attacked B-CC's administration. Our vice principal became the servant of Bob's nemesis, the fallen angel False Rob. One chapter listed the names of peers I considered to be my enemies, each of them meeting a catastrophic fate at the hands of suitably biblical torturers.

I was able, in a way, to climb up on a soapbox and scream at everyone, and it felt good. I read selections from *The Boble* in front of class, and I made Super-8 videos of these readings. I plastered the material around the school as sort-of guerrilla art pieces—scattering one-page flash fiction stories in the hallways and on the bus, and tucking them into many a library book.

I submitted my work to our school literary magazine, *Chips*, and their editorial board got used to rejecting me. B-CC was an uptight school full of proto-yuppies. Even our mascot—the Battlin' Baron—was an old white dude. Of course I had to lash out. Who in their right mind wouldn't?

The constant rejections from *Chips* finally slowed me down. I refocused my efforts—if they didn't want my writing, then I would become an editor, get on the board. I would change them. When an opening was announced in my junior year, I applied. To my surprise, they quickly agreed to interview me.

I was passionate, all smiles as I sat in the middle of a star chamber peopled by all of the *Chips* editors and their faculty advisor. They peppered me with questions—what would I bring to *Chips*? How did I see the journal evolving over the next year? What voice should *Chips* have? What were the changing elements in writing and literature that would most affect *Chips*? What was *Chips* lacking?

I cheerily told them that *Chips* was a dying zine, and that it represented only a tiny percentage of saccharine, pre-approved "literature" ("for lack of a better word," I said). This wouldn't do. I spoke of "New Writing" and the "Future of Literature" and how *Chips* could be at the forefront of all of this change, at one of the most prestigious high schools in America.

I echoed Tony Wilson's "thirteen-year cycle theory" of music, in which he said that music (and youth culture, in general) changed every thirteen years—from the Beatles in 1963 to the birth of punk in 1976 to acid and grunge in 1989. For literature, I babbled, the transformation occurred every twenty years. We had the Beats in the fifties, and then we had the post-hippie "Black Sparrow Era" in the late sixties and seventies, and then Reagan killed all that was holy. But now, as George H.W. Bush's presidency and the last vestiges of the Reagan era rapidly approached an obvious endpoint, and as the 1990s started to coalesce, it was time to found a new era of literature. We—I pointed at my confused peers, and the journal's faculty adviser, who watched me with narrow, suspicious eyes—were in the perfect position to lead the charge.

By the time I was done, the editors were staring at me with wide eyes and open mouths. After a few moments of silence, the faculty advisor laughed and said: "Get out of here."

The editors sent me a letter of rejection, which simply said "You are not for us" and was signed by the entire *Chips* staff. I flattened it out on my writing desk and stared at it for long hours while John Michael Talbot's Christian music echoed through the house at top volume, rhythmically shaking the window casements.

So *Chips* wouldn't have me, eh? The next day, I enlisted several friends and I breathlessly told them how we could make our own zine. A better zine. We could organize everyone in the school who cared and make a zine that condemned B-CC's administration and the editors of *Chips*. We could fight back. We could become the voice of the people.

Our first planning meeting was fruitful. I assigned friends to gather artwork, poetry, and writing of all genres with the promise that we would publish everything we collected, no matter the subject or quality. I named the zine *Splinters*, and, within a week, I had gathered enough material for three issues. True to my word, I published everything, lovingly laying it out and Xeroxing it. We ran angst-ridden suicide poetry, pornography, bizarre non-linear stories. We even ran a story written by a computer—someone from B-CC's small clique of computer geeks had fed random words and phrases into one of the twelve computers that the school had in its lab and let it spit out a surprisingly coherent story about youth culture gone mad.

For the cover, one of my colleagues found a picture of a naked baby happily pissing into the air. We planned an entire run of covers based on that picture—issue two would have a young boy pissing, issue three a grown man pissing, and issue four an old, decrepit man either pissing or wetting himself. Perfect! And, frighteningly, my colleague was able to lay his hands on all of those images within a few hours—cut out of magazines that his parents had. He never said what the magazines were—and nobody dared ask.

Soon, the first issue was ready for distribution. The school year was coming to a close, so we figured we'd have all summer to work on the other issues. I made fast friends with a work-study student in the library and he gave me the key to the Xerox machine's coin box. Laboriously, at odd hours of the day, with lookouts posted to actively intercept and distract any wandering librarians, I ran off hundreds of copies of *Splinters,* using the same quarter over and over again.

The *Splinters* team took false names, but that didn't do anything to conceal our true identities. Shortly before press, I was interviewed by the school paper, and I answered the questions in character as my wild and violent alter ego, Nacho Sasha, managing editor of *Splinters*.

We distributed several hundred copies in two hours. The next day, I was called into the principal's office. Another long table, but this time I sat alone at one end while, at the other end, the principal, my mother, the school counselor, and a Montgomery County police officer faced me.

The cop opened the conversation, telling me that handing out pornographic material on campus was an offense, and if I continued, I would be arrested. For an hour, the cop and our principal dressed me down. I would have to go to mandatory psychological counseling. My eyes stayed on my mother, her gaze inscrutable behind her reflective aviator sunglasses.

This time, though, she said nothing.

The beating I received that night was epic. Our battle raged throughout the house. I would escape Mom's open-handed slaps, only to have her chase me from room to room. She tackled me in the kitchen and we both went sprawling. Her head bounced off a cabinet as I caromed into the bags of trash that had piled up (and were only rarely taken out to the curb). A wet mess poured out of those bags, and I scrambled wildly to get up, as if caught in some nightmare. Mom rose unsteadily to her feet and lunged towards me. She grabbed my collar, but I twisted away and made it into the garage. On all fours, I crawled up the attic stairs as she clawed at my ankles. She finally got a grip and yanked hard. I bounced down the stairs on top of her, my chin cracking off of each step.

We both lay at the bottom of the stairs, bleeding, exhausted, and she calmly told me that my writing days were over. She told me that she had already cut up all of my floppy discs and shredded all of my printed work. Everything was gone. If I continued writing, I would be a dead man.

The way she said it chilled me to the bone.

I was rapidly approaching eighteen, and I had come to see Mom as the angry, broken, pill-addled woman she was. Yet she still had power over me. It took very little to inspire the childlike fear that gripped me in that quarry in Deep Creek Lake, or on the lake itself. Even as an older teen, from time to time I still retreated to my Legos or buried my nose in cheesy fantasy.

I went to the school-appointed counselor, but I said nothing. After three sessions, the counselor said that I was "uncooperative but otherwise very well adjusted" and I was free to go.

That same week, I applied for and got a job a short bike ride from my house. My anger, boiled away in that battle with Mom, had again been submerged. A sullen darkness clouded my mind, and I moodily returned to my countdown. It was April 1991. In thirteen months, I would be gone. I knew that if I were to leave on my eighteenth birthday, I would need money, and a job would maybe get me out of the house more easily. I stopped writing and threw myself into work, cashing my paychecks at the cash register so Mom wouldn't be able to get her hands on them. I hid the money in a duffel bag, which, in turn, was hidden in the attic above the garage.

For around ten dollars an hour, I was one of three paid employees in the bookstore of the Nature Society, which was primarily run by a horde of elderly and largely incapable volunteers. The store specialized in naturalist books and gifts—from bird feeders to identification guides to the writings of Thoreau. The birdseed was the same stuff sold at Home Depot, but marked up roughly three hundred percent. The books were boring and the idea of investing hundreds of dollars to feed the filthy birds was appalling to me. But that wasn't my problem. I happily sold it all to the yuppie suckers who came into the shop. I worked nights after school, and on the weekends, and throughout the summer, and signed up for all possible holiday hours. I supplemented my pay by mowing lawns, cleaning gutters, and taking other odd jobs around town. Anything for a few bucks, all of which was jammed into a duffel bag hidden in the attic.

I phoned in my senior year of high school and passed with a nice set of C grades. My mom, perhaps also stunned by our blowout, retreated into herself. Maybe she saw the end coming. I don't know if she cared. The distance between us had grown into a canyon, and there seemed no way to bridge the gap. That was fine with me. I took solace in the belief that I would never see or speak to her again after I left.

As 1992 approached, I still had no clear plans for what would happen after I turned eighteen. I didn't think about colleges, and my score on the SAT was appalling. I began to research what was involved in dropping out before I turned eighteen. Allen intervened before I dug myself in too deep. He said that a family cousin was the dean of Davis & Elkins College in Elkins, West Virginia.

"I've set myself up over there as a consultant for their science department," Allen told me. "That's where you're going to school."

The "West Virginia mafia," as he called it, came through for me. Allen said he would see to it that my college application was rubber-stamped. I didn't even bother to fill out the application form accurately. I left the essay section blank and I didn't send my grades in. I filled out all of the vital information in a sloppy mixture of blue and black ink, some of it fading and illegible, and messily stuffed the application into a too-small envelope, tearing it in half so it would fit. But Allen's word was true.

I was accepted at Davis & Elkins within six days of mailing the application.

The reality of the acceptance, my grandfather's increasingly domineering insistence that I pull myself together and "man up," and the knowledge that I had a place to land after I fled home, with a free ride for one semester, finally gave me a bit of a push in the late winter of 1992. I made an effort towards the tail end of my classes, though I think several of the teachers let me pass only out of pity. But I graduated on time with the rest of my peers.

May 10, 1992. My eighteenth birthday. There was no party. Nothing special happened. At the end of the day, I made the last black X in my collection of calendars and looked back through all of them, month by month, filled with black X's. Then I threw them all away.

The day before I left home I sat atop the cliffs across from the Beltway one last time. My childhood was over. I was free. But it didn't feel like it. I felt exhausted, used up, like an old man who had seen too much, fought too hard, and lost every battle. The sun set, the Beltway glowed, and I had no choice but to skitter down the face of the cliffs and go home.

PART TWO

SPLINTERS

CHAPTER THREE

VANISHING

I

In late May 1992, I packed up whatever I could carry and threw it all into the back of Allen's ice-blue 1986 Plymouth Voyager. My mother said her father had "cheaped out" when he bought it, because it was the bottom-dollar model with no back-seats—just two captain's-style chairs for the driver and passenger. Even when it was brand-new, it rattled and shook and smelled of burning rubber and oil. My grandmother told me that Allen had spent hours with the dealer negotiating over every dollar. He took particular offense at the idea of the dealer's logo appearing on the back of the car.

"If I'm going to advertise your dealership, then you have to pay me a fifteen-dollar monthly fee," Allen loudly demanded, my grandmother no doubt shrinking behind him.

The dealer refused, so Allen stood up and crossed around the desk, getting in the dealer's face. "Then you'll remove the advertisement and knock five hundred bucks off the bill."

My grandmother describes the dealer skulking away and negotiations that continued for hours. The ad was removed, but there was no savings or discount. So much work for such little things.

By the time I graduated, Allen had put the car through hell. The carpet was stained and torn, the electronics were unreliable whenever it rained, and the stereo was broken. When the engine was turned off, ninety seconds would pass before the van finally ground to a heaving, shuddering halt. Allen had to call AAA roughly once a month for a tow or a jump. Eventually, he received a warning from them that they would suspend their coverage if he didn't stop.

This deathtrap would eventually take me out of DC and climb with me into the cool mountains, leaving the boiling heat and humidity behind. But first, I spent a month at my grandparent's house, a period of stunned transition between the claustrophobic terror of Bexhill Drive and the first step into my adult life at Davis & Elkins College.

Allen appointed himself the overseer of my transition. The month was marked by a rapid-fire series of coming of age moments. First came the gift of the Voyager. The air conditioner had long since died, and we drove around Silver Spring through the July heat with the windows rolled down—but just the driver and passenger windows, since the panel windows in the back opened only a crack, and even then their latches were so loose they'd slam shut if the vehicle hit a bump. Both of us sweating, the passenger seat shuddering ominously beneath me, Allen pulled into the driveway and turned off the engine. We sat in silence, listening to it die. Then he handed the twisted key over to me.

"Your first car, son," he said.

I stared at the key in my hand, stained oily black and brown. It was still hot to the touch.

"You're gonna need something to take you to college," he continued, patting the dashboard lovingly. "This is it. Just remember—to own a car is to wreck a car. It'll happen to you eventually. Don't know where, when, or how, but you'll crash someday. So always be prepared. Always keep your shoes on so you can get out quickly if there's a fire, always wear your seatbelt." He unlatched his own seat belt then and held it out as if I'd never seen one before. "Good old Lee Iacocca invented these for a reason."

I didn't know who Lee Iacocca was, but I kept silent and tried to absorb this prediction of doom. A few days later, Allen came to my room. I was huddled against the wall, gazing out at the backyard, drifting through the summer day. He sat down on the edge of the bed.

"How much cash you got in that bag?" he asked, patting the bed with his hand.

On the floor under the bed, directly beneath where his hand lightly tapped the mattress, I'd stored my duffel bag full of cash. I shrugged.

"A real man keeps his money in the bank," he said. "The Depression's over. I lived through it. I know how it really was. It's just silly to keep your money under the mattress. What if there's a fire? What if the house burns down?"

He leaned over, pulled out the duffel bag, and then stood up. I tensed, not sure what was going to happen next, fighting the urge to lunge wildly for the bag. But he tossed it on the bed and said: "Come on."

We drove to a nearby branch of the Montgomery County Teachers Credit Union, where Allen had an account. He was still teaching chemistry at a local high school, and had been bouncing around the county as a teacher since 1970. In his current position, he was one of the lead science instructors in the county's prestigious magnet program.

Inside the credit union, he acted like a visiting potentate. He marched in and barged through the door of the nearest office, greeting the person inside using the name on the doorplate.

"Molly!" he called out in a big, booming voice, a hand between my shoulders as he propelled me toward the woman's desk. "Al Currey here. This is my grandson. We want to open an account."

Molly blinked, then started to stammer a reply, which Allen cut off immediately.

"His first account," he said, nodding towards me, as he sat down in a chair across from her desk.

"Well . . . of course . . ." Molly looked as if she wanted to run away. "We can do that for you. You'll want to go and sign up at—"

Allen leaned forward and said: "Molly, we want you to open the account. I'm bringing you new business today. You should reward loyal customers who bring new ones right to your doorstep."

I watched Molly think things through, perhaps gauging the large man in front of her. Could she win a battle of wills here? Finally she smiled. "Of course. Mister . . . Currey, you said?"

Allen barked a short laugh. "You know who I am, Molly. Now let's get crackin'." He reached down and picked up my duffel bag. She leaned back as if he'd reached for a shotgun, or a bomb. Then he threw the bag onto Molly's desk, and she jumped to her feet, eyeing it fearfully. Allen leaned forward and ripped the zipper open. They looked at the money inside.

"Um . . ." Molly said. "What is this?"

"Looks like money to me, Molly!" Allen replied.

"From . . . where?"

I finally spoke up. "Been saving it up. That's about two years of work there."

"What do you do?"

I looked down nervously. "Mow lawns. Yardwork. I have a job in a bookshop. Sometimes I help out the groundskeeper there. Trimming, clearing hiking trails. That sort of thing."

I had amassed nearly $12,000. Setting up the account involved employing a teller to count the cash. Molly and her supervisor grilled me for several minutes about my lines of work, doubtful that I had made that much at a bookstore and other odd jobs. The supervisor seemed especially reluctant to accept my money, but finally he relented.

Once the account was set up, I was given a passbook and a set of starter checks, and Allen drove me home in silence. He followed me back to my room, and then sat down on the bed in the same spot where the day had started. I perched on a stool next to the bed and watched as Allen drew a deep breath.

"Now, grown men," he began, "pay rent. Nothing's free in this world. So you'd better learn how that works. You'll only be here for about six weeks, so let's say $750 will be the rent. That's for a month, but I'm giving you two weeks free because you're learning new things, kiddo."

He showed me how to fill out a check, making one out to himself for the rent. He handed it over to me and told me to sign it.

"I know that hurts," he said, watching me write my name. "The first one always does. But, remember, I kept you alive at Bexhill Drive all those years after Bob took off. I built up a huge debt. All those Christmas presents, grocery shopping, supporting every crazy whim your mother had. I've lost my shirt, kiddo. So this is fair, even if you don't think so."

A large part of me simply didn't care. I wanted to be left alone, to go back to staring out the window. I'd taken time off from my exhausting work schedule to prep for school and get my head straight, or so I thought, and wanted to enjoy these last summer days in the DC area. But the rent wasn't enough for Allen. A week later, I walked into my room and found him on the bed again.

"Hey, old man," he said cheerfully. "Come here."

I sat down next to him.

"I'm gonna need a loan, old man," he continued. "If you don't help me out, I might lose the house. There are three mortgages on it now, all to pay for your mother's antics and your college. God knows what'll happen then."

I didn't know how to respond. I remember feeling like I was underwater, numb to everything. There was no standing against Allen, and I was already reaching for my starter checks and asking how much he needed.

"$2,500 should do it," he said.

That was the first of several "loans." By the time I was ready to head off to college, I had signed over most of my $12,000 to Allen. I went to school with a little under one thousand left in my account.

I didn't get my whole six weeks' worth of lodging, either. When I told Allen that I didn't have any money left to give him for rent, he nodded sadly and brought me back to my room again, saying gently, "It's time we talked." He closed the door and, this time, he stood and I went to sit on the bed. As soon as I did, he crossed over and sat down, pressing his back to mine.

"I guess it's time you got going, then. You can go a bit early and get settled. I've decided that forestry is the best degree for you. Already done some footwork for you over there, so they're all ready for you."

"Forestry?"

"It's a good science. Growing field. D&E has a one-hundred-percent placement rate for all of their graduates. You'll become a government man. You can travel. Just four years, a guaranteed job, and that's all she wrote."

I had told myself for so long that I was going to run and be free, and yet there I was, bled dry by my grandfather and stagnant in his back guestroom. I felt adrift. I didn't look forward to going to college. I didn't care. My mother, and my grandfather, and the world in general expected me to do certain things. I was pretty sure Allen voiced those global, universal expectations when he decided my major—go to school, get a job, work, and that's all she wrote, indeed.

I tried once, that summer, to share these thoughts with Allen. We sat back to back on my bed as I talked to the wall in front of me about my fears, and how tired I was, and how hard the last few years had been. I asked the questions I would spend a lifetime asking—why did Dad leave? What was wrong with Mom? Had I done something wrong?

When I was done, he sighed and said: "There's no time to stop and catch your breath. When you do that, you fail. You die. Life doesn't stop for you. If you can't hack it, if you can't go forward, then you're done for."

In the absence of better answers, I embraced this sad and hopeless attitude. We never spoke of my concerns again. For me, my grandfather's voice was the voice of wisdom, even if every word sounded wrong. I wanted to trust him, wanted to believe in him. Because the last eighteen years had exhausted me too much to want anything more.

I realized some of this in that small guest bedroom, when $12,000 flew out the door into Allen's pockets and I made no response. Why wasn't I angry? Why didn't it matter to me? I had nearly killed myself working for that money. Yet I never complained, never put up a fight. When he asked for a check, I quietly wrote it. I knew that I would need the money in West Virginia. But it was as if I had been taken out of gear.

Looking back, I see that a part of me then thought I deserved nothing more. After all, I had spent my high school years condemned by Mom as an avatar of my father. And almost everyone in my family routinely made the point of noting that I looked very much like him. To them—and to myself—I seemed destined for a similar ruinous end.

A few days before I left for college, a letter arrived. Without comment, Mom had forwarded it to my grandparent's address. I didn't recognize the name on the letter—Rebecca. A New York address. I opened it up and a ten-dollar bill fell out. The letter itself, written in loopy script on pink paper, was addressed to "the High Prophet Werdna Droffig."

"You don't know me," it began. "A friend gave me a copy of *The Most Holy Boble*—it's been making the rounds here—and I simply had to find you and tell you how awesome it was."

The letter talked about how she tracked me down through various bulletin boards and newsgroups, the dial-up lifeblood of the proto, text-only Internet where I had posted *The Boble*'s first chapter. My real name would have been easy enough to learn since I never really hid behind any of my pseudonyms (and my chosen pseudonym for *The Boble* was rather obvious). The money in the letter, she said, was payment for two copies of *The Boble*, signed by me.

The Boble was one of the few writings that had survived Mom's purge after the *Splinters* debacle, only because an electronic copy was still in the hands of a friend, who returned it to me when I left home. I had filed the floppy disc away and wasn't thinking about writing again, but there I sat looking at that ten-dollar bill. Money for nothing, really. Even at eighteen, I felt like *The Boble* was insane, ranting garbage written by a troubled child. But something happened when I handled that bill. Where there was one ten-dollar bill, there could be another, right?

I fished the floppy disc out of the basement crawlspace, blew off the dust, and flipped it into my computer. I reread *The Boble*, laughing. Then I printed out two copies and took them to an office supply store to be ring-bound. I signed the title page of each one, writing "thank you" beneath my name, and I sent them off to Rebecca.

A month later she wrote again. I was at D&E by that point, facing the reality that I was nearly broke, and the twenty-five dollars in her envelope fed me for a week. She had very little to say, just thanking me for the two copies and asking for five more.

I started to revise and rewrite *The Boble*, correcting errors and filling in the gaps. Between 1992 and 1994, I received occasional letters from Rebecca in New York. I ended up making $500 from her in my first semester alone.

The more copies of *The Boble* I sold, the more I began to rise above the despair. I didn't know what to do with myself, or how I could exist in the real world, but here was money from a stranger for something I had produced. Proof that I wasn't completely useless. I'd made friends, but I found the relationships more confounding than comforting. When we all split off toward college, the high school ties that bound us came undone, and almost every friendship forged in high school would meet with an ugly demise in the 1990s. I felt like there was a layer of mist between myself and every single person I'd ever met—something that I could see through, but never penetrate or overcome.

Part of me worried that what Mom had predicted would come true—that I would repeat my father's crimes. Was I predisposed, genetically, to be part of some endless cycle of evil? This fear overshadowed all of my relationships. I avoided women, I was distant with friends. Echoes of what Dad had done to us, and to Gifford's employees, played in my head. I worried that I was hurting or insulting people—forever saying or doing the wrong thing—and incapable of realizing it.

Rebecca's *Boble* orders re-ignited the spirit to run again. It was like I was back in high school, x-ing out the days on the calendar, except now I was on the larger track of life and the days I marked off were not counting down to an end, but counting away from my ugly past. Allen had told me to keep going forward, so I imagined myself again as one of those 1970s journeyman sci-fi characters. I was part of the crew of the last battlestar, I was Commander Koenig on the runaway moon, I was Doctor Who in his police box. I was running. Running and running. A fugitive from the story of Gifford's Ice Cream, a fugitive from the rage of Barbara Gifford, a fugitive from the specter of Bob Gifford. It didn't matter if I didn't quite know where I was going. I assumed Allen's simplistic attitude was correct. I would become a park ranger or a forester, I would write on the side, and then I would die and that would be that.

Running was my only option. There was no hope of therapy or healing. Allen always said that "healing comes from inside" and that therapists were "drug pushers and lie merchants." I took his advice to heart.

This was the ongoing family rule—do not talk about your problems. The moment you show weakness, you'll be betrayed, abused, taken advantage of. And, my God, I had had enough of all of those things, so the logic seemed sound to me. As my old high school friends began to slowly scatter, I saw their absence as a subtle betrayal, as proof that Allen's wisdom was on the mark. My high school friends had had inklings of my problems at home, they knew parts of the story, and this meant that I had showed them my weaknesses.

This is where my mind was on that first solo drive to Elkins late that summer. I left DC, went up I-270, and connected to I-70 West at Frederick. To get to Elkins, I had to pass by Deep Creek Lake, the dark body of water that still starred in my drowning dreams. I rattled over that old steel girder bridge and zoomed past the quarry, past Alpine Village and the liquor store, over roads and paths visited every childhood summer, all largely unchanged. It took only ten minutes to clear Deep Creek, but I still couldn't help running into ghosts—even my own. I saw the boy I once was and heard my mother's voice, felt her diamond-bladed spanking. At one point I had to pull over and catch my breath.

But I made it through. I pulled my old minivan up toward the mountains and left that cursed lake behind. I had faced down a fear Allen didn't know about—no one did. I've never spoken about my fear of that place until now. In later months and years, I passed Deep Creek Lake several times on lonely winter nights as I drove to or from school. Just once, I stopped the car, got out, and walked to the shore to stare in the moonlight at the icebound mountain water.

II

The road that took me from Deep Creek to Elkins was old US 219, one of the so-called "blue highways" that predates the interstate era. It ran from Lake Erie to middle Virginia, weaving through Appalachia and little towns long forgotten. Elkins itself was an old train town, its main street a choked thoroughfare of big trucks and travelers desperately working their way to points north or south. For many miles, US 219 followed tracks that once carried the railroad to its now-dilapidated downtown. The train station perched on cinderblocks and rotting wood, the tracks overgrown with weeds. Its downtown looked like the center of every Appalachian town—mostly rundown and ramshackle buildings around the glittering Davis Trust Company bank. An old hotel was more halfway house, grim and dark even in the brightest summer sunlight. Businesses were boarded up, and chain stores slowly encroached into strip malls on either end of town. There was no bookstore, just two diners and a bar on almost every block.

My first impression of Davis & Elkins was a smell. A good smell. The crisp mountain air that, even on a hot summer day, reminded me of wet leaves and cool forest. The wooded mountains rose up all around me, and as always there was the sense that, in West Virginia, the sky is awfully small.

Davis & Elkins College perched on a hill overlooking the town, with a scattering of traditionally collegiate brick buildings. Two mansions—Halliehurst and Graceland—stood at the crest of the hill. These were manor houses of the wealthy elite for whom the town was named. One was in disrepair, and the other was being remodeled to house the college's administrative staff. The combined student body was smaller than my graduating senior class at B-CC. Though the school had only a few hundred students, it had been built for nearly two thousand. An entire dorm building lay completely abandoned, and the active dorms—three co-ed and two for women—were full of empty rooms, suites, and halls.

Allen's new job at D&E was unclear to me. He said he was helping to "network the campus." And he talked quite a bit about remote teaching. I think he was also working to hook up classrooms in the local prison. The school claimed two hundred more students than it actually had on campus and, for the most part, I gathered, those were prisoners earning distance-learning degrees.

The way Allen outlined his plan, it sounded like D&E was poised to become a distance-learning tuition mill that would serve students around the world. He said that this was the goal of Lawrence Kudrow, a cousin of Allen's who was dean of students and, according to Allen, the one who really ran the college.

"The president's a drunk," Allen said. "Old Lawrence is the man behind the throne. He's a real bastard—all those old hillbillies are—but he's our bastard."

Allen never seemed to work at his job, though. He only came to campus about once a month and, for the most part, stayed in Maryland and kept at his regular teaching jobs. Everyone in the family joked that he was a man who would go to West Virginia just to get a cup of coffee. And, indeed, some days he would arrive at noon, having driven 250 miles, have lunch with Kudrow, then turn around and drive right back home. I began to suspect that Allen had simply called in a favor with Kudrow and lied about his gig with the college.

The D&E administration, as Allen hinted, was in turmoil. I first met with the director of financial aid, to get my tuition bill sorted out. It was all part of Allen's paycheck, but, on paper, it was explained in a byzantine manner as a sort of scholarship or loan. The financial aid director—a short man with a long beard and slitted, dead eyes—stank of scotch. In fact, at eight in the morning, his entire office smelled like scotch, and he slurred half-finished sentences my way as he clumsily shoved papers at me to sign.

Next was the registrar. When I arrived at her desk to ask for my schedule, she couldn't parse my name. We went through multiple alternatives—Griffith, Grifford, Guildford, Guilford, and Clifford. Finally I spelled it for her and she sounded it out slowly: "Giffff-fffford." She looked up at me and said: "Is that one of them Muslim names?"

The school was small enough to defy the common nightmare of getting lost on my first day. Most classrooms were squeezed into three buildings—the liberal arts in two buildings, science and math in a third. I had a functioning map of the campus in my head by the end of day one. Because my declared major was forestry, my first faculty advisor was a science teacher. When I walked into his office, the first thing he said was: "Whose side are you on?"

I blinked, uncomprehending. He was looking down, scribbling senselessly on a piece of paper. When I didn't answer, he looked up.

"Faculty or administration?" he demanded. "Whose side?"

I shook my head. Speechless. He nodded judiciously.

"You have to choose sides quickly here," he advised. "You're either with the faculty, or you're not." He tapped his pen against his bearded cheek. "You look like a soldier."

"I do?"

"Yes. The faculty needs soldiers in this battle against Dean Kudrow."

Then he sketched out the battle lines. With the president in a stupor, war had erupted between the college faculty and Dean Kudrow. I thought, *oh dear*, but said nothing. I knew to keep silent about my family relation to the dean.

"A librarian!" my advisor continued. "They make a librarian dean! To do what? Make sure all of our books are shelved?"

He leaned forward, his eyes drifting over my shoulder. I glanced behind me, but saw no one. My advisor continued to rant for several long minutes against this massive injustice. I waited patiently. I needed his advice. What classes should I take?

"Oh, that," he said, indignation rapidly giving way to boredom. "Don't sweat it."

Then he signed me up for some core classes—most of them a sad repeat of my last years of high school, right down to the books and projects assigned. My first semester, I often recycled old high school papers. I probably could have skipped the lectures, too, if I didn't find the diatribes my professors carried on against Kudrow so oddly entertaining.

I had a hard time understanding the issue the faculty took with Kudrow. A huge bearded bear of a man, Kudrow was indeed a hillbilly, though a dandy one in his pink and purple shirts. I watched Allen run rings around him. Even I could run rings around him. So why would professors fear him?

Kudrow enjoyed taking my grandfather and me for rides around the countryside. If we came upon a construction zone and saw workers toiling over hot asphalt, Kudrow would pull his Mercedes to the curb and watch them for several minutes. Then he would laugh heartily and say: "Look at 'em. Look at the poor sons of bitches."

Then he would turn around and take us back to Elkins, chuckling the whole way.

It was almost too surreal to believe, and this lunacy reenergized my writing. I started scratching out short stories peopled with a wealth of characters from my classrooms and my dorm.

There was the kid who only lasted half a semester, sequestering himself in his dorm room with a Nintendo and a TV, curtains drawn tight, subsisting entirely on sandwich bread and Mountain Dew. Instead of using the communal bathrooms, he would piss into the empty soda bottles, a pile that grew for weeks and weeks until he finally decided to drop out.

There was the brand-new English professor who fell on his first day of classes, shattered his knee, and spent the rest of the year confined to a wheelchair. He became embroiled in a bitter legal battle with the school that would occasionally seep into his lectures, and, in his second year, he was caught red-handed having sex with one of his students. Rumor said that the girl was riding him in his office as he waved his crutches in the air. Apparently, a janitor investigating "cries of agony" caught them. The anti-

Kudrow bloc, of which this professor was a member, insisted that he'd been set up by the administration.

The school's dorms hosted three fraternities and two sororities, the members of which lived together with the ordinary students. My first dorm room was right next to the TKE hall, and TKE members—all upperclassmen—were intermingled with the freshman population. Most of the time these organizations were allowed to run wild, as if we had all been thrust into a 1980s comedy. They ruthlessly pranked us, once leaving a severed deer's head in the clothes dryer. Cows were slaughtered or abandoned on roofs. Marijuana was grown in the forest around campus. Stills operated in dorm rooms.

The only one of my core classes that first term that I could not call forgettable was history. An admittedly tedious introductory course, it was nonetheless enlivened by Dr. Royal, a troubled, amoral genius. He took me for my first real drink at Captain T's, the bar near the school whose owner allegedly had the police in his pocket and would serve copious amounts of alcohol to minors. For Dr. Royal, history seemed to be a gleefully dark celebration of the insanity and evil of mankind. Dry, antique texts came alive in his lectures. It was the only class I looked forward to.

Socially, I was hopeless. I tried to go through the correct motions. What would be expected of someone who led the simple life of school, job, and death that Allen had described to me? Should I fake my way through love? Friendships? Whenever I tried to make new friends, I felt that same impenetrable film between us. I couldn't tell them what I was going through.

Despite the free ride on my tuition, my debt mounted. My meal plan covered only weekdays, and textbook prices were marked up to an extraordinary degree—for English class, a paperback copy of *Of Mice and Men* with a list price of $5.99 was sold in the school bookstore for $25.

I decided to turn away from it all and throw myself into my fledgling publishing and writing career, which was being subsidized by a stranger's money mailed from New York. The floppy disc that had survived Mom's purge didn't just contain *The Boble—*

it also contained the contents of unpublished issues of *Splinters*. As I sat in my dorm room, the crisp West Virginia autumn outside the windows, I flipped through those unpublished issues—collections of poetry, surreal short stories, and a few strangely powerful literary gems. I thought, why not? And so I started to work at reviving *Splinters*.

In fact, I thought: why not go bigger? *The Boble* was making money, and I had enough material between the archived *Splinters* submissions and my own writing to put together three or four sixty-page chapbooks. It took nothing to start a publishing company. Just print the books, draw a logo, and say I was the CEO. I stayed up until dawn editing the first chapbook—*Elegra*—a collection of short stories by me and several friends who had worked on the second issue of *Splinters*. My first venture into publishing, and it happened overnight.

At the end of the semester, Allen quit his job in a huff. He never said why, and no one would ever talk about it again. He simply had a falling out with Kudrow, told me that the guy was a bum, and then drove off. That was the end of my free tuition. If I wanted to come back to D&E for a second semester, it would happen entirely on my dime.

I returned to my grandparents' house in Silver Spring and went right back to working at the Nature Society bookstore and helping out the groundskeeper. Money was my only way out. I needed it to return to college, I needed it to live, and I needed it to fund my new publishing company. So I decided to work as much as humanly possible and restore the nest egg that Allen had confiscated. I spent the five weeks of my break working every day and late into every night.

III

I named the publishing company Purple Publications. My favorite color. When I returned to Elkins for my second semester, I was still short on money. Tuition cost thousands of dollars, textbooks were murder, and every tank of gas yielded fewer miles from the decaying Voyager. I picked up a weeknight catering gig in Elkins. Weekends and holidays, I drove back to DC to work at the Nature Society's bookshop. I also worked as manager for rental events at the Society's mansion—a job with shifts that stretched ten hours, policing clients, caterers, and a bevy of vendors.

During a typical month, I hammered away at classes Monday through Friday, spending several evenings catering low-grade special events at the Elks Lodge or someplace like it. Then I drove the 250 miles to suburban DC, where I spent my weekend either at the Society's bookstore or managing the mansion for an event. Sometimes I also picked up the odd job landscaping for Allen's neighbors or with the Nature Society's groundskeeper, who was always happy to hand off his duties.

A normal weekend day saw me in the bookstore from eight in the morning to six at night, when I would move to the other end of the mansion to run an event until two in the morning or later. I slept at my desk, or in the store, or curled up on a couch in the mansion's third floor. The third floor also had a shower, and I could cook meals in the full service kitchen, often using leftovers from the events. When other staff members were working in the mansion, I hid. In the grungy basement, I used the groundskeeper's washer and dryer to do my laundry. Sunday nights, as soon as my shift ended, I drove back to Elkins and started all over again.

In this way, I avoided staying with my grandparents as much as possible. Allen always imposed rent, even if I was in town for just a weekend, prorating the monthly amount down to the hour. And I loathed his house. The belching steam furnace answered to no thermometer. In the winter, a humid, wet heat boiled from it. The furnace had two settings: on and off. The damn thing would crank away all day and all night, the radiators spitting and leaking brown, steaming water that stank of rust and rot. My grandfather kept it running with parts salvaged from junkyards and condemned buildings. Sometimes the furnace would explode, spraying boiling water across the basement, and he would march downstairs to unintentionally and humorlessly reenact the epic battle between father and furnace from the film *A Christmas Story*. Even in the deepest freezes, the house would maintain itself at a steady ninety degrees as the incessant humidity warped wood and fogged glasses.

What remained of the Gifford's equipment in the garage was like a forgotten shrine, its once-shiny stainless steel lost beneath layers of dust and grease. Tools and junk covered displays and freezers as Allen puttered around with his many experiments and business ventures.

The Gifford's specter seemed to always hang over us. Perhaps it was haunting by association, but I felt like the longer I spent cooped up with my grandparents, the more Gifford's burrowed under my skin and destroyed me, as it had them. Working—and practically living—at the Nature Society's old mansion was relaxing, comfortable, and so much better than the claustrophobia of my grandparent's house.

Most of the property around the mansion was wooded, ten or so acres of once-manicured lawns and ornamental gardens that were now covered by underbrush. The Society's goal was to create a nature preserve in the middle of bustling suburban sprawl. They kept the lawns mowed, so as to begrudgingly rent the house out for special events, but otherwise lived hand to mouth off of bequests and membership fees while the rest of the acreage went wild. Visiting the grounds just off of the screaming highway felt like arriving suddenly and wonderfully at a remote and densely forested island. Fox and deer ran through the parking lot into the woods, hawks wheeled in the afternoon skies, bats swarmed across the face of the full moon. At night, when the property was closed, it was almost primeval.

In the bookstore, in the long hours between customers, Purple Publications came together. My writing flourished and soon my catalog had thirteen titles. Sometimes, I wouldn't even tell Allen I was in town. I became a ghost at the big mansion, creeping around the basement, avoiding staff, living off of cast-off food, drinks, and clothes. I wandered the grounds after hours, when nobody was around, and pretended that I was the lord of a tiny fief. Looking back, it's alarming to see the parallels with my father's last days in the Gifford's store. Was every Gifford boy doomed to become a ghost at his place of employment? I slept in the bookshop, in various offices, and, in the summer, on the roof under the stars.

The strange and twisted adventures of the Society staff, at least the part not made up of old ladies, became a fascinating lesson in office relationships. I watched romances play out, sometimes pathetically. I lost count of how many people had sex on my boss's desk. Corruption was rife. So many books went missing from the bookstore that one of the revolving-door parade of managers started spending the night behind the cash register, hugging a baseball bat to her chest. Another co-worker received regular shipments in boxes addressed generically to the store, no return address, full of cassette tape cases packed with pot.

The most outlandish scheme, though, involved a government-sponsored pilot composting program, back before composting was trendy. As I understood the arrangement, the head of the program made a deal with my boss to sell cheap little plastic composters through the store for ten bucks a pop, cash only. Then they embarked on a massive advertising campaign. Sales were extraordinary. A truck would arrive on Friday and dump the composters outside the store and we wouldn't even bother straightening them up because they'd be gone in forty-eight hours. Thick envelopes piled up in the back of the cash register as thousands of composters moved through this anonymous cash system. Certain employees took a regular, undisclosed sum off the top, but, of course, everyone helped themselves to a little bit.

Even the government worker heading the program would pocket all money from sales during his frequent "compost demonstrations"—hour-long classes about how, exactly, you should go about dumping your shit into a plastic bin. How much was this knowledge worth? When a co-worker started giving the class, he told me he made a thousand dollars in sales each time, and since I was the one counting, I knew that far less than that amount actually made it into the till.

As if that weren't enough, I watched people drive up at night and fill their cars with compost bins after the store had closed. Sometimes they put money into the little mailbox beside the store's entrance, but usually they just stole the bins outright.

Even with this rampant theft of the merchandise and profits, the composters made so much money that we had to haul the envelopes of cash upstairs to the safe multiple times each day. For almost a year, several thousand dollars of untraceable income passed through our hands every day.

And the composter scam was only one of many. Some of my coworkers were literally selling the property's trees. They'd cut one down, have the dopey old volunteers chop it into firewood, and sell it by the truckload. One employee made so much money off this scheme that she was able to put her three kids through college with her profits.

It seemed that the whole world was mad, with nothing clearly and purely good. I learned to despise the customers—the wealthy elite seeking status through bird feeders and generic birdseed that cost twice as much per pound as a gallon of gas. My coworkers were often nuts. One went through the trashcans every night, noting what had been eaten or drunk, even restoring shredded notes. When I clocked in each morning, he prided himself in constructing a detailed Sherlock Holmes-style analysis of my previous day's activity. In response, I began to write random words and nonsense sayings on scraps of paper, after which I'd tear them up and deposit the scraps in multiple trashcans. I wrote short absurdist poems and filled up one sheet of paper with: "Should I do it? YES! Should I do it? YES!" written over and over in an increasingly crazed scrawl.

I poured all of this material into my stories for Purple Publications. In the new writing, I rediscovered the passion I'd felt in high school when I stumbled across my first zine.

Early in my second semester at D&E, I blared music at all hours and started to skip classes to focus on writing and laying out chapbooks. Slowly, my GPA ratcheted down to a C—about as low as it could go at D&E, where professors seemed, largely, unwilling to flunk anyone. I asked Dr. Royal if there was a place where I could get chapbooks printed on the cheap.

"Chapbooks?" he asked.

"Yeah, short collections of—"

"Goddamnit!" Royal barked. "I know what chapbooks are. What are you doing writing them?"

I told him about Purple Publications and that spilled into a story about my hopes and goals and the insanity around me at school and at work that had found its way into my writing. A slow, dangerous grin split his weathered face.

"You want Shirley and Matt," he said.

He wrote their names and a phone number down on a scrap of paper and slid it across his desk. I reached out to grab it, but he held it pinned to the table with his fingers, fixing me with a grim glare.

"Don't share this number with anyone," he added.

I called the number from the dorm payphone. The phone rang seven times. When a man picked it up, the first thing he said was: "How did you get this number?"

I told him that Dr. Royal had given it to me.

The man was silent for a few heartbeats, then he sighed. "Are you good?"

"Good?"

"Yes. Are. You. Good."

"I . . . yes?"

"Is it time?"

"I was told that you could help me print some chapbooks that I—"

"Oh. Yes! Of course."

He laughed nervously, then rattled off some directions and told me to spin by for dinner.

Shirley and Matt's printing press was located forty minutes away, deep in the woods outside of Parsons, West Virginia. I piled into my rattling minivan and headed out to meet them. I couldn't see anything of their property from the road other than the start of a gravel driveway and a rusted metal gate emblazoned with a large black and white sign warning that trespassers would be summarily executed. There was no mailbox, no address, no other sign of life. The directions provided relied on landmarks and mileage more than anything else—"go precisely 7.8 miles past the diner and look for a rock formation on the right side of the road, then turn at the first left. You'll see a pile of railroad ties . . ."

I pulled to a stop at the gravel road beside those railroad ties, as instructed. A bald man in khakis emerged from the forest. His neck and arms sported curlicue tattoos that I couldn't identify. He stepped up to the driver-side window, standing slightly back and sideways like a cop.

"Gifford?" he asked.

I nodded and he demanded ID. I showed him my driver's license. He walked around to the back of the car, writing down my license plate number in a little book, then he came back to the window and handed my license back. Without a word, he went to the gate and hauled it open. I caught a glimpse of a shoulder holster under his camouflage jacket and my blood started to chill. I should have probably started to second-guess my desire for a cheap and reliable book printer, but a publisher takes whatever charity he can get.

The gravel road turned a couple of times, working deep into the woods before finally opening up into a large clearing around which five buildings clustered. One building was a proper farm-house, while the others looked like World War II-style POW barracks. Several women and children wandered around, chickens ran aimlessly through the yard, and two German Shepherds chained to a rusted-out pick-up truck barked themselves stupid. I sat in my car wondering what I'd wandered into.

Another man walked out of the house. Tall and barrel-chested, he sported a long, white beard, jeans, and a T-shirt with no sleeves. An SS tattoo blazed on one of his bare arms, and on the other was a sleeve tattoo with the same curlicues I'd seen on the guy at the gate. He walked up to the passenger-side window and knocked twice. I reached over and rolled it down, nervously introducing myself. In reply, he nodded and said: "Welcome to Free Mill Creek, brother."

This was Matt, the man I'd spoken to over the phone. His wife, Shirley, was much less imposing. She poured me lemonade and talked about the nobility of the Indians who once "ran free through these hills." She walked me through their printing press, in one of the big sheds behind the main house, and told me what they were capable of printing. Tattooed, bald-headed workers all labored away, none of them looking up at us. Behind the shed, Shirley showed me her "shrine"—a pile of rocks, with various herbs planted around it. Dangling above it were medicine wheels, feathers, and bird skulls, suspended from a web-work of strings.

"When the Indians were here," she said, kneeling and laying a hand on the pile of rocks, "they would worship right here. Free Mill Creek is built on a ley line—do you know what that is?"

According to Shirley, a mystical alignment ran through West Virginia, a "track of power" that crossed right beneath our feet at Free Mill Creek. It was because of this alignment that people had been coming to West Virginia even before the Indians. The Templars had come here to hide their treasure, the Vikings had come here and built stone huts and left cryptic runes, and others had been here—"ancient builders" who developed several local caves into "temples to forgotten gods."

"The Indians were merely the caretakers of this tradition," Shirley told me, "and now it's up to us here at Free Mill Creek to preserve this tradition and protect it from the government."

I nodded politely, spoke when spoken to, and listened attentively. I wanted to hurry up and get down to business.

Back in the house, over more lemonade, I outlined Purple Publications to Shirley. The first thing they would print would be a professional version of *The Boble*, and we spent an afternoon poring over paper and layout options.

Within four days, Shirley delivered the first bound and official print run of *The Boble* to my dorm room. When Rebecca's next letter with *Boble* orders came, I sent her a lengthy reply detailing the three new chapbooks and explaining the sudden change in *The Boble*'s quality. I told her I'd like to raise the prices for each item, but the decision was ultimately hers.

Her reply came a month later—an order for ten copies of each of the chapbooks and, as always, more copies of *The Boble*. Without comment, she included $7.50 for each item. Nearly $300 in flattened bills from New York City. A king's ransom that, in one swoop, paid off the printing fees from Free Mill Creek.

As Purple Publications "boomed," my relationship with Shirley and Matt also grew. I visited them only twice more, a bit spooked by their compound of radical isolationists. But Shirley seemed happy to deliver the chapbooks to my dorm. She sat with me and we drank coffee, using my oversized dorm fridge as a table, and she told me that what I was doing was very important.

"*The Boble* is going to change the world," she said. "We've all been reading it, and we think it needs to get out there."

She mentioned a distribution plan, which Free Mill Creek would undertake. I shrugged and said that I usually got $7.50 per sale from a girl in New York. Really, what Shirley offered was a trade. If I let Matt and her take over distribution and sales of *The Boble*, they would use the proceeds to pay for printing it, as well as my other chapbooks. If there was a profit, then I would get fifty percent of it. Perfect! No cost to me and maybe some cash on the side. I shook on it.

In the meantime, the middle of the semester was approaching fast and I had barely attended any of my classes. I had befriended many of my professors outside of class, though, so most of them gave me passing grades anyway, and my GPA never dipped below an already pitiful 2.0. My second semester was still a ridiculous echo of what I'd learned in high school. I still recycled old papers and reports. It seemed I could pass at D&E even without trying. Even without showing up.

But the warnings had started. Even my staunchest professorial allies told me I would have to shape up if I wanted to come back the following year. All the admonitions fell on deaf ears, though. I had found my love—writing and publishing.

What my professors and a handful of friends called reckless, I considered inspired. I was going to live off *The Boble* and the rest of the Purple Publications catalog. I didn't need to follow Allen's simplistic worldview anymore. I felt high and alive on this newly found freedom.

In March of that year, 1993, the "storm of the century" hit, dumping more than three feet of snow on West Virginia and cutting off Elkins from the rest of the world. For a week, crews tried and failed to dig us out. With almost all roads closed, the town ground to a silent, moody standstill. With our classes canceled, I turned those snowbound hours into a writing marathon, working round the clock on Purple Publications.

Outside of my dorm room, the snowdrifts rose over my head. I flung myself into them from the third story balconies. The sensation was spectacular—the bright white snow enveloping and suffocating me as I desperately fought my way out. I felt like the snow was cleansing me, freezing and choking out everything bad. Again and again I hurled myself off the precipice into the drifts, laughing, gasping, racing back up the stairs to do it again.

IV

When the semester ended in May, I left college with no real desire to return. Dean Kudrow had made it clear I wasn't welcome back, anyway, with a few snide comments delivered in the privacy of his office. But tuition was astronomical, and I could already see the beginnings of an income from Purple Publications. Disillusioned and uninspired by the college experience, I decided it made much more sense to develop what I still saw as money for nothing.

Writing came easy to me, publishing even easier. And there was the promise of money in publishing. But the old adage hung in my mind—to make money, you have to spend money. And I'd been living a variation of that adage all semester, working locally during the week and going back to DC every weekend to work even more. Now, without school to worry about, I could live near my DC jobs again and let my work schedule go wild.

Back in the guest bedroom at my grandparents' house, Allen was less than pleased with my decision. He said I was a "drop-out." But he seemed happy enough to see what were now $900 monthly rent checks resume. A ridiculous sum for a rented room in Silver Spring—even today—but I didn't have the will to fight Allen. I never did.

At the Nature Society bookstore, I took over most of the duties that an assistant manager would perform—assuring myself six shifts a week. The groundskeeper then paid me to patrol the forty acres of footpaths at night and to clean the mansion in the early mornings. Throughout the day, on lunch break from the bookstore, or whenever it was closed, I did odd jobs, from painting to gardening. Occasionally, I finished cleaning up after a weekend rental event just minutes before it was time to open the bookshop in the morning.

Since I spent many nights at the mansion, I often observed my co-workers after an event, when they thought the house was empty. They would undo each other's closing-down checklists. These were weekend-only workers. Since our boss hired more staff than needed to cover a weekend, they were trying to sabotage their co-workers and gain a larger number of these lucrative shifts.

Co-workers also collected "trophies" from each event—items stolen from clients, like the tops of wedding cakes. But there was theft at every level, from bottles of wine to cars. Because I rarely slept, I often worked back-to-back twelve-hour shifts. One of my colleagues would even "sell" her shifts to me for a small finder's fee—I would pay her a quarter of my earnings, or, more often, steal a certain amount of booze for her. All of the jobs were ninety percent downtime, really. I had to always be "on," in case something happened, but I spent most of the time writing and working on publishing assignments. I even fleshed out my downtime with freelance writing assignments for business magazines. I could put together three or four assignments, each paying $150 a pop, during one rental shift. With tips and all the jobs combined, I could clear a thousand bucks a weekend.

My savings grew, and soon I had tons of disposable income on hand. I began to pay bills in advance. I wrote a check for twelve months of rent to my grandfather, hoping a $10,000 check would shut him up. He replied by raising my rent to $1,000 a month and saying I owed him the extra in back rent. I ignored this demand, finally making a meager stand against him, and used the rest of my earnings to pay my car insurance and credit cards in advance. For a year, I had no bills.

My handshake agreement with Shirley and Matt, the West Virginia printers, was still in place. As the Purple Publications catalog grew, I sent new files to them for printing. They sold them all under the same deal as *The Boble*—a fifty-fifty split of the net profits. The occasional check from them seemed like proof that I had discovered what was really important in life.

But I was naïve about running a business. They were the publisher, not me. I called them my distributor, but the fact is that I was focused on the writing side of things and not on the business of running a publishing company. My lonely, zine-like, ranting screeds were going into chapbook after chapbook and all I got in return was a check and no explanation. Money for nothing is how I always felt about it, anyway. And the money coming in soon felt more important than the art it was supposed to serve. I became addicted to the cash and, inevitably, I once again drifted away from my own writing, losing interest and time.

I had thought I'd escaped. That was the point, after all. That was the theme of my life—run away and bury myself in anything that could erase thoughts about my family and Gifford's Ice Cream. Purple Publications and getting paid for my writing meant nothing, really, except yet another excuse to fill every waking moment with a screaming, blinding distraction.

Allen expressed increasing concern about me. But, when he sat me down for a heart to heart, it wasn't to encourage me to return to school, nor to ease up on my work schedule. It wasn't even to challenge me on the boxes and boxes of ill-gotten alcohol and wedding supplies building up in the basement. He had another mission—to kill Purple Publications.

For an educated man, my grandfather had a bizarre hatred for literature. In his house, I wasn't allowed to read openly as a child. If as an adult I took a seat in the comfy living room chairs and kicked back with a book, he would attempt to distract me with a movie or a chore. If I sat out in the yard on a glorious day to read beneath a tree, he'd devise some sort of yard work. I was even forbidden to read in the bathroom, and Allen policed this. If he saw me leave or enter the bathroom with a book, he'd upbraid me about my bad habit.

"Writing," he said, "is for faggots. This little thing you have going on with your writing is a stupid waste of time and money and you should be focusing on your jobs."

Part of me knew that Allen was way off base. But another part took his words to heart. Talking to him, or rather being talked at by him, I started to feel an old, familiar exhaustion. It didn't take much to slow me down. In just eighteen months after leaving college, I had worked myself to the point of collapse.

I never understood then how much my mother and Allen were alike. They seemed very different—he was big and set in his ways, but, for the most part, he seemed to care about me. I think, though, that I didn't know what being cared about really meant. My only benchmark was that he didn't prank me or deliver punishments on the level of those meted out by Mom. Looking back now, I see so clearly that they both suffered from the same spiritual and mental illness. But then, at Allen's urging, I made one of the worst decisions of my young life.

Near the end of 1994, I shut down Purple Publications.

I returned Rebecca's latest chapbook order and the $250 she'd sent with a note saying, "Purple Publications is no more. I'm very sorry. Thank you." I never heard from her again.

I sent a similar letter to Shirley and Matt—"It's all over, I'm out." I never heard from them again, either—though I did find out, many years later, that they continued to produce and distribute (and, no doubt, profit from) the Purple Publications catalog for nearly a decade.

I dedicated myself completely to my jobs. I thought that I could somehow learn to like them. That I might somehow inherit my managers' positions when they retired or left. My life became a blur, surrounded by the excesses of my co-workers and the transgressions of my bosses.

The blur didn't last long, though. It vanished, replaced by a new and welcome clarity, during one winter wedding in early 1995, only a few months after my fateful decision to kill Purple Publications.

Winter weddings were especially boring—with the mansion overheated and damp, and the client bound by a strict maximum occupancy, events were too small and too stuffy to get really raucous. Around ten at night, I was spinning around in my office chair, music blasting through the walls as the DJ tried to enliven the evening, when my breath caught and I stopped. My vision clouded, sparkly and black on the edges. I had been struck many times with the urge to run. But this was the most powerful such urge I'd ever felt.

I had to run farther. I had to leave the country.

That night, I decided that I would go to England—a country that felt close to me, if only through the lens of imported Britcoms. I made a second promise, as well. I would spend a couple of months in England to restore my sense of myself, and then I would go back to school.

I went home and re-applied to D&E because I felt like I should finish this chapter where it started. A month later I had in hand an acceptance letter from D&E and tickets for a six-week adventure in England.

For a few blissful months, then, it seemed I had a life plan, a goal, an idea of where the future would take me. Was I running simply for running's sake? I didn't care. Focus and clarity had returned, and that was enough.

I meticulously planned my trip, relishing this new lease on life. A sea change would happen the moment the wheels touched down at Gatwick. I applied for my passport, held it like an amulet when it arrived. I made exhaustive lists of places to see, ranking them from must-sees to secondary stops.

I knew the money would dry up the moment I went back to school in the fall, so I wanted to build as large a nest egg as possible. I kept working, steadfastly refusing Allen's "requests" for back rent and loans, right up until it was time to leave.

Armed with a Britrail pass, I experienced the bustling wildness of London, dipped my toe in the British Channel, and gorged myself on English breakfasts. I was introduced to fine single malt Scotch, and stood on the shore of Loch Ness, trying not to compare it too closely to Deep Creek Lake. I even walked in the footsteps of Patrick McGoohan from *The Prisoner* at Portmeirion in Wales.

Finally, in a small northern town called Brampton, I began to realize that I couldn't keep running.

V

I was comfortable on trains in the UK, watching the countryside pass outside the window. Able to hop on and off with my pass, I would detrain at random small towns and wander, anonymous, through the streets. I'd buy the local papers, drink at the local pubs, and sometimes go for days without speaking to anyone. My vacation was marked by the rhythmic rattling of train cars and the smell of summer rain.

Every moment felt free. I soon forgot what day it was. There were so many towns that they started to bleed together even as I tried to journal my thoughts. The farther north I went, the more lonely the countryside became. But no one asked me about Gifford's Ice Cream. No grueling job waited just around the corner. That old world felt like a dream, remembered with less and less clarity as the days wore on.

I didn't plan on visiting Brampton. Hadrian's Wall was on my list of primary stops and I selected to stay in Brampton because it was roughly halfway between Carlisle and Newcastle, the Wall's two end points. Lonely Planet demanded that I stay at Hexam if I wanted to do anything involving the Wall, dismissing Brampton in two sentences. But looking at the map, my heart told me to make it my base.

The train from York took me to Newcastle, where I got on a little one-car commuter train that looked like it had rolled out of the late 1960s. After the big Inter-City trains, experiencing this model was a quaint thrill, and the fact that it was a single car was enormous fun. Only four other people joined me on board, and we made rattling, old-world progress west, the countryside quickly rising up around us.

After a couple of hours, the train stopped at an unmanned platform in the woods. A few spray-painted signs indicated I was at Brampton, but I saw no other sign of civilization. I had gathered my bag and started for the door when the conductor looked up, gave me an "oy," and asked where I was going.

"I'm for Brampton," I said, pointing out the window.

He and the passengers stared blankly at me. The conductor asked: "What's in Brampton?"

The driver stuck his head out of the front cabin and said something, and the conductor shouted back at him in his thick Geordie accent. Everyone laughed.

"You're the first person I seen get off here," the driver shouted down the aisle to me.

I shrugged. He shrugged back. As I bounded onto the platform, the driver honked his horn several times, then the train slowly rattled off, curving into the distance. I stood in the quiet country calm for a few minutes, utterly alone but for the gentle lowing of cows somewhere nearby. I found a bench at the platform and sat, reading my guidebook, imagining myself the last man at some post-apocalyptic outpost. It was the quietest place I've ever been.

A rusting, antique sign tilted in the mud near the train platform. Eventually, I leapt down and walked over to it. It read "Brampton, 1 mi." and pointed towards a deep, dark wood. It was like finding the lamppost in Narnia.

I threw my travel bag over my shoulder and leapt down off the platform. The footpath weaved through a quarter mile or so of thick, sun-dappled forest before it approached a busy road, its traffic the first sounds of the human world I'd heard since the train rattled off. The path went underneath the road, curved again, and the sounds of civilization were lost as the countryside rose around me once more.

After what felt like much more than a mile, the footpath emerged between hedgerows into a clearing that overlooked the tiny village of Brampton. All at once I felt something—a shiver, a certainty I was being followed. The feeling was so strong that I spun around, ready to confront whoever was there. But the path stretched away, empty. A chittering, mindless sort of panic insisted I was being followed, pursued. I stood there a few more minutes, looking back along the path, a terrible fear settling over me.

And then it occurred to me: I was 3,300 miles away from my parents, but there was no escaping their ghosts. The wounds were lodged in my soul. I carried them wherever I went. Old Andrew was following me, the Andrew I thought I'd left behind in the dark-paneled rooms of the Society mansion or the stifling back bedroom of my grandparents' house.

Entering Brampton, I found a town with one butcher shop, next to one bakery, next to one pub—the White Lion, which had a room for rent on its second floor. That first day, I sat in a corner of the bustling pub and drank a few pints, people-watching and soaking up the atmosphere, trying to forget that dark feeling on the footpath. The next morning, I rose at dawn and hit the local co-op, where I filled my backpack with sandwich makings, a six-pack of lager, and some water. Then I set out on foot for Hadrian's Wall.

The start of the path was marked by a grassy hill that used to be an Iron Age fort, though it was now just a tree-covered slope with a statue of the seventh Earl of Carlisle at the top. From there, a three-mile hike would bring me to the Wall just east of Housesteads Mile Fort.

At first, the path was comfortable, passing through a gentle meadow before skirting along the edge of a sheep farm. I stepped carefully around sheep shit, my jangled nerves anticipating a farmer's gunshots cracking through the air to warn against my trespass. But it never came. I was in the English countryside, far removed from the rat racers in DC and the well-armed folk in West Virginia.

The path eventually descended into a small river valley, and rose up again near the grounds of Lanercost Priory—a beautiful church that had managed to survive the worst of the Reformation. The old church ladies had put up a display for the tourists, selling drinks, snacks, jams, and gift items. Welcome refreshment after the first mile of my hike.

The way continued along a bridle path, then into a dark forest, where it wound precariously along the banks of a rushing stream. The first evidence of Hadrian's Wall—a crumbling pillar of rock about two feet high and signposted—sat along this trail. Not long after loomed the Wall itself, a stark low ridgeline about six feet high, with a one-lane road hugging its curve. To imagine it nineteen hundred years ago, twenty feet high and topped with legionnaires, was awesome.

I spent two hours there enjoying my lunch and soaking up the atmosphere. Then I clambered back to the path and began hiking along the Wall, covering several miles before I felt like I was being followed once again. I spun around again and, this time, there was someone there. A black-haired woman of my mother's build and height.

I felt an old fear rise in me.

She was maybe fifty feet behind me, and she came to a stop when she saw me looking back at her. We stood there, both of us unmoving, and I tried to make out her features. But she wore a large, pulled-down hat that cast her face in shadow. Then she turned, walked to the edge of the Wall, and looked over it.

I jogged away, putting some distance between us. After a few minutes, breath heaving, I checked behind me and saw that I was alone once again. Nervously, I climbed to the far side of the Wall and hid myself among the stones, waiting for perhaps an hour. Was Mom following me? Maybe she had found out about the trip and was stalking me?

Or was I insane?

After that encounter, I resumed my hike to a museum along the Wall, then in the later afternoon turned around to head back to Brampton. When I passed the spot where I had seen Mom's twin, I paused. When I turned to look behind me, she was there again, well back this time, sitting on a rock and facing me.

Now I was certain I was being followed. I continued walking, determined not to run, and checked over my shoulder periodically. She followed, carefully maintaining her distance. She stopped when I stopped, started up again when I did.

I had misjudged the time and, when I reached the path to Brampton, dusk was settling in. I nervously kept an eye out for Mom's twin, but she held back and vanished from sight before I turned and left the Wall. It was fully dark when I arrived back at the White Lion, which was wild with village youths. I grabbed a pint, went up to my room, and lay there for a day in something of a fugue state, Mom's twin still on my mind.

Was I seeing things? Had my troubled past been given form by a brain swiss-cheesed from anger, confusion, and overwork? After a few restless dreams, I rose for a late snack and then let myself sink into the bed again in my tiny guestroom. Soon I stopped thinking about the woman at the Wall, and everything else. It was just me in that room above that pub in Brampton. Some of my sense of hope returned—I still had a long leg of my trip through Scotland to look forward to. But I feared that Mom's twin would always be there.

I've had a hard time deconstructing my experience at Hadrian's Wall and in Brampton. The feeling of being pursued by whispering ghosts, of glimpsing a freedom I couldn't quite grasp. I've returned to the spot many times since 1995, walking again and again in my own footsteps to sit with my back against the Wall, gazing across the moors below, the summer sun (or rain) beating against me, the makings of a sandwich waiting in my backpack, my feet bleeding and blistered from the hike.

Though I didn't know it at the time, my mother had vanished during most of that summer of 1995. She had taken leave from her job and driven into the sunset, dropping in and out of touch with friends and family as she slowly made her rambling way across the U.S. Though she eventually re-emerged in San Francisco, her strange journey remains shrouded in mystery. In later years, this eerie coincidence has made me look back at Brampton and wonder if my younger self was right—could Mom have followed me? But how? She didn't vanish as neatly as Dad had—there were sightings of her as she travelled west. It's unlikely she was actually there in Great Britain, but I still wonder.

I went home that summer with a heavy heart. I didn't want to leave England. But I had promised myself more than just a vacation. My life change wouldn't be complete until I returned to Davis & Elkins and proved to myself that I could get a degree and live a simpler, better life.

So once again I made that long country drive to the tiny college in the mountains. This time, I had a new advisor: the grinning, mischievous Dr. Royal, who had been so inspirational my freshman year. I sat down with him in a reading room in the school's glittering new library. In the hushed silence that all libraries impose, even when full of chattering students, Dr. Royal stared at me without speaking for a full minute, his face solemn. Then he shouted, in a thick southern drawl: "You're a history man!"

His laughter echoed off the high ceiling, and students and faculty all turned to stare at us. I smiled to myself. I had loved history. So, of course, I became a history man. But I told him that I was determined to earn my degree as quickly as possible and, ignoring his counseling, I signed up for twenty hours of classes— two credits over the maximum. Half of my tuition was covered by student loans, but my previous year's income meant I didn't qualify for more. So I put the other half of my tuition on credit cards.

With history came heavy-duty writing assignments and fewer wasteful core classes, but I took to the schedule happily. I spent weekends researching in the library, reading ahead, and using the primitive Internet of 1995 to supplement my studies. For some classes, I turned in the entire semester's worth of assignments a few weeks after classes began. This bought me enough free time to resume my local catering job in addition to my usual routine where I ran back to DC on the weekends to work my multiple jobs. This time, though, the money was all poured into tuition.

Thanks to Dr. Royal, I began to learn to find some joy in life. He dragged me out to the bars in town and there his lectures would continue, in hushed tones, over countless drinks. At night, we'd go back to his house and listen to old vinyl records, continue drinking, and discuss college politics.

Dean Kudrow's star was falling by then, and rumors of his departure were circulating. With what would turn out to be remarkable prescience, Dr. Royal predicted how the faculty would turn on each other to fill the power vacuum Kudrow would leave behind. It wasn't that he liked starting fights, but his fascination with history was largely a fascination with the human tendency toward conflict, so watching it unfold in front of him was a professional delight.

I filled the next two years with as many credit hours as possible, working multiple jobs all the while. By the start of my senior year, only one foreign language credit and ten self-study credits remained. But I had earned a poor reputation on campus. I hung out with crazy people. I fought bitterly with the administration, and worst of all, I'd managed to get myself banned from the library.

One night as I'd sat and worked on a research project in the library, I listened to a night clerk harassing one of the Japanese exchange students. He had her pinned against a wall and was slurring all sorts of terrifying sexual threats. I got up, stalked over, and shouted him down.

The next day the chief librarian (a man known to colleagues and students only as "Edward") sent me a letter saying that I was barred indefinitely from entering the library. I disobeyed this rule and was ejected several times. Librarians—even those I had befriended—were forbidden to allow me to check out books. I had to ask my professors to check out books on my behalf. At one point, I disguised myself with sunglasses and a hat, hiding in a group of students, and slipped past the sentries. I filled my backpack with the books I needed for class and snuck out through the service entrance. I never returned them.

I was sick of D&E by that point.

I appealed to the dean's office to let me finish my final credits back home—the one class at the University of Maryland, and the self-study on my own—and Kudrow was glad to see me gone. When he signed the paperwork approving my move, he shoved it across his desk and said: "Good riddance."

I finished my studies in Maryland and graduated. I returned to D&E to walk the stage in May 1998. When my turn came, Kudrow mispronounced my name—"Guildford"—and refused to shake my hand when I marched across the stage and took my degree. When I got back to my seat and opened the folder, instead of finding my degree, I saw a note saying that I owed twenty dollars in overdue library fees and that my degree would not be officially conferred until I had paid off the debt.

I did so without complaint.

As it turned out, Kudrow had been burned in effigy the year before I graduated. Not long after my convocation, he resigned in disgrace.

In 2007, Edward contacted me and told me that he had been pressured by Kudrow to ban me from the library. He apologized profusely and said that if he had refused to ban me, Kudrow would have fired him. He said it was one of the things that he felt "most guilty about" from that era. I learned some years later that he died a few days after that apology.

My B.A. in History and Political Science felt tainted by all of these antics. But I'd done it. I'd fulfilled the promise I'd made to myself on that lonely night in early 1995.

My victory, though, was short-lived.

Gifford's

Ice Cream and Candies

Menu

Sundaes, 95c

Gifford's sundaes are always a generous treat—excitingly made with fresh toppings from our own kitchen: Two scoops of ice cream topped with the sauce of your choice, real, old-fashioned whipped cream and a Maraschino cherry.

CHOCOLATE	**MAPLE WALNUT**	**RASPBERRY MAGNIFIQUE**
CHOCOLATE-MINT	**STRAWBERRY**	**WILD CHERRY**
PINEAPPLE	**MARSHMALLOW**	**CHOCOLATE-MARSHMALLOW**

Jumbo Sundaes, 1.15

A sure hit with the person who wants that something extra: Three scoops of ice cream topped with your choice of the above sauces, whipped cream and a Maraschino cherry.

Enjoy the sundae of your choice by adding that extra touch of the true ice cream aristocrat: Crunchy Chopped Nuts, Old World Spanish Peanuts, Extra Long Shredded Coconut, Old Dominion Water Blanched Peanuts, Tender Supreme Pecan Haves, Exotic Oriental Cashews, Golden Gate Almonds.

ANY OF THE ABOVE SERVINGS 20¢ ADDITIONAL

Sodas, 95c

We believe our sodas are unique . . . made the old-fashioned way, with sauce, soda water and ice cream blended to give that rich, creamy flavor: finished to perfection by the addition of two scoops of ice cream, whipped cream and a Maraschino cherry.

STRAWBERRY	**CHOCOLATE-MINT**	**RASPBERRY MAGNIFIQUE**
CHOCOLATE	**COFFEE**	**VANILLA**
PINEAPPLE	**ROOT BEER**	**WILD CHERRY**
MINT		**MOCHA**

Jumbo Sodas, 1.50

A real find in the tradition of the heroic ancient flagon: Four scoops of ice cream, your choice of any of the above flavors of sauces, whipped cream and a Maraschino cherry.

Gifford's Summer Features

FRUIT FREEZES A refreshingly delicious combination of pure fruit ice and chilled soda water: Orange — Lime — Raspberry — Lemon **75c**

FRUIT ICE COOLER A smooth blend of our pure fruit ice and extra rich ice cream with just enough carbonated water to make it a cool and refreshing summer drink: Orange — Lime — Raspberry — Lemon **75c**

FRUIT ICE BOWL Three scoops of your favorite fresh fruit ice with strawberry or pineapple sauce: Orange — Raspberry — Lemon — Lime **80c**

PARFAITS The gem of the ice cream connoisseur, parfaits are colorfully attractive with layer upon layer of our rich ice cream, sauces and whipped cream — STRAWBERRY — NEAPOLITAN — CHOCOLATE **1.00**

CANDIES

Sheer elegance of the art is demonstrated! Our chocolates are hand dipped by artisans of experience. Did you know the swirls on the top indicate the flavor? Observe the different designs on each chocolate. Better yet, try some. Also, wedding mints so delicious to the taste that your friends may forget who is getting married.

BE SURE TO STOP BY OUR SUB-ZERO DISPLAY CASE AND SEE OUR LARGE EXHIBIT OF EXQUISITELY DECORATED PARTY ICE CREAMS.

We are glad you came in —

Giffords Famous Features

SUPER BANANA SPLIT Nominate yourself king for a day and enjoy a king size **1.55** serving of royally prepared ice cream and sauces: Made with a whole banana, three scoops of our ever rich ice cream, a ladle each of chocolate, pineapple, strawberry sauces and regally crowned with whipped cream, crunchy chopped nuts and a Maraschino cherry.

CHILDREN'S BANANA SPLIT Two scoops of ice cream: vanilla and chocolate; **1.20** one-half banana, chocolate and strawberry topping, nuts, whipped cream and a cherry.

SWISS SUNDAE Made with three scoops of our delicious ice cream, topped with **1.40** Swiss sauce (thick, creamy, chocolate flavor), whipped cream, chopped nuts and a Maraschino cherry.

JUMBO SWISS SUNDAE Four scoops of ice cream. **1.65**

ALPINE SPLIT Deliciously made with two dips of ice cream, half a banana sliced **1.25** lengthwise, topped with our ever rich, creamy Swiss sauce, whipped cream, chopped nuts and a Maraschino cherry.

BIG TOP For the connoisseurs of ice cream who love generous portions: Generous **1.95** serving of sponge cake smothered with strawberries under a blanket of vanilla, chocolate and strawberry ice cream and topped with chopped nuts, whipped cream and a Maraschino cherry.

HOT FUDGE SUNDAE We are especially proud of our Hot Fudge sauce which is **1.10** made in small batches from an old Dutch recipe—a delectable blend of extra rich cream and smooth Dutch cocoa: Two scoops of ice cream, Hot Fudge sauce, whipped cream and a Marashino cherry.

JUMBO HOT FUDGE SUNDAE Three scoops of ice cream. **1.35**

HOT BUTTERSCOTCH SUNDAE Our smooth and creamy Hot Butterscotch sauce **1.10** is a natural for the appetite that enjoys the best in life. Processed from the finest of ingredients it fittingly tops the finest of ice cream: Two scoops of ice cream, Hot Butterscotch sauce, whipped cream and a Maraschino cherry.

JUMBO HOT BUTTERSCOTCH SUNDAE Three scoops of ice cream. **1.35**

DELMONICO SUNDAE The gourmet's delight: Made with two scoops of New-Old **1.00** fashioned Delmonico ice cream, refreshing Claret sauce, and topped with whipped cream and a Maraschino cherry.

Bicentennial Specials

NUMBER 49: ALASKA GOLD There's gold in them thar mounds of vanilla ice **1.10** cream. Butterscotch syrup adorns this strike. Dig under the glacier of marshmallow and whipped cream to find it.

NUMBER 50: HAWAIIAN DELIGHT Go with our version of Hawaii 5-0! An **1.10** exotic blend of pineapple, papaya, guava, cherries, passion fruit; and of course, slices of banan-o! All covering two scoops of pineapple ice cream in a tulip glass topped with whipped cream and a cherry.

MOUNT VERNON REFLECTIONS George Washington and the cherry tree and **1.10** then on through history to the White House. Gifford's reflects with two scoops of whitehouse ice cream covered with wild cherries, topped with whipped cream and finally adorned with, what else, a cherry.

DISH OF ICE CREAM (Three scoops, without syrup) **85c**

MILK SHAKES, all flavors . . **85c**   **MALTED MILK SHAKES** · · · **90c**

JUMBO MILK SHAKES · · · **1.45**   **JUMBO MALTED MILK SHAKES** **1.50**

Come back soon!

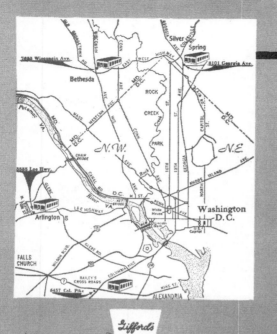

SILVER SPRING STORE

8101 Georgia Ave.
Silver Spring, Md.

BETHESDA STORE

7623 Wisconsin Ave.
Bethesda, Md.

ARLINGTON STORE

5555 Lee Highway
Arlington, Va.

BAILEY'S CROSS ROADS

5834 Columbia Pike
Bailey's Cross Roads, Va.

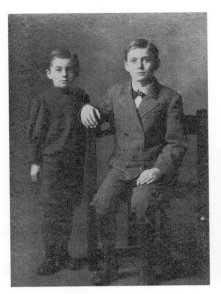

John and Leroy, ca. 1910

Mom riding a Newfoundland dog, ca. 1958

John Nash and Mary Frances Gifford in the backyard at the Kensington House, 1960s

Me and Dad, ca. 1977

Mom and Dad, 1973

The Gifford house in Kensington, 1980

At Deep Creek Lake, 1979

Me and Dad, 1984

With Tom Baker, the Fourth Doctor, 1986

Allen Currey, ca. 2010-2012

Harmony Grove, ca. 1986. Allen has asked me to pose on my future grave

Leaving home, May 1992

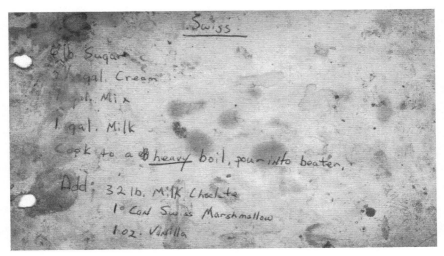

Recipe Card for Swiss Chocolate

CHAPTER FOUR

TRIGEMINAL INTERLUDE

I'm afraid to talk about trigeminal neuralgia. With every word I type, and every thought I have about this period in my life, I feel like I'm summoning a demon. I feel like I'm inviting the pain to come back.

But I have to talk about it.

The trigeminal nerve is a major trunk nerve in the face. It starts behind the ear and branches out towards the eyes and across the cheek, nose, and jaw. These branches are the nerves that control all facial movements—every blink, every smile or frown. In most cases, like mine, trigeminal neuralgia is caused by an artery enlarging or wrapping itself around a section of the nerve. With every heartbeat, the nerve's pain receptors are triggered. Sounds simple. But the disease can be elusive. It's hard to diagnose and even harder to treat. More often than not, there's very little a doctor can do to bring permanent relief.

The majority of sufferers experience pain through the cheek, nose, and jaw, and it's a pain that goes beyond description. The nerve misfires like an explosion of electricity in the face. Sometimes, for me, that electric explosion was so strong that I crumpled to the floor or lost my vision. I would claw at my face and writhe. Even writing this brings an ache to my jaw. My eye twitches, my hand moves to my cheek and massages a ghostly pain.

Sometimes, if I held my hands just right, pressing hard into my cheek, the pain would relax. I would press my face against the wall, or pull at my cheek like a cartoon character, and then freeze the moment the pain stopped, contorted in some bizarre position, my breathing labored and rattling my chest.

For a long while I found myself trying to tell the story of my family and Gifford's Ice Cream without talking about trigeminal neuralgia. My actions and reactions to the events between late 1995, when the pain started, and April 19, 2007, when I was cured, are recalled through the lens of this horrible disability. I was under its spell for the largest chunk of my early adult life.

It used to be that this story was the story of Gifford's, and what I discovered about my family later, with a huge gap in the middle. Dad vanishes in 1985, and then suddenly, in the 2010s, I begin to figure it all out. In between lay just a quick, glossy recap of work and school. My voice and tone shift away from reality. Many elements of the story take place during the trigeminal years, but for so long I could only speak of this time, think of this time, like a news reporter: Barbara Gifford did this, Robert Gifford did that, and that's all she wrote.

The pain started small. In late 1995, I began to experience what felt like a toothache. The ache became so severe that regular pain medication did nothing and I started to experiment wildly. I ground up Tylenol and aspirin and formed a hot compress that I pressed against my gums. While D&E students were chewing tobacco and spitting into bottles all through class, I was chewing on my homemade compresses, deadening my gums and cheeks and stripping away my ability to taste anything. (A side effect I exploited as a party trick in the late 1990s, mixing dreadful alcohol concoctions out of food and liquors and drinking the shakes down to the amused horror of other guests.)

At first, the bouts of pain came about every other month. They began and ended mysteriously, without any sort of trigger or timeline. As the 1990s drew to a close, the bouts became more and more frequent and severe. One minute I'd be talking happily, and the next I would be unconscious.

Drugs can't really touch this pain. By mid-1996, I couldn't shave or brush my teeth without experiencing a pain so sharp that I'd be in danger of passing out. Taking a shower in the morning sapped my strength; I'd scream when the water hit my face. Once I woke up on the bathroom floor, wrapped in the shower curtain, the hot water long since gone cold and chilling my legs. At night, if I turned onto my right side, contact with the pillow would send me scampering out of bed as if I'd been bitten.

For many, this incurable, unstoppable, unmanageable pain leads to severe depression. Trigeminal neuralgia has earned the nickname "the suicide disease," and I'd be lying if I said that I wasn't close to that ultimate solution a few times.

By 1997, my world was a living nightmare, a hazy, strange, distant dreamscape that I can barely recall, that clouded my life for a decade. Everything that happened in those years happened as if at the far end of a tunnel—a life of echoing voices and shapes barely discernible against the harsh daylight outside. Snippets of memory come through, loosely tied together with the cold and clinical narrative of my life. I worked, I slept, I ate, I huddled against the pain. It all feels empty, like I'm relating the life of a stranger.

And yet so many things happened in the pain years. I started a new publishing company, and the ghosts of my childhood finally came roaring back into my life. Monumental life changes played out, yet I kept myself distant. I felt nothing besides the pain. I felt no joy, no freedom, no life. Eventually I felt there was no future, no point. I existed simply because I had no choice. I became a ghost haunting my own life.

When I talk about trigeminal neuralgia, I usually talk about what it is. A clinical description, a reiteration of a Wikipedia page. I don't talk about my experiences with it. I don't try to deconstruct the years of my life lost to it, or the choices I made while under the influence of the pain and, eventually, the even more ruinous treatment for that pain. I self-medicated with alcohol. I lied, cheated, and robbed my way through work. I dismissed friends and lovers with a shrug. There was no room for other people. Chronic pain erases all humanity, all kindness, all hope. I lived for the pain, I lived to control the pain. With my family's bizarre paranoia coursing through my veins, I lived also to hide the pain. I saw the pain as weakness, and I didn't want my co-workers or friends to see weakness because I feared I couldn't trust them. In pain, my childhood lesson returned: trust no one.

In fact, I worry, sometimes, that it was my mother's voice in my head that kept me alive through those years. Not a voice of support or love. Not an idealized image of Mom. This voice was snarling and vicious, filled with a hateful anger at the entire world and at me. It kept me alive because my reaction to it was defiance.

"You've lost," that voice whispered. "Go ahead and give up. Once a loser, always a loser. No one will miss you. No one will care."

After many years, I recognized this voice in my head as my own, the cries of a forgotten Andrew, locked away behind the pain like a prisoner, echoing what his mother had always told him.

The doctors had no clue what to do. I saw allergy specialists, ear-nose-throat doctors, orthodontists, dentists, psychiatrists, and, finally, neurologists. Twelve doctors in all, and each had a different diagnosis and a different remedy.

My dentist assumed it was the aftereffects of an old injury to my mouth I'd received horsing around with a friend, so she sent me to an orthodontist. Between them, I had root canals in both of my front teeth and underwent a painful surgery in which the orthodontist dug into the roof of my mouth above my gum line. Then, when the pain didn't ease, they figured that the root canals had gone wrong and went into my front teeth again.

The allergy specialist said I had a chronic sinus infection and, after proclaiming that she didn't believe in drugs, prescribed me antibiotics . . . and kept refilling the prescription for nine months. When these did nothing, she told me that I was imagining the pain and accused me of trying to scam more drugs out of her.

All the while, every day, the pain got worse. I was often unable to eat properly or sleep. Sometimes, I couldn't even drink water. Allen would jam a straw into my mouth and yell at me until I sucked on it.

Still, the doctors shrugged and said that I was either crazy or lying. A psychiatrist wanted to put me on Prozac after concluding that the pain was clearly a manifestation of my parental issues. After a long line of western doctors dismissed me, I sought remedies in alternative medicine—Chinese medications that stained my face orange and burned my skin, acupuncture, acupressure, meditation, even a Buddhist retreat and a dodgy purification ritual.

Nothing worked. I became an odd, part-time invalid—a shut-in, but only after work. I had no choice. Besides Allen's extraordinary rent, I was giving my Chinese doctors hundreds of dollars a month. So I struggled through the day and came home exhausted and defeated, sealing myself in my grandparents' back bedroom.

I began to drink heavily, partially as self-medication but mostly to get away from the pain-fueled voices in my head telling me to end it all. I buried what little free time I had with repeats of sci-fi shows, fantasy novels, and booze. Eventually, even the ever-present specter of Gifford's Ice Cream didn't bother me. That was out there in the real world. I was in exile.

Nor did I socialize. Though I had a small group of friends, all of my relationships were strained. I simply couldn't speak or interact without some degree of pain. The majority of my friends grew distant as time wore on. I couldn't kiss a woman without star shells of pain driving me to the floor in a boneless heap. Trigeminal neuralgia was the perfect excuse to stop talking, to leave suddenly if I felt awkward at a party, to not engage in anything or with anyone.

I was glad to be alone. I even became obsessed with the idea that the pain was my only companion—the only one I deserved. I called it my "wife." The fewer friends the better, I thought. I still haunted my old Bethesda neighborhood bar, Flanagan's, located in a gloomy basement along pre-gentrified Old Georgetown Road. Down there, nobody talked to me. There were no overheard snippets of conversation where Gifford's was mentioned. Flanagan's wasn't the place for ice cream talk, or any talk. The patrons all drank in the gloom and nobody knew anyone's real name. The bartender knew me as Jack and Coke, the trucker guy down the bar as MGD, and the guy who sat in the shadowed booth as Vodka Straight.

Embracing the disease, at the time, seemed the only sane path. It was the perfect escape from real life. Fantasy books ended, TV shows got cancelled. Those old childhood escapes always had harsh re-entry into the real world looming at the end of the program, or just past the last page. But the pain was forever. I was exempt from trying to achieve anything. I was too tired. I'd become tired before I turned eighteen, and that feeling had never left me. But now it felt deeper. I wanted to give up, and the pain was a wonderful excuse for doing so. Talking was hard—so I never had to tell my story. My writing was nearly non-existent, except for freelance business stuff, which was empty and soulless. Just like me.

I was a dying man, I was sick, and there could be no greater relief from my story than to simply be driven mad and killed by the pain. With my death, I decided, Gifford's Ice Cream would finally die. I was what kept the legacy alive, simply because I was my father's son.

I fantasized about suicide. I planned it out. Something dramatic. Maybe throw myself in front of a train, or simply let go of the wheel of my car. On the Metro platform, I rocked back and forth at the edge and imagined myself letting go. Just a blink of an eye away from doing it. I felt my body drawn to the train as it rushed out of the tunnel.

I blacked out often, and, when I woke up, I was always disappointed to still be alive and in so much pain.

I feared my commute to work. Each day, I left ninety minutes early. I took the train only twelve stops, but at each stop, I had to get off. The pain from the movement of the car sent me into barely concealed fits of agony. At least once a week, I passed out at a Metro station as I sat, trying to recover, preparing myself for the next leg of my trip.

Every effort went into hiding this affliction. I created a construct made of what I wanted people to see. Most of the time, when I forced myself to go out and socialize, my brain was dulled by weird Chinese herbs or simply overwhelmed by pain, no longer processing what was going on around me. I simply muscled through it. Showing no weakness, grimacing a gritted-teeth smile, eyes tearing up. I'd laugh, pat friends on the shoulder, and glide into the bathroom, where I'd either pass out or dissolve into a sobbing, gasping mess.

When people suffer from chronic pain, there is never relief, but there is great comfort in routine. Managing pain is also about managing life, down to the minute. No surprises, no emergencies. Problems? Just walk away from them. Preserve the routine at all costs.

I think I survived trigeminal neuralgia simply because I came to feel that I deserved the pain. If this was a punishment from God, then my Catholic upbringing had taught me that there was also redemption at the end of the road. I felt responsible for the actions of my parents, and the fall of Gifford's, but now I had paid for their crimes. I was ready for redemption. Like Job, I would ultimately be rewarded for my long suffering. I came to believe that the pain was, indeed, a sort of purification. This was the last step in moving beyond Gifford's Ice Cream, and Mom, and Dad. There was no more room in my mind for their story.

In 2002, after suffering for seven years, I was finally introduced to a neurologist who diagnosed me—within minutes. A dozen doctors, years of agony, so much shoulder shrugging and guessing wrong, and this guy had it figured out almost before I finished introducing myself. I couldn't believe it. My agony, my impossible inexplicable punishment, was given a name: atypical trigeminal neuralgia. Textbook case.

Unfortunately, though, naming my demon didn't kill it. The neurologist put me on a wicked cocktail of drugs. He told me there were very few options to treat trigeminal neuralgia, so he would use a combination of pills to try to dull the pain. Trileptal was the king, an anti-seizure drug that deadened all of the nerve impulses. It transformed the pain from a flaring, screaming sunspot to a steady, bone-deep agony that felt like walking around and using a broken arm while never seeking treatment. The Trileptal was backed up by a standard muscle relaxant and the occasional "OxyContin as needed," which, as so often happens with OxyContin, soon became always.

The drugs left me in a dream state. With dull eyes and an even duller brain, I recall the years between 2002 and 2007 as hazy and distant. Sometimes I forgot where I was, or where I was going.

On the train, I stared out the window, unaware of the passage of time until day turned to night and the scenery changed enough to break the spell. At least twice a week I forgot which Metro stop was mine and rode, in a state of Alzheimer's-like confusion, to the end of the line.

I reached the maximum safe dosage of Trileptal, and still the medication was doing very little for the pain. In early 2007, I blacked out in my grandparents' house and fell to the floor. While unconscious, I writhed and screamed and clawed at my face with such force that Allen had difficulty holding me down. I went to my neurologist to demand alternative treatment. I sat in the waiting room clutching my face, unable to speak. The other patients moved away from me, huddling along the walls. My neurologist came out into the waiting room and squatted down in front of me.

"It's that bad?"

I nodded, fighting back tears of pain and exhaustion, unable to voice my reply.

"I don't think there's anything more I can do for you," he said. "We're going to have to explore surgical options."

He and a nurse helped me stand up, and they walked me back to his office, where he gave me an OxyContin and tried to calm me down. He quietly explained the next steps, and I saw no choice but to move forward toward the next dim, impossible hope.

My neurologist referred me to a doctor who advocated percutaneous denervation, in which the patient is put under and the doctor injects glycerol or alcohol into the Trigeminal nerve sac, just behind the ear. This effectively deadens the nerve and, in many cases, leads to relief from pain. This relief is often temporary—when the pain returns, the patient has to go through the procedure again. An imperfect remedy, it's often preferred to more invasive surgical options. I would have volunteered for anything—even experimental surgery—but my doctor said massive, invasive surgery wasn't worth it.

So I took the Metro down to George Washington Hospital and went through the usual surgical routine—the long wait on a gurney; the false, patronizing cheer of the anesthesiologist who swears, this time, I won't get sick from the drugs (I always do); the doctor who swans in, all business, and mutters platitudes before vanishing.

The first operation lasted four hours. I woke up, the pain from the neuralgia worse than before, my neck stiff and unable to move, a purple bruise along one side of my face. The doctor swanned in once again and I told him, through gritted teeth, that the pain was unbearable. He shrugged and said that it might take a few days before I felt better. Then the nurses took me out to the front doors and left me there, alone.

I worked my unsteady way to the Metro and went home, getting off two stops early to dry heave onto the station platform. With my hospital wristband, green soap and bandages on my head and neck, drooling from the post-anesthesia sickness, I must have been a sight.

The pain didn't stop, so the surgeon suggested that I try the same operation again. A month later, I once again took the Metro to GW and checked in. Again, the anesthesiologist came in, offered the same patronizing lies about not making me sick, and shot me up with his pre-surgery drugs. He left and a nurse ducked in. She told me that the doctor was stuck in traffic and might be late.

I lay there for an hour, the anesthesiologist's drugs working their magic, and slowly the pain faded into a background hum that I hadn't experienced in months. It was still enough to make me cringe, twitch, and claw at my face. But it felt like the sweetest, most powerful relief compared to the pain before.

When the doctor finally showed up, he asked how I was and I dreamily replied that I was fine. The pain had receded.

"Wait . . ." he said, stepping into the cubicle where I was lying flat on a gurney. "You mean the pain is better?"

"Yep . . ." I slurred.

"Damn. Then there's no point in the operation." He threw the curtain aside and called a nurse over. "We're not doing it today. He's improving. Get his clothes and let's get him out of there."

The doctor glared over at me and shook his head, as if disgusted, then stomped away. I was discharged, the pre-anesthesia drugs still roiling in my system, and I dizzily walked back to the Metro, this time almost tumbling down the escalator. I clung on to the handrail and giggled, then sprawled onto a seat in the train and fell asleep until we hit the end of the line and a cop woke me up with a gentle hand on my shoulder.

I returned to my neurologist and told him about the cancelled surgery. I also said that he should try and do a bit better with his next referral. Without comment, he picked up the phone and called Ben Carson's office at Johns Hopkins University in Baltimore, Maryland. Before his political aspirations made him a national figure, Ben Carson was a gifted and pioneering neurosurgeon. He was also a kind, gentle man. As a Marylander, I knew his name and his stellar reputation at Hopkins. He'd performed miraculous surgeries on the poor and the wealthy alike. My time with him would be punctuated by the arrivals and departures of other patients who warranted Secret Service protection and bodyguards, patients who arrived in their own helicopters. Yet he never treated me as if I were less important.

The next, and last, surgical choice was MVD—micro-vascular decompression. My neurologist told me that he had wanted to avoid this procedure, but my case was especially severe. MVD carries with it all of the dangers of brain surgery. A hole is drilled into the skull behind the ear, after which the doctors push the brain aside and remove the vein from the trigeminal nerve, then splint the nerve with Teflon or, in my case, muscle from my neck. The procedure takes more than six hours and the risks are great, including stroke, hearing loss, brain damage, and death.

Dr. Carson explained the surgery, exuding calm and patience. He said I could take all the time I needed to think about the operation, but I said yes right away. I had to stop the pain at all costs, and nothing he said really scared me. I knew that the next blackout was just around the corner. One day, I might never wake up again, or it would happen while I was driving, or God knows what. Once I was given a realistic promise of relief, I didn't care about the cost. I left our first meeting certain that this man could give me my life back.

On the morning of April 19, 2007, I drove up to Johns Hopkins with my uncle Richard. My mother's only brother, he had recently returned to the DC area from New Mexico. We were taken to a small, windowless waiting room. A young couple sat holding each other, eyes downcast, crying softly. Dr. Carson's assistant came in and asked if I was ready. I said yes, and she reached out for my hand. I waved weakly at my uncle and allowed myself to be led away.

Stripped onto a gurney, the anesthesiologist went through his pandering routine, promising that I wouldn't be sick when I woke up, and I was out by the count of three. When I woke up, I was in a head vice in the neurosurgery intensive care unit. Dr. Carson stood on one side of the bed, his assistant on the other. They greeted me with smiles.

"Welcome back," Carson's assistant said softly.

She reached down and pinched my cheek, holding it for a few long seconds between thumb and forefinger as I tried to jerk away. The vice, which had been drilled into my skull, held me steady.

"Feel any pain?" she asked softly.

I didn't. Not a twitch. The pain was gone. After twelve years of suffering, it was gone.

I was awake and alive. I spent three days in the hospital, three months recovering at home, six months getting off the drugs, and a year before I believed my life was real and I wasn't caught up in some sort of *Jacob's Ladder* death dream.

I felt like I had gone to sleep one day in the mid-1990s and had woken up to find that it was summer 2007. I looked back anew on a lifetime that had been informed not only by the pain, but by my parents and the legacy of Gifford's Ice Cream. Now that I wasn't ensnared by the drugs and the agony, I started to ask questions. I wanted to talk. What had happened? Why did it happen?

I was asking these questions far too late. By 2008, both of my parents were dead.

CHAPTER FIVE

HARMONY GROVE

I

Mom took her own life on August 15, 1999. She was forty-seven.

It took the coroner ten days to identify her body. We went through the latter half of August ignorant of disaster and assuming Barbara Gifford would outlive us all. She would always be there, the unstoppable, angry force that had scarred three generations of my family.

I hadn't seen Mom since I left home for D&E in 1992, intentionally keeping my distance. I'd put the life she represented squarely in my past, out of sight and out of mind. I didn't feel any sort of disturbance, no awareness that Mom was no longer part of the world. I didn't feel anything but the trigeminal demon, searing my face.

On the day we learned of her death, I came home from my pain-addled commute, sweating from the heat, to find my grandparents sitting on the couch. The TV in front of them was silent. With no Food Network blaring at top volume, I knew that bad news was coming.

My grandmother was crying gentle tears, her face upturned and regal. There were no tears from Allen. He looked up as I came through the front door and without any preamble said: "Hey, kiddo. Your mother's dead."

I blinked. Mom had been estranged from all of us for so long that it took several seconds to parse that simple declaration. Allen stood up and put a hand on my shoulder.

"The police just called," he said. "It was a car accident."

With that he returned to his seat on the couch. The manner in which he looked away implied that I should simply go about my business.

This was one of the many times when the trigeminal neuralgia "saved" me. The news of Mom's death washed over me, and then I put it out of my mind as I went through my troubled sleep routine—making sure that the pillow wouldn't brush my cheek, my breath shallow, trying not to move.

The next day, Allen shook me awake and spurred me to action. I had to take control. I was the next of kin. Allen said there was "no walking away from this." And then he said: "There's going to be a lot of money coming your way."

A puzzling comment. My understanding was that Dad had left Mom high and dry. But I now think Allen had always known more than he was letting on. Not until recently, clear of the trigeminal haze, have I been able to reconstruct the last days of Barbara Gifford. Even now, though, trying to retrace her last steps raises as many questions as answers.

A couple of days after we received the news, I was contacted by the only person who really knew my mother—her lover, a woman who feared outing her even posthumously. But news of Mom's sexuality didn't surprise me. Mom added enough lurid details to the rape stories I heard as a child that it was pretty easy to see she felt no attraction to men. After Dad left, all of her friends were women. Their carefully secret intimacy was clear to me even as a boy. While she never came out to my grandparents, they'd always assumed, as I later discovered.

This latest lover told me she and Mom had been in a very serious relationship. But then, in Mom's final months, she started to distance herself from this girlfriend for no clear reason. Mom was trying to quit smoking and seemed to have curtailed her drinking, though her girlfriend was convinced that she was still sneaking out for drinks. Mom had sought professional help for depression and was given several prescriptions that seemed to be working. She had a good job, the respect of her co-workers, and as far as anyone could tell, she was fine. In fact, better than usual. More engaged, more cheerful.

A few days before her death, she called her girlfriend and said that she was going on a pilgrimage to Walton's Mountain in Schuyler, Virginia—the hometown of Earl Hamner, Jr., who was the creative force behind the 1970s TV drama *The Waltons*. Hamner grew up during the Depression in what was then an isolated village in western Virginia. In the 1950s, he turned that hardscrabble country suffering into a successful writing career. His book *Spencer's Mountain*, inspired by his Appalachian youth, follows the trials and tribulations of a down-on-its-luck family, crippled by alcoholism, cheating husbands, and poverty. The novel reads like something a first-year creative writing student might produce if asked to "try and write like Faulkner," but it occupied a rare niche in literature: honest Appalachian story-telling. It spawned a movie with Henry Fonda and, eventually, a TV show, which removed all of the realistic elements of the book (and the Fonda movie). Instead of a family of brutal alcoholics crushed by poverty, the Waltons were a huge family living in an awesome house on a mountain named after them, with a small town down the road where everyone treated them like royalty. Supposedly they suffered from the Depression, but 1970s TV veered away from all of the pain and somehow made it seem noble.

Mom watched the show, and the reruns, religiously.

The popularity of *The Waltons* remains strong with many fans. Schuyler, Virginia capitalizes on it. What must have been, in the 1920s and 1930s, a slice of Appalachian hell is now home to the Walton's Mountain Museum—something of a mini-theme park, with Earl Hamner's boyhood home as the central attraction. The museum boasts more than 100,000 guests per year, many of them on a pilgrimage like the one Elvis fans take to Graceland. Like the one Mom took now.

She went up to Schuyler on a Saturday, spent the night, and then headed back late Sunday night. The road home took her onto Virginia's scenic Skyline Drive and, by the time she weaved down that narrow road, trees looming up on each side, she was all alone. Probably the only car on the road for miles.

The police and the coroner were able to piece together her final moments. A representative of the sheriff's office relayed them to me in staccato sentences. She was traveling at high speed. She went off the road. She hit a tree. She was killed instantly. The car burst into flames. There was very little left of the driver. It happens sometimes.

Her death was listed as accidental. I paused over the word. An accident? On the phone with the sheriff's representative, I demanded some logic. He sighed over the line and broke out of his matter-of-fact speaking style.

"Look, son, there were no skid marks. No sign that she braked or swerved to avoid something. She wasn't wearing a seatbelt, nor did she have any drugs or alcohol in her system. In my experience, this wasn't an accident. I'm sorry. But it's best for everyone if we rule it as one."

He went on to tell me that if there was any doubt, officials would customarily rule a death accidental and not suicide. Why should the family suffer more? There would be no insurance money or peace from a suicide. The trooper told me this with a deep sadness in his voice. I sat clenching my teeth against the neuralgia. But his honesty worked. I stopped asking questions.

Mom's girlfriend gave me the key to Mom's townhouse in Frederick, Maryland. I stepped inside with my grandfather, expecting to find a hoarder's paradise. Instead I found a humble, well-kept home. Her favorite easy chair, in front of a shrine-like entertainment system, was worn through. Her girlfriend told me that Mom often slept there, spending all her free time parked in front of the TV. Plagued by depression and insomnia, Mom spent more time in that chair than in bed. Her kitchen cabinets held more prescription bottles than spices. True to form, Allen swept the bottles into a trash bag before I could read any of the labels.

On the kitchen table, Mom had organized all of her paperwork and personal effects. Her purse, wallet, and IDs were laid out neatly, as well as banking information, insurance details, important contact numbers, and her address book. The house had been thoroughly cleaned. Just days before her death she'd paid off most of her bills and her rent and utilities for three months in advance. On a pad of paper, she listed the location of her retirement accounts, passwords, and who to contact at her office. Her entire townhouse had been converted into an efficient suicide note.

A dark cloud now settled over the family. Allen and my grandmother, who had been estranged from Mom for years, blamed themselves. I left them to sort through Mom's belongings while I moved into the legal mumbo jumbo of death. They packed her entire world into boxes, my grandmother weeping, my grandfather a dark, roiling cloud in the corner of the room. In her belongings, we saw a tableau of a sad, wounded woman: Gifford's Ice Cream nostalgia, all my childhood toys, and countless journals and file folders containing every scrap of her life after Dad left—every letter, every email, every newspaper article, everything to do with the family or the business.

I was pretty sure that I was the one who had wounded her the most. It seems strange to say that, given what I'd gone through at her hands, but whether as a result of my misguided Catholic upbringing or something else, I always felt guilty—always felt like I was responsible for everything my parents did and for the punishments I received. Besides, no matter the troubles of the past, she was still my mother, and I wondered if we could have—should have—met in the middle at some point. I wondered if I could have saved her. Suicide is hard on the survivors, even those of us who were estranged. Even those of us who have entertained the idea ourselves.

In the bank, Mom had about $5,000. In life insurance, she had $40,000. The rest of her estate, containing the last few Gifford family antiques, was valued at $6,000.

This is what it comes to when we die. A tallying of worth, lifetimes and memories reduced to a spreadsheet and glanced over by appraisers and lawyers. Everything we cherished thrown into a box, wrestled away by movers to be sold off or stored in a forgotten basement somewhere. Mom's entire life fit into a single U-Haul, and I had it sent to a storage unit in Germantown, Maryland. I didn't want to go through the boxes. I didn't want mementos. I didn't want memories. I put all that was Mom into a concrete and chain-link corral, padlocked behind an aluminum door, and I didn't look at it again for fifteen years. In 1999, wracked by pain and guilt, I wanted everything to end. I wanted Mom in the ground and I wanted to walk away forever.

But her death wasn't as simple as that. Two months into the probate, my lawyer called me in for a meeting. She had found an account in a second bank with $130,000 in it. In doing so, she'd stirred up the feds. The IRS swooped in and sued the estate for $170,000 in back taxes and penalties.

We soon discovered that Mom hadn't paid income tax since 1995—the year she sold the house on Bexhill Drive. While I was hiding from her doppelgänger along Hadrian's Wall, Mom had come into money. The records suggested that she had received roughly $550,000.

I was flummoxed. For at least a few days in 1995, she had half a million dollars. My lawyer suspected that there may have been much more, but that most of it had vanished. The paper trail showed that, in the summer of 1995, Mom cleaned out her accounts, bought a new car with cash, and then disappeared. She stayed off the grid until 1996, when she reemerged in a humble rented townhouse in Frederick, Maryland. Her records, at that point, show that she had only a couple thousand dollars to her name.

The IRS said it would clean out the estate and that any remaining debt would pass on to me. My lawyer warned that tax debt was, in fact, inherited. For several agonizing months, it looked like my life was over. I'd owe the IRS nearly $50,000 in Mom's back taxes while I was crippled by trigeminal neuralgia and barely able to work, my meager income steadily sapped by Allen's extraordinary rent.

When I complained to Allen, he shrugged and warned me not to be greedy like my father. I had to contribute if I was living under his roof. I asked my lawyer if my estrangement from Mom would give me the chance to walk away from all of this mess unscathed—reject all of my claims and let the estate go to the government. She said that that was impossible. I would have to face this tax debt.

It felt like Mom had finally gotten me. What looked to be a sad but orderly chore—close out a dead woman's humble estate—had turned into a disaster. In despair, I gave up and went along. I accepted the burden of Mom's estate, including all of her debts. But I had enough sense to tell my lawyer that we should at least fight for something a little more fair.

The probate lasted for fifteen heartbreaking months, with all the twists and turns of a TV legal drama. At home, my grandparents avoided the topic entirely. I sleepwalked through my job and slept in a bed often covered with Mom's paperwork. As the months passed, I felt like I was being infected by her, like she was taking me over. I spent sleepless nights weeping like a child.

In the fifth month of the probate, after countless meetings, we entered the new year. The calendars flipped over to 2000, and on a cold January morning, I headed to my increasingly flustered lawyer's office once more. She sat opposite me at her long table and said: "I'm your lawyer, not a psychologist. Do you understand?"

Confused, I just nodded.

"I'm going to tell you something, and then I'm going to leave the room and let you digest it. Okay?"

She was speaking to me like a child. I nodded again. My lawyer took a deep breath, and then she told me: "Your father has filed suit to take over the estate."

On May 10, 1985, I had been the last person to see my father, Robert Gifford. His last words still echoed in my head—"I'll be back Monday." That last moment in the Jhoon Rhee parking lot had travelled with me for almost fifteen years. In my mind, May 10, 1985, was also when Dad effectively died. How could he be suing me?

But apparently he was. He was unable to come to Maryland, she said, but he had hired one of the area's most powerful attorneys. My lawyer looked at me and said: "Frankly, I'm scared. I don't think we can win this."

Then, as promised, she stood up and walked out of the room, leaving me alone with an army of ghosts.

II

With Dad's return, the IRS now seemed like a small problem. In fact, my lawyer said that I'd been given a way out. She told me to let Dad take the estate and the debt. She was terrified of Dad's lawyer, almost as much as she was terrified of the IRS, and she advised me to roll over at every turn. But, I argued, what if there was more money? We'd found only a fraction of the money Mom supposedly had. Might there not be more? Wouldn't I be surrendering that to Dad, too? My lawyer only repeated her refrain: give in to Dad, give in to the IRS.

Indignation crystallized in me. A pure and brightly burning rage. I had been asked to suffer the debts of a woman I hadn't spoken to in seven years, and now I was being asked to bow down to a fugitive deadbeat father.

Enough.

I told my lawyer to fight. I told her to double down on her efforts to research the money trail, to create a fuller narrative of Mom's final years. We would battle it out in court against the feds and against Dad, no matter the cost. She shook her head sadly, but she didn't refuse.

Tracking the money, and Mom's actions, was difficult. The story we eventually pieced together was based on hearsay and guesswork. Lovers, friends, and family tried to fill in gaps. Even then, the people she saw on her long journey west had differing versions of the same story—as if they were each talking about a different woman.

The thousand faces of Barbara Gifford.

There was usually something in common—interests, hobbies, her sense of humor—but then I'd try to tease out true, real personal details from the people she'd visited, and what became clear was that Mom was a secretive, suspicious woman. One who told some of her story but never all of it.

Her trail west had indeed been erratic. She'd showed up, often unannounced, at the homes of people she'd befriended online through newsgroups and bulletin boards. One of these people met Mom online in a genealogy newsgroup.

"During your mother's trip west, she visited us," she told me in an e-mail.

One night, Mom had showed up on this family's doorstep during dinner. She introduced herself, and they spent an awkward evening talking about Dad. Mom asked to spend the night, and, in the morning, at breakfast, she signed over a cashier's check for $9,000.

"I tried to refuse," this astonished hostess wrote. "I handed it back. But your mother was insistent."

Mom told her that she had come into a lot of money, and $9,000 was nothing. She had to split the money up and she was giving it to friends for safekeeping. If she kept it, she said: "Bob will get it. Bob's watching me closely."

Her fear that my father was just a step behind her was palpable enough that this stranger, this online friend, spent the next few weeks glancing over her shoulder and jumping at shadows. She clearly felt that my father was a dangerous and violent criminal. And the money? She apologized profusely. It was gone, she told me. Her husband had lost his job in 1997, and the $9,000 had been used for house payments and food money for months while he looked for a new one.

I related this story to my lawyer. She replied that, yes, she believed that Mom had skipped town with a bag of cash. But that cash was impossible to trace, especially if she'd scattered the money among friends and acquaintances in this way. My lawyer sounded her familiar refrain: there was nothing I could do.

In early 1995, Mom had showed up at her brother's doorstep in Albuquerque, New Mexico. She flashed wads of money and her new car, but wouldn't otherwise speak of her windfall. As I dissected her life one night over drinks with my uncle Richard, he told me about that strange visit.

Mom had acted cagey, and she'd avoided personal topics. Yet she threw money around like she was made of it. Very unusual for Barbara Gifford. So my uncle kept pressing for details. What's with the money? What are you up to, Barb? The more questions he asked, the more squirrelly she got. Finally, after a couple of days, she left in the early morning, leaving a note on the kitchen table to say goodbye.

She ended up in San Francisco, where she stayed with her oldest friend for several months. The new year passed, and in early 1996 she returned to the DC area and resumed a normal life, picking up the thread again as if her year-long hiatus from the grid had never happened. Mom's last girlfriend, my lawyer, and my dad's lawyers all agreed that the old friend in San Francisco most likely received the bulk of Mom's money—an unknown amount that could have been as high as $250,000.

Mom's lovers and friends and co-workers were able to patch together her final eight years for me, but no one could paint a complete picture. She remained a cipher. Even those who knew her intimately couldn't answer the larger questions. My lawyer and I were scrabbling. She hoped for a windfall, but I was less concerned about finding more money and more concerned about defeating the government and my father.

The probate passed the one-year mark. The math of Mom's estate never added up, and that drove my lawyer crazy, but I didn't care. The math of my life was simple. I lived in between pain episodes, self-medicating as needed. My life inched forward hour by hour, with no room to think about the future.

At one point, it seemed like we would lose everything to Dad. As it turned out, he and Mom had never divorced. He was officially the next of kin. We also discovered that my parents had maintained a steady communication after Dad supposedly vanished. Mom had always known where he was, and they wrote each other frequently. Their contact even seemed amicable.

In no way did this fit with the reality I had experienced. I let that information wash over me. It was too much to even imagine. What had been the point of all the madness and turmoil for all those years if Dad was in touch—and, by all accounts, sending a regular income? There were hints, though no details or proof, of a private deal between the two of them.

From 1986 on, he'd sent her an undisclosed monthly stipend. Considering that fact and the sudden glut of money from the house sale in 1995, why had she bled Allen financially? Or maybe she hadn't bled Allen. Maybe he had bled me without cause. After Allen died, the realtor who sold his Silver Spring house said that Allen had "made off like a bandit" in the sale. The realtor suggested that the house had been paid off, and that there hadn't been multiple mortgages.

Always against my lawyer's wishes, we continued to fight Dad. The IRS, perhaps sensing that the pot wasn't as juicy as they hoped, settled for a lump sum payment of around $70,000. The remainder of the estate stayed on the chopping block, and we spent months engaged in a legal battle with a man who, in my mind, was little more than a ghost. By the time we hit court, the probate had stretched out for a ridiculously expensive period, and Dad and I were fighting over almost nothing after all the fees and expenses were counted.

Finally I met my father's proxies in court. My lawyer was also there, with Dad's team of attorneys. They filled a row of seats across from us, like a scene from a court procedural TV show— young, well dressed, Ken-doll good looks.

Three judges presided. Unable to speak through the trigeminal pain, I wrote my statement on scrap paper and had my lawyer read my words aloud. The judges asked her to stop and demanded that I tell my own story, in my own voice. Through clenched teeth, I haltingly spit out my story, clutching the right side of my face. Only a few minutes passed before the lead judge stopped me, shook his head, and then ruled in my favor. He pointed at my dad's lawyers, who seemed ready to appeal, and said: "Forget it."

The Ken-dolls nodded politely and filed out. I sat there reduced to tears by pain and relief, while my lawyer stood awkwardly next to me. One of the judges approached and hugged me, telling me to "stay strong" and "keep fighting." In my darkest days to come, this display of warmth from a stranger in judge's robes often gave me hope.

At home, my grandparents never asked how my day at court had gone. My family didn't care.

After that courtroom drama, it finally felt like Mom was dead. The probate was over. Her belongings were mothballed in a storage shed. The madness of that fifteen months convinced me that I was correct in trying to put the family behind me, in disowning everything about them, living or dead. I suppose I had all the answers in front of me, but in 2000, I didn't care.

III

What do I talk about when I talk about Barbara Gifford? She's like a comet, plowing wildly around the sun, slamming into anything in her way, and leaving us all staring in wonder up at the long, bright tail as it works across the skies. People love her or people hate her, and there aren't many in between.

After a lifetime of tragedy and heartbreak, the tattered remnants of my family hold onto Mom's memory only with fear and confusion. Yes, she was beautiful, she was strong, she was wickedly intelligent. But she was also angry. Always so terribly, violently angry. A woman smiling from a snapshot in one moment and trying to tear down the world around her the next. Her lifelong battles with Allen, from childhood to adulthood, were epic. Confrontations between them half a century ago are still recounted, in harsh and frightened whispers, as if the molten bitterness between them still lingers in the next room.

I've tried to use Mom's death to understand her life, but that has proven impossible. Even those with whom she was intimate don't seem to have known her. She was indeed a woman with a thousand faces. I've talked to her friends and lovers—some who had known Mom her entire life. I've asked these people who knew her so well, who loved her or feared her so much, who grew up with her, to tell me who my mother was. I talked to her co-workers, her neighbors, her doctor. And always it seemed like every single person was talking about a different woman. Even Mom's hobbies and personal interests would change with each story. I once talked to someone who told me Mom said she was Jewish.

Paradoxically, she was also a woman with one face. Every

one of her stories shared a through-line. The art of a lie is that it should be built on truth, it should come naturally, it should be easy to remember. The through-line, as I compared all these stories of Mom, was heartbreaking. I saw in there the kernel of Barbara Jean Gifford: a troubled, brilliant woman, always at odds with the world around her, seething with rage at the cards she'd been dealt.

Her life borders on legend. Her death left nothing but questions. I try to write about the woman she was and the woman she became. I try to write about her last, fatal, lonely night on Skyline Drive and what happened. I get nowhere.

Then, in October 2014, Allen died. And his death opened yet another door on the story of my family and Gifford's Ice Cream that I was always afraid to investigate. I realized, as my shoes slowly sank into the wet clay of the family cemetery at Harmony Grove, West Virginia, beside his open grave, that in order to tell Mom's story, we must begin with Allen.

IV

Just over an hour south of Morgantown, West Virginia, lies Bridgeport, a crossroads town—a small rural oasis where you can get real coffee, crash at a Hilton, and get a good meal. It's also headquarters whenever someone in my family dies. We all gather, solemn and quiet. The teetotalers hold hands and pray, the others creep into bars and drown their sorrows as a NASCAR race blares on a TV. In black suits and dresses, hats and veils, we follow a hearse deep into the hills north of Bridgeport. We've done this many times. We're no strangers to this grim caravan that crawls along switchbacks and hairpin turns into the high, lonely forest.

After World War II, Mom's grandfather Everett Earl bought a cemetery plot at Harmony Grove, about ten miles outside Bridgeport. He wanted the family to be together, always. He bought six plots, and his son, my grandfather Allen, later expanded that to ten. To get to the cemetery, we must follow a torturous mountain road, dodging the occasional rockfall.

The graveyard crawls clumsily over a ridge, an erratic mismatch of stone markers that vanish into the surrounding woods. A dilapidated one-room church, propped against the mountainside atop jacks and stacks of cinderblocks, stands guard over two hundred years' worth of our loved ones and neighbors. In recent years, the desolation of the spot has been interrupted by the sight of happy little split-level homes. The suburban sprawl of Morgantown and Fairmont seems incongruous with the spooky, mist-shrouded Appalachian woods.

The clay soil is somehow always slick, even on warm and sunny days. Our family plot straddles the crest of the hill, with the most recent graves dipping down the shadowy side opposite the old church. A fence separates the graveyard from the surrounding forest, but foraging through those woods I've found old stones, the names long since worn off, nearly obscured by the gnarled trunks and loam of the forest floor.

My maternal family's plot holds three generations and, surrounding it, the extended Currey family stretches back through the nineteenth century. Everyone in the ground at Harmony Grove is related in one way or another.

When I was not yet a teenager, Allen took me to Harmony Grove and walked me around the plot. We had told my grandmother, back in DC, that we were going out for a "boy's day," and three hundred miles later, the sharp mountain air around us, he paced out the borders of the plot. He pointed to where Everett Earl and his wife were buried, and then he pointed out all of our graves.

"This is where your grandmother and I will be buried," he said, straddling the ground beside Everett's grave. "And there," he pointed beside his future grave, "is where your uncle Richard will rest."

He named everyone, finally coming down to my generation. He crouched in the second row of empty graves and patted the ground lovingly.

"This is your grave," he said.

It didn't quite end up that way. Mom died out of the expected order. We buried her before we buried my grandparents. So now, as we slowly fill that plot, we're aware of Mom's grave beneath us. If something goes wrong at a funeral—a chair falls over, a sudden gust snatches at the tented covering, or there's a technical error with the casket, those of us gathered turn to each other, smile, and joke that "Barbara did it."

Barbara did it. Fractious, angry, feisty, and a cruel prankster from her earliest days. In so many ways, she was her father's daughter, perhaps more so than her siblings. She and Allen shared the same physical traits—tall, dark-haired, lanky—and also the same emotional fault lines. Both were often irrational, tempestuous, and mercurial. Both were masters at holding a grudge, incapable of meeting anyone halfway, dissatisfied with what life had given them.

Father and daughter were so much alike that the rest of us sometimes felt that we were simply bystanders (and occasional victims) in the endless war between two great titans. I can't believe Mom's attitude and approach to life were hard-wired genetic quirks, though. Allen fostered and helped create the monster within her because, I think, something in him had stopped working when he was very young.

Born in 1925 in Shinnston, West Virginia, near Parkersburg, Allen was the heir apparent to Everett Earl's empire. The young Everett Earl was a wild man, deeply involved with local organized crime. He never left home unarmed, running his own small version of the mafia from his house on the hill.

As well as running several legitimate businesses, Everett Earl was primarily a bootlegger, and perhaps a pimp. Allen always claimed that he had worked for Everett Earl as a roadcutter for bootleggers during prohibition, carving out highways through the fields and valleys for the trucks as they worked their way down from the north. Since he would have only been a small boy at the time, just about everyone in the family looks doubtful when I relate that story.

Everett does appear to have dabbled heavily in the sex industry. And while Allen probably wasn't cutting roads at a tender young age, he seems to have been the "delivery boy" for Parkers-burg's small red light district. Hard evidence is difficult to produce regarding a pseudo-criminal in a small mountain town in the early years of the twentieth century, but Everett appears to have owned quite a bit of property in the red light district, and Allen's "news-paper route" in this hard-bitten section of town is an interesting coincidence. Though I have my doubts about his story, Allen once boasted that "all the girls" knew him by name and would invite him in for snacks. He told me that he stopped in this way, every morning, at several houses. Rather intimate and inefficient for a paperboy. When it came time for the girls to pay their subscrip-tion, they would hand over blank envelopes full of cash. Allen remembered that, by the end of his route, the envelopes weighed almost as much as the newspapers he had just delivered.

Everett Earl enjoyed his booze and his women a little too much, so he couldn't keep either around for very long. The clear signs of alcoholism are present in every story about Everett. But that hadn't really mattered when business was good. Then, in 1929, the banks went bust and America dissolved into the Great Depression. Everett Earl—who literally owned the local bank and kept all of his gains, ill-gotten or otherwise, in its vault—lost ev-erything overnight. He would never recover, and up to his dying day he would reminisce about this disaster. Decades later, he told my uncle: "Every penny I had was gone like smoke on a breeze."

By mid-1930, he had lost his house and his wife. He took a factory job and worked for a little under twenty dollars a week—much of which he spent on whiskey. In the midst of Everett's im-plosion into alcoholism and depression, Allen's sister Evelyn, ten years his senior, developed what some in the family believe was mastoiditis—an infection in the bone behind the ear, often the result of an untreated ear infection. I find her symptoms disturb-ingly familiar—an intractable, tough-to-diagnose, and agonizing pain in the head, neck, and face.

Her condition rapidly worsened, so Everett Earl medicated her the best way he knew how—with whiskey. But this medication soon graduated into drug use, and by the 1940s, she was dead. The circumstances of her death are horrific and heartbreaking—those of the family who are still around can't bring themselves to talk about it. Right up to his final days, Allen was barely able to speak Evelyn's name without bursting into tears.

For Everett, Evelyn's death had been yet another psychic body blow. He began binge drinking to the point of blackouts, blaming himself for his daughter's demise and often clutching a photo of her, sobbing uncontrollably.

As Everett fell deeper and deeper into his own downward spiral, Allen tried to pick up the slack. But when Allen was around ten or eleven, several years before Evelyn's death, Everett found himself unable to handle the responsibilities of parenting. Allen was sent to a boy's home, where he witnessed, and probably experienced, routine beatings. After a year, Everett picked him up and took him home again, and no more was said about this strange interlude.

Everett provided no clear explanation to Allen and, when pressed to theorize on his father's actions, Allen always shrugged and claimed ignorance. Was Everett trying to dry out? Had he left town? Some suggest he may have been in prison. The most Allen ever said was: "My dad couldn't take care of me. He had no money, even to feed me. He had no choice."

What really happened, and why, is buried with both of them in Harmony Grove.

As so many did at the time, Allen fought in World War II, with the Navy, though he escaped serious action. He caroused in San Diego, and ended the war guarding German POWs in Banning, California. He'd often talk wistfully of these "noble warriors." He'd tell me: "The Germans were a real fighting machine. They were huge, disciplined, and terrifying. The only reason we won was because we were lucky."

After the war, Allen earned his degree in chemistry on the GI Bill. While on leave toward the end of the war he had met and married my grandmother. They had their first child in 1949. My mom followed in 1953, and my aunt in 1956.

Allen was a strange, domineering, and unpredictable man. He was never happy in one place, never happy at work, and never happy taking orders. Without warning or explanation, he would quit his job and move the entire family to another town. From 1949 to 1970—except during the Korean War, when he was called back to duty—the family didn't live in one place, nor did Allen hold down a job, for more than nine months at a time.

But Allen was never a drifter, and his family never suffered. He always had a new job lined up. Yet the upheaval of constant moving took a toll on my grandmother and the children. They reached a point where they stopped unpacking. My uncle and my mother isolated themselves socially—what's the point of friends when you'll be gone by the end of the school year? Like clockwork, they always were moving again shortly after the last day of classes.

Sometimes the moves would be small—from rural West Virginia to rural southern Ohio. Sometimes they were bizarre. One took the family to Goose Bay, Labrador, where Allen taught chemistry at a high school on a military base. Even then, in the wilds of Canada, Allen was restless, and he soon moved to another school on another military base in Newfoundland.

In the late 1960s, he brought the family to another job in Silver Spring, Maryland and, after a few local moves, my grandmother finally put her foot down in 1970. Move again and she was done with the marriage. The family would stay in Silver Spring.

Kept from pursuing his wanderlust, Allen seemed to seethe. He turned his energy toward various get-rich-quick schemes. He went into hock to start Currey Radio and TV Repair, painting the logo and his home phone number on the side of a panel van that was the family's only car. He taught chemistry to high school students all day, then he went out on repair calls all night. The company quickly tanked and Allen filed for bankruptcy.

The cycle repeated with the Currey Silver Company of Canada, Ltd. This company specialized in reclaiming silver from various medical and scientific instruments. Allen imagined that this residue, once collected, would add up to a huge payday. But it was simply impossible to reclaim enough silver to pay for the cost of the reclamation itself. Another company gone bust, another bankruptcy.

Next was Currey Scientific Instruments, as Allen set out to build computers in his workshop and sell them to customers. He imagined himself as a rival of Texas Instruments and IBM, but it didn't pan out, and everything went bust once again.

Then came the goose with the golden egg—mumbling, stumbling, apparently dim-witted Robert Gifford. From the moment I was born, Allen concocted various schemes to install himself as the head of Gifford's Ice Cream.

V

Of Allen's three children, Mom was the most vocal and the most dissatisfied with their strange, nomadic lifestyle. She tormented her siblings all the time. Her default mode seemed to be picking fights, most dangerously with Allen, whom she usually saw as an enemy. Even then, she often referred to him in those terms—"the enemy," "the devil," or "Satan." Allen once told me: "Barb was born into the wrong family."

From day one, she was a terror, and absolutely brilliant. No one could keep up with her, and when they couldn't, she took the time to cut them down. She'd go out of her way to make life as difficult as possible for everyone around her, driven by a mischievous streak that bordered on homicidal. At the age of nine, she held her six-year-old sister by the ankles from the Parkersburg railroad bridge, high over the wide Ohio River. Friends who had been crossing the bridge with them turned and stared in horror before trying to stop her. Calmly, she kept repeating to her terrified sister: "I'm gonna drop you."

Then, with a laugh, she hauled her sister back over the rail and put her down. Just a game. Just something to break up the day. When I ask about Mom's childhood, I hear nothing but stories like the one of that day on the bridge.

She was a tomboy, she tortured everyone close to her, she was violent. She searched for everyone's buttons and, once she found them, she pushed them relentlessly. My uncle remembers a time when Allen, enraged by her taunting, picked her up and threw her against a wall.

Even her beloved grandfather Everett Earl had run-ins with her. Mom told me that she was his favorite, but the rest of the family told stories that suggested otherwise. Mom once drove Everett Earl so crazy that he threw a wet sponge at her with enough force to knock her down. What was she doing? Teasing him. Relentlessly. This man she said she loved more than anything on Earth, and there she was, a child, mocking him for using a cane, for being bald, for being old. Her cruelty knew no boundaries.

The first time Mom ran away from home, she was four. She tried it again periodically until, finally, at sixteen, she succeeded. She moved in with her best friend, Fran, and quickly entered a cycle that was uncomfortably similar to Evelyn's downward spiral. Dropping out of high school (Mom would never earn her degree), she fell into alcohol and drugs. There were rumors of heroin use. In 2000, one of Mom's childhood friends told me that Mom and Fran had become involved in some sort of home-spun prostitution ring to pay for their habit. I've heard that same story from other sources, and Allen was convinced of it.

But this could easily have been another of the thousand faces of Barbara Gifford. Other contemporary friends tell me that Mom was virginal, pure, even nun-like. There's no common theme to those stories. Only two wildly opposing sides of the spectrum: Mom was a prostitute and on serious drugs. Mom was clean, sober, and a wide-eyed innocent virgin who only ever slept with one man.

The truth is in there somewhere but probably known only to those in the ground at Harmony Grove. Shortly before Allen died from cancer in 2014, he told me about the incident with Fran. How one night "things went too far" and Mom called home. When Allen went to pick her up at Fran's basement apartment, the two of them were with several men, all near naked and passed out, and Fran had "overdosed on heroin."

But I don't think Allen can be believed, either. He was as guilty as Mom when it came to reimagining reality. It's my own theory, as I've spent time trying to deconstruct Mom, that she and Fran were lovers. That perhaps that episode ended simply due to a quarrel. Mom's life ended in a same-sex relationship, one of a string of intimate female friends after Dad left. Neither did she and Dad have anything close to a romantic relationship—I can't recall one instance when I saw them kiss or even hug.

She started working at Gifford's in the Silver Spring store in 1972. She would have been nineteen then, and she was lovely. Her hair shines black in every picture, her skin clear, her eyes bright. On the rare occasions when she didn't assume the garb of a confirmed tomboy, her figure was stunning. It's no wonder that she caught the eye of the owner's son. By the end of 1973, she was pregnant with me.

But there was none of the usual courtship. There's no tale of a love affair. I talk to employees and friends and the picture painted of Dad in the 1970s is startling. He was working his way through the waitresses at the Silver Spring store, with a strong preference for tall redheads. Former waitresses he'd chased have sent me pictures of themselves in the store back then and they're almost identical—lean and narrow, long red hair sweeping around delicate faces and soft eyes. I ended this line of research when the sexually harassed redheaded waitress brigade reached six members.

Dad's standard routine was to awkwardly pen the waitresses into a corner and, between nervous laughter and idle conversation, stammer: "You know, my favorite flavor is vanilla. I'll be back in my office."

And then he would amble away. Some waitresses brought him that cone of vanilla. Some were wise to such clumsy tactics. Some have told stories about abortions and illegitimate children. My ghostly half-siblings.

The reconstructed story of his courtship of my Mom is downright creepy. One of her co-workers told me that Dad took an interest in her and one day left a musty-smelling artificial flower on her car. One of the horrible, mildew-covered decorations rotting in the terrifying basement of the Silver Spring store.

Nevertheless, the flower earned Dad a date, on which he "convinced" Mom to have sex. This one sexual encounter—Mom's first, according to a friend who subscribes to the chaste-virgin school of thought—resulted in her only pregnancy, which resulted in me.

There's an attempt by some people to cast this rapid courtship in a sweet light. Poor introverted Bob and shiny, happy Barb. But it's hard to know what to believe. Allen, shortly before his death, described a very different scenario: Mom, resistant to Dad's advances, "felt pressured to give in." Allen's implication was that Mom had been raped, and he told me that he had no choice but to act in my favor and force them to get married or report Dad to the authorities.

This implication made more sense after my uncle related other events he'd witnessed. According to him, Dad was brought to Allen's house in Silver Spring and confronted with all of Allen's towering, broad-chested menace. Allen ranted and pointed fingers, telling my dad that he would marry Mom to make an "honest woman" out of her. There's an "or else" strongly implied. Dad's reaction was, to my uncle, puzzling. He sat pensively on the couch, eyes averted, and simply nodded his head. He seemed guilty, shifty, strange.

"Yes, Allen, yes, Allen," was all he said.

Meanwhile, John and Mary Frances didn't approve at all. Mom, Allen, and even Dad admitted to this. Dad was nearly disowned by his parents. In Mary Frances' will, I am referred to only as "Robert's child."

Allen always claimed to have known John very well, though any discussion of my paternal grandfather was prefaced by something like, "He was an asshole!" But Allen's stories about his counterpart on the Gifford side of the family tree tended toward the same bizarre flavors as the stories Mom told me growing up. There were the various takes on the little blue men and the naked march down Georgia Avenue with a gun. I heard how John Gifford was running prostitutes out of the store, how he behaved generally like an outlandish *Batman* villain.

But shortly before his death, Allen confessed to me that he had only met John once, and that they'd exchanged few words. He said the Giffords wanted nothing to do with the Curreys. He'd never spoken at all with Mary Frances.

I like to think that Mom and Dad had a marriage of love, after a fashion. In some ways they were well suited for each other. Both loved pranks. Both loved to play people. And they were both brilliant. But the battling began right away, Mom raving at Dad's nodding head. The way my mother fought was legendary in the family. The story of my first Thanksgiving is still told regularly.

It was 1974, and I was only a few months old. An unusually quiet baby in the corner. The family gathered around the dining room table at Allen's house, a scene I can picture very clearly since nothing changed in my grandparents' house in the forty years they lived there. The dining room was windowless, with dark-paneled walls, feeling all the more closed in by the wet, oppressive steam heat. A low credenza took up one whole wall. I was probably sitting on top of that credenza in a baby carrier, as many babies on my mother's side of the family have done.

The dining room table would have been covered in one of my grandmother's garish tablecloths—red-and-white-checked gingham plastic. The food was always amazing, home-style country cooking that my grandmother and the other matrons in the family slaved over for days. There would rarely be alcohol—the family drink was my grandmother's iced tea, so heavily sweetened that even hummingbirds would have complained.

We were never a formal family, but there was a feet-on-the-ground Protestant seriousness that settled on us during the holidays. I never found these occasions to be joyous, and I don't think that anyone else did either. We sat, talked little, and mainly tried to hurry up and eat, after which we peeled away as quickly as possible.

No one recalls the cause of the argument between my mom and Allen that Thanksgiving. Mom had been moody, Allen critical of something. No one remembers if Dad was there—Bob Gifford could fade into the background at will. He must have been there, though.

The fight escalated rapidly. Mom stood up, Allen did the same, and for several tense moments they verbally battled across the table. I started squawking in my baby carrier. The family sat frozen—once again, bystanders caught unawares in the clash of these two angry comets. In our collective memory, four decades later, no one is able to remember anything that was said. So often, the fights between Mom and Allen felt to others like they had walked in on a shouting match between two strangers.

Suddenly, in a few quick strides, Allen stepped around the table, closed in on Mom, and grabbed her. Then he ripped off her shirt and tore it to pieces. Mom, standing in her bra, barely even reacted. She continued to unleash a torrent of vitriol, and Allen, too, returned to shouting. They stood like umpires, nose-to-nose. Grandchildren and sudden wealth did nothing to curb the Allen and Barb show.

I would like to believe, deep down, that Mom couldn't have been a truly bad person. I look through snapshots of her from the 1970s and I see someone young and carefree. The darkness that surrounded her is absent, the weight of all the terrible family stories drops away. I see a beautiful young woman, smiling at the camera, or gazing with a studious expression and bright eyes into the distance. In one, she looks cheerful in her yellow bikini, a wave crashing around her legs on a beach. Her arms are in the air and her smile is wide and bright. I gaze at that photo and I wonder:

What happened to you?

VI

It was a rainy, cool October afternoon when we buried Allen next to Mom. Mist shrouded Harmony Grove, the wet clay underfoot threatening to pull us down into the muddy graves. A wind blew down into the little hollow, the flimsy tent over the grave shivered. As a group of elderly Masons performed their ritual over Allen's coffin, the remnant of our family huddled under black umbrellas. My aunt, uncle, a few cousins, and I were all that remained. A row of rickety folding chairs, all attached to each other, sat on a strip of Astroturf beneath the tent. The men yielded the chairs to the women and the infirm. I stood behind my aunt, the rain pattering against my umbrella. Beneath us was Mom's grave.

The coffin shuddered and the funeral director reached out a hand to steady it. I tried not to laugh, recalling similar scenes from film comedies—the coffin's moving! Then, without warning, the ground beneath the chairs shifted, sinking onto Mom's muddy grave, and came dangerously close to sliding down the hill. I reached out and steadied my aunt and she turned to look up at me, smiling sadly. Her voice was soft, just above a whisper: "Barbara's here."

It's taken a lifetime to achieve some distance from Mom. Now her death is fuzzy, cloudy. Memories from a different Andrew. A stranger. So many of the years spent under the influence of trigeminal neuralgia are remembered through distant eyes. It all ends so humbly there in the soil of Harmony Grove. Mom died with her story largely untold. Many people would disagree with me, but, the truth is, none of us ever really knew Barbara Gifford. And maybe that's exactly how she planned it.

PART THREE

HEIR TO A SCANDAL

CHAPTER SIX

ANATOMY OF AN EMPIRE

Jack nearly screamed, "I never want to see ice cream
again as long as I live. A terrible thing, ice cream.
The most terrible thing in the world."

—Anthony Burgess, *The Land Where the Ice Cream Grows*

I

John and Mary Frances Gifford are like strangers to me. Yet
they are inextricably dynamic and powerful forces in my life. It
is a fact that my grandparents were the architects of Gifford's Ice
Cream. I have also come to believe that they fostered whatever
madness it was that drove my father to destroy it.

John died in 1976. I was two, so I do not remember him. Allen told me that John bothered to see me only once, when I was
an infant, and even then he refused to touch me or get too near.
Though not even this much may be true. Friends of the Gifford
family have told me that my grandfather never visited me, or even
acknowledged my birth.

His wife, Mary Frances, died in 1980. She'd been crippled by a
stroke in 1977, her mind and body no longer of much use to her. I
saw her three times that I can remember, terrified of her contorted
appearance on each occasion. The exact date and circumstances
of her death would remain a mystery to me until 2014.

Growing up without either paternal grandparent, I stopped car-
ing about them. The more Mom elaborated her frightening stories,
the less I wanted to know about John and Mary Frances. By the

time I turned eighteen I wanted only to get away from my family and its dark legacy. I kept running for nearly twenty years. But I am still the heir to that dark legacy. I can't run away from my name.

In writing and revising this memoir, I've struggled to find who was at the heart of all the evil I witnessed. Mom was plagued by madness. Could she really be blamed? Allen was crippled by greed. Maybe he was the bad guy? Or was it Dad who was the criminal—the one who vanished with our fortune and our hope? Yet looming over them all hovers the ghost of John Nash Gifford. I see its shadow fall across generations of Washingtonians. Forty years since he died—and still people try to reboot Gifford's Ice Cream, clinging to the name with a dark and greedy obsession. John Gifford's complicated legacy seems inescapable.

So who was he?

There's not much to go on. For a long time, I had only three photographs of John. One I found in a random Google search. Another is a professional portrait, taken when he was maybe about fifty-five or sixty, which would place it around 1960 or so. He's wearing Harry Truman glasses, he's bald, and he stares stoically into the middle distance over the photographer's shoulder. In the other picture, a snapshot, he's a little older, perhaps later in the 1960s, sitting in the backyard at Bexhill Drive, which was eerily unchanged from the backyard I played in years later. Seated in a chair, he wears a napkin on his head and smiles slightly as Mary Frances stands behind him in a tasteful frock, hair perfectly coiffed, grinning malevolently at the camera as she dangles a butcher's knife over his head.

The picture I found online was from the *Tiptonian*—the high school newspaper in Tipton, Indiana. The caption explains John entered with the class of 1915, "ever quiet and studious," but by virtue of extra course work, he would graduate in 1914. Then it goes on to say: "John is the youngest member of his class and although he has not decided what profession he will take up, we predict nothing but success for him."

In fact, by 1925, John had gone on to play a crucial role in revolutionizing industrial, large-scale ice cream production. He was among the pioneers in that field, and he was good friends with the inventor of a process that made mass production possible, the process that paved the road for all major ice cream brands, including Gifford's. But how he got from the "proficient book-keeper" reported by the *Tiptonian* to a pioneer of industry is a hard trail to follow.

Eventually I found more photos through websites and from shoeboxes of Gifford's memorabilia maintained by strangers. One snapshot, from around the time Lindbergh made aviation history in 1927, shows a biplane barreling through a grey sky. The handwriting on the back says, "John's Plane." So the quiet, studious boy and steady, determined worker had become a skilled pilot, too. Many of the stories about him claim that he was an adventurer, a reckless barnstormer. The more I researched, the more that photograph of "John's Plane" seemed to typify the man. There he was, all alone, watching the small world below him spin and twirl away.

II

Gifford's Ice Cream & Candy Co. was founded in 1938 by John Nash Gifford. In the same year, he opened the first Gifford's on Georgia Avenue in Silver Spring, Maryland, where he sold his six original ice cream flavors. In 1940, he opened a second location on Wisconsin Avenue in Bethesda, Maryland. Today, with five locations, Gifford's stands by its family traditions.

For so many years it had seemed that everything I needed to know about the family history was contained in that brief paragraph from the menu. Even in my teens, when I questioned the history, my effort was half-hearted. I knew early on that any family history gleaned from Mom, Dad, and Allen was probably not entirely true. I never stopped to think about the actual truth until after 2008, clear of the trigeminal pain, when all of the Giffords were dead and buried.

Getting to the bottom of that truth was difficult. As the back of the menu implied, there seemed to be no family identity beyond the business. My mom's sister worked there, my mom's best friend worked there, my parents worked there, my maternal grandparents worked there. The demands of the company, the ever-present swirl of duty and management that consumes everyone who is in business for themselves, shaped our lives. Seven days a week, the store was open. Seven days a week, there were staffing issues, money issues, supply and equipment issues. Things could and did go wrong. Even Willy Wonka went mad from the pressure. Sadly, there was no Charlie to shake sense into John or Robert Gifford. Their consumption was complete.

Until recently, I didn't know where my grandparents were from, or what the names of my great-grandparents were, or where anybody in my family came from. Mom embellished John's and Mary Frances' lives in such a theatrical way that it was impossible to hammer out a nugget of truth from her stories. So are they the real villains in this tale?

In my research, I kept returning to that grainy snapshot of John's biplane, taken over ninety years ago. In its sepia tones, his world looks calm, almost quaint. John frozen forever, wheeling through the sky. From what facts I could uncover, he sounds a lot like his son—quiet, reserved, distant. Another man who wanted to get away from it all but never succeeded in achieving that dream.

Aviation in America went through a fascinating downturn in the 1920s. With a Luddite attitude, the U.S. turned its back on the industry, even though it had proved itself with deadly efficiency in the First World War. The armed forces scaled back their programs, junking planes and firing pilots. Though KLM and other European-based carriers were running passenger flights as early as 1919, America didn't embrace the technology until the 1930s. Even the Wright brothers quit designing planes and concentrated instead on engines.

So there were no flight schools, just as there was no need for regulations or laws. Anyone who could afford a plane could buy one, but that didn't include a lot of people. Most pilots—like Charles Lindbergh—were self-taught. Their planes were often no more than tent fabric stretched over plywood. With an unreliable water-cooled engine and a tank of gasoline pressing against their backs, they took to the skies.

There was little hubris involved. These early aviators weren't naïve. They knew the dangers. Aviators died all the time in pursuit of what seems to be one of the most deadly hobbies in modern human history. They were crushed by the gas tanks or burned to death. Surviving a crash landing then involved even more luck than it would now.

Some of these pilots were entrepreneurs. They'd make money on the side delivering mail or dusting crops. Others learned stunts and put on airshows. Some of the stunts were alarming. In his book on 1927 America, *One Summer*, Bill Bryson describes a barn-stormer who could pick up a handkerchief off the ground with his wingtip while flying at top speed. On more than one occasion, fatal crashes also involved members of the audience.

So while that image of John wheeling in the sky seems lazy and peaceful when captured by an ancient camera, it's anything but. Here was a man with money enough to buy a plane. A man with an adventuring spirit who taught himself how to fly and performed stunts to wow those on the ground. He even flew his plane to work. John was well-heeled and successful by the time he was twenty-five, and by the evidence of his hobbies, he seems vibrant and alive. Yet he died hated by his son and brother, and friends and co-workers remembered him only as "dour, moody, and quiet." This seems to be a tradition in my family: nobody is what they seem.

In 1916, John enrolled at the University of Chicago to pursue a degree in political economics, which he received with honors in 1921. So his family had enough money for higher education. A family member sent a snapshot showing John in a World War I army uniform, yet his college transcripts don't reflect that he ever left school to go to war—which, for America, would have been 1917–1918.

Then, as I tore through boxes of rotting memorabilia, half-convinced that I should simply destroy everything I found, a folder emerged with publicity stills of ice cream logs and fully-laden candy counters from the Bailey's Crossroads store when it was shiny and new. Tucked between these glossy photos were John's war records.

On September 27, 1917, he had indeed entered flight school as a cadet. Twenty-one years old, he listed his interests as swimming and tennis. The intake form describes his temperament as "quiet." It also notes that he already had seventy hours flying experience, and that he had even flown across country—an extraordinary feat at the time, especially for someone so young. (If this is true, John, by 1917, had almost as much, if not more, flying experience than the Red Baron and most other World War I aces.) But there was no hint of any wartime action. No further details.

After the war, John went back to school, quiet and unremarkable until graduation in 1921 when, once again, he drops into obscurity. The only clue I had to his early post-college years was the fictional biography my father put on the last Gifford's menu. In 1981, Dad upgraded the menu and dramatically reshaped the story of the family's past:

> *In 1921, upon graduation from school, John Gifford went to work for an Ohio-based ice cream company. Devoted to producing ice cream of superior quality, John was content until the day he was ordered to lower the butterfat content. John Gifford, uncompromising in his standards, left to make his own ice cream, Gifford's Ice Cream.*

Ohio? My childhood had been warped by tales of vengeful dairy farmers from New Jersey. Yet here was a very different story. By the time that alteration on the menu came around, I was so exhausted by the swirling madness that surrounded my parents that I didn't even think to question them.

"The Gifford's Saga began in 1922," a 1981 article in *Regardie's* magazine recounts, "when John Gifford, recently graduated from the University of Chicago, began the Franklin Ice Cream Company with two partners, in Toledo and Cleveland, Ohio. The company prospered, and within a few years, John opened five stores and a plant in New Jersey."

But as vice president of operations in Newark, he was far from the Ohio offices where decisions were made. Over his "strongest objections," the butterfat content of Franklin ice cream was reduced from its original seventeen percent to twelve percent. John, along with a coworker named George Milroy, eventually quit, leaving New Jersey in March 1938. The article contains quite a bit of Dad's menu revision, along with some obvious contradictions. The company was headquartered in Ohio, but made its ice cream in New Jersey? John was a co-founder, but also an out-of-touch VP hundreds of miles away? Then I found a history of Franklin Ice Cream and, with it, I picked up the trail of John Gifford.

Franklin Ice Cream Company's headquarters was an abandoned World War I airfield, which made John's commute easy. The records don't show John as a founding partner, or even as a mover and shaker. He appears to have been working with the accounting and day-to-day operations at the Toledo headquarters, after which he does, indeed, end up in Newark. Franklin's parlors seem to have multiplied wildly throughout Ohio before expanding into New Jersey. John may have been the company's ranking representative there, though the records are unclear.

Shortly after the Jersey expansion, the company made overtures to sell out to United Dairy. Things were getting ugly at Franklin and John was unhappy both in his work and his locale. A friend's son told me that Mary Frances—a native Washingtonian—despised New Jersey and was pushing John to move to DC. Mary Frances had a mother and an older sister who lived in Silver Spring, and they undertook the preliminary scouting for the new company's location.

The deciding factor in the move, it seems, was Dad. My father was born on February 5, 1938. One month later, John quit his position at Franklin without notice. Leaving with him were George Milroy, who also appears to have worked in the Newark plant, another man named Leslie Daley, who looks to have been involved in the corporate side of things, and John Tillotson, who was the real ice cream man.

Deep in my mom's archives, which I emptied out between 2013 and 2014, I found the original incorporation documents for the company. They were preserved at the bottom of a box—a packet of tissue-thin papers in a pale blue folder the size of a regular envelope: "The Articles of Agreement between John Gifford, George Milroy, John L. Tillotson, Leslie J. Daley, and Mary F. Gifford for the formation of Gifford Ice Cream Company."

The date of the agreement was September 11, 1939, with a note that the business had officially opened on May 22 of that year. Signed, witnessed, notarized.

John Tillotson has a patent on file: "(A) computing scale, patent number US 1498938-A, a weighing apparatus for ice cream manufacturers for ascertaining the percentage of overruns." I contacted an ice cream expert at a local creamery and we talked at length about Tillotson's invention. He explained that "overrun" is a measurement of the volume of air, expressed as a percentage of the volume of actual ice cream mix. Ice cream mix that is half air has a one-hundred-percent overrun, which is also the legal maximum. He said: "Overrun is a reliable indicator of value."

This is because the lower the percentage of air in the mix, the higher the butterfat content. A lower overrun reflects a higher-quality product, and vice-versa. Without Tillotson's patent, there'd be no way to gauge the butterfat content of the ice cream, and it would be impossible to mass produce a premium product. It would be like cooking without knowing all of the ingredients.

My contact knew Tillotson and some of his history. He told me that by creating an accurate method to measure the butterfat in a base mix, Tillotson helped to usher in an ice cream revolution in the early twentieth century, with Franklin Ice Cream at the forefront. Yet this revolutionary inventor left Franklin Ice Cream without warning when John jumped ship. He moved from New Jersey to a rented house just blocks from the first Gifford's location in Maryland.

With Tillotson on board, it was possible for John Gifford and the other partners to undertake what some have called an insane adventure: to buy an old feed warehouse in Silver Spring and turn it into a gigantic ice cream factory, with a one-hundred-seat parlor in the front and twice as much space in the back.

The early sales figures are impressive. In 1940, the population of Montgomery County, Maryland, was around 83,000 people, compared to more than one million today. John and his partners took a gamble by opening shop in a place that was still semi-rural. But they soon realized that they had a mega-hit on their hands. Demand for their ice cream was so high that a second location was opened in Bethesda before the end of 1940. By 1946, the two locations were selling up to 90,000 gallons of ice cream every week.

By 1956, the Silver Spring store was supplying four other stores and countless high-profile private accounts, such as the White House kitchen and the kitchens serving Walter Reed Hospital and the Bethesda Naval Hospital. By then, Gifford's was moving millions of gallons a year. John and his partners were practically printing money. They had doubled their investment within six months of opening the doors at Silver Spring, and it was still paying increasing returns years later.

Tillotson's share of the partnership was relatively tiny. He controlled 9.5 percent of the company with a start-up contribution of $1,600.80, the equivalent of more than $26,000 today. John controlled 55 percent, George Milroy 21.5 percent, Leslie J. Daley 9 percent, and Mary Frances 5 percent. The overall investment of the five partners totaled $20,000, or about $347,000 in today's money.

Tillotson and Daley seem to have been silent partners. Daley died in 1946, and it looks like George Milroy acquired most of his shares at that time to bring his stake in the company up to 25 percent. In 1941, both Tillotson—a Marine veteran from the First World War—and Milroy enlisted to fight in World War II. Tillotson returned from the war no longer a partner at Gifford's, though I couldn't find a reason. His shares appear to have gone to Mary Frances. As of 1946, the only partners remaining were John, Milroy, and Mary Frances.

When Milroy returned to his position at Gifford's after the war, he and John immediately began looking at new locations, opening a third store in Arlington, Virginia in 1948 and a fourth at Baileys Crossroads in Virginia in 1956. Milroy, as vice president of the company, was responsible for the development, opening, and management of each new store, while John took care of the finances.

The Gifford's cachet was extraordinary. During the JFK years, Jacqueline Kennedy held White House balls at which ice cream specially made by Gifford's was colored to match her gowns. Mamie Eisenhower was a regular at the Bethesda store. J. Edgar Hoover often waited in his car outside the Silver Spring store for his agents to return with a scoop.

John Gifford had beaten the odds—he had built a million-dollar business. He had maintained that business, emerging from the war years with more money and local power than he and his partners knew what to do with. And he wasn't done. During the following decades, Gifford's became practically synonymous with ice cream in suburban DC. John had built an empire, seemingly from scratch. His legacy survives today. It will survive me.

The ability to create this kind of business and keep it afloat for thirty-five years is impressive to me. This man and his staunchly loyal supporters—Mary Frances and George Milroy—did something that seems improbable when you put it all down in print.

So what went wrong?

III

Allen always told me that, after John and Mary Frances could no longer run it, the company was supposed to pass to me. The story—and Mom backed this up—was that my grandparents despised Dad, so when John died in 1976 and Mary Frances was too ill to take control, I had actually inherited Gifford's Ice Cream.

As the three-year-old president (Mom used the word "king"), I was supposed to be supervised by a "council of elders," of which Allen would be the "leader." Dad, however, was constantly maneuvering. According to Allen, Dad and his team of lawyers stole the company from me but kept me on the books as president. Mom and Allen both said that everything that went wrong at Gifford's had actually happened in my name.

Like my mother, Allen was a powerful storyteller with a flair for the dramatic. He used to tell me that no one understood that I was the president of Gifford's—the "council of elders" protected me—until Mary Frances was "out of the picture." This was the only time in my youth that anyone—beyond Mom, with her wild horror stories—gave an account of my grandmother's death. But Allen was elusive about the date, variously placing it between 1978 and 1981, and both he and Mom would also sometimes imply that Mary Frances was still alive and had been kidnapped by John. Either way, he said, there was no hiding the fact of my "regency" once she was "gone."

Allen conjured this big reveal like something out of a soap opera. The family gathered by Mary Frances' bed as machines measured the slowly failing heartbeat of our dying matriarch. He told me that "a final gasp punctuated the room right before— *bweeeeeeeeee*—the flatline." The family bowed their heads. The piercing sound of the monitor played loudly as the scene faded to black. The scene was so over-the-top that, even as a child, I could tell it wasn't entirely true.

Later, in a lawyer's office, the will was presented. Allen described the office down to the last detail—the wooden partner's desk, a well-used fireplace roaring in the corner, mahogany-paneled walls hung with expensive, antique pictures. The family had gathered, framed perfectly in Allen's shot. The different factions clustered in their separate groups. My mother and father stood off to the side, behind a couch. Allen and my maternal grandmother were on the opposite side of the room. For the sake of completing the scene, Allen said that my aunt and uncle were also present, though they had no relation to the Giffords and didn't rate any blocking or stage directions. The grey-haired "solicitor," as my grandfather called the lawyer, sat behind his big desk, watching the family over the top of "half-moon glasses."

As Allen told and retold this story, perfecting it through my high school years, I could almost hear the music cues. In later tellings, the lawyer's role became more of a cameo, but when I first heard the story, Allen went off on a tangent about him: "He was a shyster who robbed the family blind for decades and was slippery as an eel."

When I asked for the lawyer's name, Allen laughed and mentioned the firm: "Dewey, Cheatum, and Howe."

I loved his telling of this story, even as it went through its many changes. Allen, for all of his faults, could be entertaining and funny. One thing that didn't change was the pivotal scene, when the lawyer prepared to read the will aloud. It was at that point when Allen's face would become very serious. Act two of the tale then began after a long silence.

The lawyer cleared his throat and began reading the last words of Mary Frances Gifford. Here, Allen spoke in a deep, officious tone, "To the assembled family . . ." To the horror of all gathered, the lawyer declared that the sole heir of the Gifford fortune and company was—

Allen always paused here. Then he'd reach out and either prod me in the chest or pat my head: "Andrew Nash Gifford."

Allen told me that he'd known exactly what to do when he heard that. He moved fast. He knew that my father would destroy Gifford's, and that the "council of elders" couldn't maintain authority with Mary Frances gone. So he tried to take over the company, to act as my "regent."

"Bob would have rolled over, too," he said of my dad. "He was weak. He didn't care. He wanted out, anyway."

"So what happened?" I asked.

Allen blew a raspberry. "That damned lawyer! He forged a new will that left the company to your Dad."

I asked how he could forge a will if he'd already read it out loud to everyone, but Allen told me that wills change all the time.

"A will is just a suggestion," he said. "In reality, you can't skip an heir. So all Bob had to say was 'give me the company' and he got it."

"Even though he wanted out?" I asked.

Allen shrugged. "He had a screw loose."

Much of Allen's story was backed up by Mom. Unusually, though, she didn't provide her own take on it. The only addition she made was to say that, after Dad had won his battle against his mother's will, he was the one who ruled as "regent" in my name.

"Your father has left you holding the bag," she once said to me, in one of the rare moments we talked about Dad's absence. "They're gonna blame you. You are Gifford's Ice Cream."

But I could get off the hook, she said, if I became a priest. "If you marry Jesus, then the debtors can't come after you."

As it turned out, every single aspect of Allen's story was fictional. In reality, John left the company to Mary Frances, and her will, written in 1977 shortly before her stroke, stipulated that the company go to Dad, with a very large trust fund set up for "any children Robert may have." That trust fund was then emptied out by Dad—part of the plunder with which he would vanish in 1985.

None of these stories, however—true or untrue—told me what I needed to know about John and Mary Frances. Okay, he flew planes, she was from Silver Spring, they were ice cream gods and made some serious cash. But who the hell were they?

I searched high and low for people who knew John and Mary Frances, for anyone who could shed light on them or my family's history. The story had to be out there somewhere. After all, here was the founder of an ice cream empire, a big name in the DC area, a man who entertained DC's elite. This was no bizarre shut-in, like Howard Hughes. Eventually I pieced together a life that appears to be exactly the one expected of a 1940s millionaire. People remember parties at the house on Bexhill Drive—delicate china laid out, champagne served in crystal, a bustling staff bringing out tray after tray of delicacies.

Both party guests and family friends describe my grandfather as a quiet man with a dry sense of humor. When his university friends occasionally came through the area, John would shut down the main Silver Spring store and lay out an ice cream banquet for them, using the family's finest crystal and silver spoons.

These people praised him as the most generous man they knew. A child of one of John's friends said that John paid for his college tuition in the 1960s. He owed "a debt of everlasting gratitude" to my family.

Gifford's employees I've interviewed seem less sure that John was such a great guy. Some recalled him as a dark cloud, stalking the halls of the Silver Spring store, firing people on the spot for minor transgressions. They described a loner, a quiet man who stayed in his office most of the time.

But other employees loved him.

"The brains of the company," one employee said. Another told me that she accompanied John, once a week, to the Walter Reed Military Hospital in DC, where he would hand out free ice cream and "sit and talk with wounded veterans for hours." She stood by, eyes averted, serving as personal secretary for his needs during these visits.

Was John a dark presence to be feared? Or a kind-hearted and extraordinarily generous man who loved everyone? Like the stories about my mother, every story about him tended to rest on one end or the other of that spectrum. And both types of stories had an anecdotal feel. Were both somehow true?

When I pressed for more details—when I asked who this man was, what he was like—the storytellers all came up blank. People who said they had known my grandparents for decades all stumbled when asked to describe the finer points of John or Mary Frances. There seems to have never been any true personal contact. What I heard most often was:

"It was all business."

"We never really talked."

"He always kept to himself."

Many employees said they rarely knew if John was even in the building. But they agree on one thing: Mary Frances ran the show.

The partners who survived the 1940s—John, George Milroy, and Mary Frances—all seemed to have specific roles. Milroy was the operations man. Besides managing the stores, he also controlled a fleet of trucks that supplied locations outside Silver Spring. Milroy was the man in the field, a general making sure the entire system worked like a well-oiled machine. He was gregarious and loud, a strong presence screaming over machinery, dealing with Teamsters, and running the intricacies of a busy retail ice cream chain.

Each store relied solely on the ice cream made at the Silver Spring plant under John's strict supervision. The other stores did not make ice cream on the premises, or have the equipment to do so. This was John's way of controlling quality. His role was a combination of the quiet, withdrawn man behind the scenes keeping the business part of things running and the front-of-house personality for showier events.

Mary Frances was the heavy, the hatchetman. She had full power to hire and fire at will. She was a constant presence at the Silver Spring store, always watching, always quick to anger. Employees and customers alike recall incidents when Mary Frances kicked Dad's girlfriends out of the store or publicly fired waitresses involved with him. But she also once fired an employee whose teenage brother wrote a disparaging review of Gifford's in his school newspaper. I spoke to one waitress fired on the spot for not wearing correct shoes, and another waitress let go when she ruined her uniform and couldn't afford to replace it. An accountant was sent home for wearing tight jeans. And fifty years before widespread smoking bans, God forbid that Mary Frances caught an employee lighting up anywhere near the building.

One former waitress told me that she could never escape the gaze of M.F., as she was commonly known. She had an eerie habit of appearing, silently, to observe someone's worst mistakes. That waitress said: "It always felt like, whenever I did something wrong, I'd turn around and find M.F., arms crossed, narrowed eyes, watching me."

A former candy lady said she would look up from her work and see M.F. lurking nearby "like some sort of ghost."

The men running the giant mixers on the floor of the Plant would turn to get ingredients and find her checking off a tally, or just watching carefully. Delivery truck drivers would load or unload their goods as she stood, tapping her foot, always keeping count. Besides enforcing the dress code and smoking violations, an ex-employee told me that M.F. once fired someone because she discovered that the employee's distant relation worked at a rival ice cream parlor.

The roles were reversed at home. I tracked down old neighbors in Kensington who said that all they ever got from John, outside of social events, was a wave or a nod of the head. If they tried to engage him in conversation, he would go quiet, blank, mumbling an agreement or nodding anxiously as if he couldn't wait to run away. Neighbors who were children in the 1960s and 1970s said that they always avoided the house. That lines up with the quiet, dour man at the store. But then I kept hearing another word when I asked people to recall their childhood memories of John from Bexhill Drive.

"Scary."

Once, John confronted a neighbor whose son had kicked a ball into the backyard. The boy's mother apologized profusely and asked for the ball back, but John punctured it and threw it away. He warned that worse would happen if anything like that occurred again. Then he leaned back, cleared his sinuses, and hocked into the mother's face. That boy, now in his fifties, sat with me in a bar and broke down into tears as he related the story.

Another individual told me how John tried to convince him to write a favorable feature on Gifford's in a local newspaper. John's negotiation tactic involved placing a pistol on the table and idly playing with it as he made his request.

Very few neighbors or friends could recall any details about Mary Frances. She faded into the background when at home. Evidence of her life outside Gifford's is frustratingly obscure. I dug through public records, finding not much more than hints and scraps, even with her birth certificate in hand. Her family and her life are largely undocumented.

The picture of her—and of my grandfather—is all over the place. Generous, domineering, sensitive, insane, dangerous, violent, prudish, terrifying, shut-ins, party animals, loving, kind.

Every story contradicts the one before. So perhaps their actions should speak for them?

John was a member of the Rotarians for three decades, and a founding member of the Citizens Building and Loan of Silver Spring, once the DC area's largest and most prestigious savings and loan organization. From 1946 on, in addition to his visits to hospitalized veterans, John donated his time and his ice cream to handicapped orphans and other disadvantaged children. In 2008, I spoke to a ninety-nine-year-old former candy lady who praised John as a "great man" and a "benefactor." He regularly sent large donations to the American Cancer Society and other charitable organizations. He helped build his adopted town of Silver Spring, riding a post-war boom of gentrification in the 1940s and 1950s, into a powerful regional retail market.

In 2013, a real estate agent and long-time native of Kensington, Maryland, sent me a copy of the deed to the Bexhill Drive house from 1977. I discovered then that Mary Frances had "sold" the house to my father for ten dollars. She signed the deed with an "X." That's also how she signed her will, and other corporate documents. Her trail is cold. There's no sign that she was involved in John's philanthropy or interests.

But John's family still had a surprise up its sleeve.

IV

My mother once told me that the Gifford family could only ever have one heir. I was an only child, my father was an only child, and John was an only child. But that wasn't all true.

One day in 2005, I got a phone call. A man on the other end asked if I was Andrew Gifford, and I replied that I was. The caller took a long, slow, breath, and then said his name was Leroy Nash Gifford Junior.

"My father was Leroy Nash Gifford," he said, "your grandfather's brother."

I had never heard the name before. John had a brother? That had never come up. I listened to Leroy Jr. as he told me about his father, whom he called "co-founder" of Gifford's Ice Cream. What emerged was a dark tale of betrayal and abandonment that played out while John Gifford and his partners made a fortune. The story, according to Leroy's family, was dramatically different than anything I knew at the time.

For the first time, I learned the names of my great-grandparents—Stella Nash and Carl Gifford. Carl died very young, leaving Stella to raise the two boys. When she died, she left the family farm to her two sons, John and Leroy. Between them, they were supposed to split roughly $75,000. But John took it all to start Gifford's, drafting his brother Leroy as "co-founder and equal partner."

The company struggled, however, and Leroy had to find another job, moving to Kentucky while John ran Gifford's. Then, in 1949, John contacted Leroy and said it was time for him to come and help run the company as co-president. On Christmas Eve, Leroy set out for DC. But his car crashed on an icy road. He was hospitalized with severe injuries that would haunt him for the rest of his life and leave him forever on crutches.

In the hospital, he also developed a drug habit, which he later replaced with heavy drinking. Shortly after the accident, John and Leroy had a feud and John disowned Leroy so completely that no record of his branch of the family remained. Theirs were the names so brutally obliterated in our family bible. Leroy died in 1977, still hating his brother and blaming John for stealing that long-ago inheritance.

So why was Leroy Jr. calling me now? He said that it had taken him a while to track me down. He told me that my mom had contacted him out of the blue in 1995, shortly before she took off across the country, and shared her own research and stories about the Gifford family, saying that she had become fascinated with genealogy. I shared this story with Allen, but he had never heard of Leroy either.

After Mom's death and her probate, when I was back in touch with Dad occasionally, I challenged him about Leroy's story. Dad sighed over the phone and said: "Here's what really happened . . ."

The story he spun was a variation of the familiar New Jersey tale. The two Gifford brothers spent their listless post-college years on a dairy farm in New Jersey. It was the 1930s, a hard time for many of their peers, but the brothers came from a wealthy family and weathered the worst of the Depression. I stopped him to mention John's plane, and said that I had a photo of him flying it. Dad replied: "That's ridiculous. He never flew. There weren't even planes back then."

Then he continued his story: both brothers had cars and bright futures. John had an economics degree from the University of Chicago and was "free from worry or want."

"What brought them to New Jersey?" I asked. "Did they live there? Were they born there?"

Dad said yes.

"Did John steal the recipes?"

"Yes!" Dad wheezed, sounding excited. "Oh, yes. But you have them now. Your legacy."

"So what happened to Leroy?"

Dad coughed, and I almost repeated the question as the silence stretched out into several long moments. Finally Dad replied: "Whatever Leroy Jr. told you is the truth."

After that he clammed up. The conversation was over.

Desperate for information, I contacted Leroy Jr. with more questions about the founding of Gifford's. I asked about the feud—what did he know about the split between the two brothers? What did he know about the money John stole from Leroy?

Leroy Jr. told me that there may have been a third partner, but he wasn't sure. He thought the third partner was "the real ice cream man" and that John's original investment was $75,000. He remembered, as a child, his parents fighting John for their portion of the payment after his father was ousted from the company. He blamed his father's drinking for the split, saying that Leroy became a severe alcoholic after the car crash. With Leroy's exile and alcoholism, he said: "The family went from comfort to poverty."

That third partner sounded like Tillotson, but the timing and the situation didn't make sense. Why didn't Leroy take a role in the company sooner? According to Leroy Jr., Gifford's had struggled until 1949. The company couldn't manage to bring on another officer.

Years later, when my research led me to the incorporation papers, the original partners, and John's history and background, Leroy Nash Gifford was missing from all the records. Not a hint or mention anywhere. Leroy remains elusive during all of this long history.

But he was there. I have a photo of John and Leroy together from around 1910. The blacked-out names in the family Bible speak of a terrible break in the family. But those are the only clues I have. What happened? In some sort of rage, did John erase his brother so completely that even Leroy's past was obliterated? Did John go back and alter records somehow?

The story just didn't add up.

Why did John wait until 1949 to summon his brother? Gifford's was booming in the 1940s. Where was Leroy during the Franklin Ice Cream years? Why would John steal Leroy's inheritance when John made his first million by 1940 and had a gang of partners to help fund his initial investment?

I brought my research to Leroy Jr. and he asked his sister for more details. Her response brought yet another spin on the story. She remembered how, when she was ten, the family struggled with a decision to sell the inherited Indiana farm. Her father, Leroy Sr., was very stressed and "hated to let it go." But John and Mary Frances forced the sale during a heated visit.

After some angst, Leroy Sr. bought into Gifford's Ice Cream in the late fall of 1948, she said. Initially, Leroy did work at the stores. It was during the winter of 1948–49 when Leroy Sr. had his accident, but he kept pushing forward, according to his daughter.

"We moved to DC in May of 1949," she recalled, adding that "Daddy was one of the founders of Gifford's. Andrew's research may be a little faulty."

But John had plenty of money by then. In 1948, Gifford's was well established with three operating, fully-equipped stores. The next store wouldn't open until 1952, and Milroy took charge of all that. Leroy Jr. surmises: "Everyone in my family has always believed Gifford's was founded by John and Leroy Gifford. That was my father's claim. Your research makes it look like that had been a promise more than a fact. My father either stretched the truth, or he was deceived. Or both."

Leroy's family knew nothing about the partners named on the articles of incorporation, or Franklin Ice Cream, or even John's life in the 1920s. Had John cut off Leroy far earlier than anyone knew?

Neither Leroy's family nor I will ever know the real story, sadly. But the extent to which John went to ostracize Leroy is shocking. How can two brothers fall so far away from each other? There's no hint of an attempt at reconciliation. Leroy has simply been erased. Yet he and his family lived no more than fifteen miles from Bexhill Drive's front door, watching Gifford's Ice Cream thrive decade after decade.

I wonder if Leroy felt the way I do. I wonder if he got that same question—"Gifford? Like the ice cream Gifford's?" How did he respond? His family says that he died angry, bitter, and broken. The younger brother, always in the shadow of John Gifford.

It took some digging, but I eventually found my great-grandparents. Carl Gifford was a small-town lawyer in Tipton, Indiana with the firm of Gifford and Fippen. A stern-faced man in all of the pictures I could find, he still seems like someone who should be reasonably happy. Carl, Stella, and two bouncing baby boys are the very portrait of the American dream.

But then disaster struck. Carl died at the age of thirty-seven, in 1904. John was six, Leroy only four. The two young brothers were abandoned by their mother, Stella, who vanished until 1929, when she died on the operating table in a Denver hospital during a surgery to remove a benign tumor from her thyroid.

What happened to Stella, and her life between 1904 and 1929, remains a mystery as deep as most of the others in this story. Once again, there are no records, no clues, no witnesses. Once again, accounts conflict. John and Leroy, in 1929, were contacted out of the blue as the next of kin and thrust into the business of her death much as I was with my mother's.

The boys were raised by an uncle, and, for John, at least, his childhood was never a topic of conversation. Before his death, my dad struck up an e-mail correspondence with his first cousin, Leroy Jr. In one e-mail to Leroy Jr., my dad wrote: "Our fathers being raised without a father and mother, I think, explains some of my dad's eccentricities and his reluctance to talk about family or deal with family matters."

For all the searching, all the research, all the questions, the tragic story of Carl and Stella is probably the best glimpse we'll get of whatever made John Gifford the man he was.

V

By 1980, the Plant at Silver Spring was producing and selling 200,000 gallons of ice cream a month. That's 2.4 million gallons per year. By comparison, in 1995, Ben and Jerry's cranked out 10.1 million gallons, for global distribution. Gifford's, by contrast, had only four outlets, and no distribution or presence in supermarkets. 2.4 million gallons is an extraordinary amount of ice cream for a local operation.

But by the early 1970s, John was already planning to shut down the parlors, to close every store except for the Silver Spring store, which would be remodeled to provide a larger manufacturing plant. The front parlor would be halved in size. John—always of a pioneering mind—wanted to develop a fleet of food trucks. Gifford's would go on the road, chiming through neighborhoods in the area. So long, Good Humor Man. Gifford's would also hit the store shelves. John was negotiating with all of the major grocery stores in the area. By the time I was born, Gifford's was poised for a sea change.

But then something happened. Someone very close to John told me that "something went wrong with John Gifford around 1974." He and Mary Frances began hoarding ice cream at the

Bexhill Drive house. Except they weren't storing it in a freezer. They put gallon and quart containers on the shelves, eventually outgrowing the kitchen and storing ice cream on book shelves, in the basement, in the attic. When my parents took over the house in 1977, they had to clean up this sour, stinking mess of years-old melted ice cream.

The descent into madness of the elder Giffords put the new plans for Gifford's Ice Cream on hold. In 1976, John died. Six months later, in 1977, Mary Frances had the stroke from which she would never fully recover. Confined to a hospital bed, she inherited John's shares and the entire estate, placing George Milroy in nominal control as president of the company.

The story of the business gets cloudy at that point. Officially, Milroy ran the company until 1980, and Dad had no control at all. Still, Dad was a constant presence at the Plant, and some of the administrative employees remember Dad taking over portions of the day-to-day operations. One former employee told me that Dad was the store manager, serving under Milroy. Dad's official position is not recorded in any corporate document, nor does he appear to have been on the payroll. Despite Dad's daily presence, it seems that Mary Frances, through Milroy, was trying to keep her son at a distance.

So Allen's theory that Mary Frances hated my father seems to have some credence. In 1977, Dad was thirty-nine, a Harvard graduate with an accounting and business degree. Why didn't he take up the reins when John passed away? What made his mother find him so unfit? An answer may lie in complaints I heard from many ex-employees. As one woman told me: "I found your Dad a little creepy. He walked around in what I joked were crepe sole shoes."

As he crept around, she often found him standing behind her as she worked. "Maybe he'd been there for five minutes or thirty," she continued. Unnerved, she demanded an explanation. "[But] you know he had that way of sort of stuttering when he was nervous. Not exactly stuttering, but sort of fumbling with words to try to answer."

Caught red-handed, my dad could say only that he "wanted to see what people were up to." This serial stalking of waitresses became a commonplace in my research.

At home, Mom was raising me, all of us now in the big house on the hill as Mary Frances was sequestered in a nearby nursing home. Meanwhile, at the store, Dad worked his way through waitresses with abandon, and he didn't stop with redheads. Everyone was a target. I spoke with fourteen and only three said that he didn't hit on them, creep about, or outright force them into sex.

Mary Frances lingered until January 22, 1980. She died at midnight, which is probably the reason that her death certificate lists both the 21st and the 22nd as the date of death. The cause of death is listed as pneumonia, from which she suffered for three days.

Seeing her death certificate threw me back to that moment I was left alone in the house, spooked by *The War of the Worlds* and huddled under the bed as I imagined Martian warriors stalking me. For three days, my grandmother had suffered alone. My parents didn't visit her or talk about her. She had no other visitors I know of. She died alone, choking on the fluid in her lungs.

I have never visited the Gate of Heaven Cemetery in Aspen Hill, where she is buried next to John. In fact, I was always told there was no permanent gravestone. Only in 2016 did a stranger inform me online that this isn't true. John's name is on a stone, though an empty space beside his name remains blank. So Mary Frances was interred, and my parents never added her name to the stone. What passed between mother and son to justify this unmarked grave? I recalled Mom's stories that it was Mary Frances who abused my father. Whether or not they were true, I realized that Dad had spent a lifetime hating his mother.

Her grave wasn't the only slight to her memory. With Mary Frances dead, Dad took over the company and immediately purged all of the administrative staff. He stopped paying the bills, taxes, and vendors. He set about dismantling Gifford's.

In 1980, Gifford's was clearing a net profit of $1.3 million a year.

By January 1981, the company was embroiled in countless lawsuits.

By March 1983, thirty-eight months after my dad took over, the company was on the verge of bankruptcy.

By April 1984, Dad was in hiding and Gifford's was in Chapter 11.

By May 1985, Dad had vanished and Gifford's was gone.

Robert Gifford was a chameleon. He moved in shadows, watched from a distance, faded into the background. Family, friends, and employees alike say: *Poor Bob. He just couldn't handle the pressure. He was in over his head.* After all, this is the man who lost the golden egg, the DC icon painstakingly built and maintained for two generations by John and Mary Frances Gifford. Poor Bob. He was so clueless.

Or so people thought. They saw a sad sack who mumbled his way through life. A Harvard business graduate without any business acumen. Robert Gifford, the scrivener. But I believe that's exactly what Dad intended. Because the best thief is the one you'd never suspect.

The sheriff, the lawyers, and a horde of jilted investors agree. They see a very different Robert Gifford: a criminal, a fugitive, a man who pulled off one of the greatest heists in DC history. A man who vanished with somewhere between two and ten million dollars. A man who systematically, and with malice aforethought, dismantled and destroyed Gifford's Ice Cream. Who outmaneuvered everyone, especially people—like my grandfather Allen—who thought they had Bob Gifford in their pocket.

People ask: why? I think I saw the answer in those mysterious scratches in the laundry chute at Bexhill Drive. The same answer so crudely described by Howie the handyman as he pinched my leg. It was an open secret for decades. Dad was a victim of childhood abuse, and he wanted revenge. He could not kill the people who had abused him, so he aimed to kill their legacy instead. And whatever the public thought of that legacy didn't matter. Bob Gifford never saw us. He never thought about us. He never cared. He was on a mission.

CHAPTER SEVEN

SELLING LIES

I

March 1938. On what appears to be partly an impulse, John Gifford moves to Kensington, Maryland, with his wife and one-month-old son. Kensington, nestled in the cool forest of Rock Creek Park, was then a small whistle-stop village about to boom as a wave of suburbanization washed over the ring of small towns around DC. The Gifford family home on Bexhill Drive had just been built. With four bedrooms, four and a half baths, on just over a quarter of an acre, the white-brick house stood on the hill and proudly faced the world. Mary Frances exercised her green thumb, planting rows of tulips and prize-winning rose bushes in an immaculately sculpted garden. The Gifford manse was designed to impress from day one.

Young Robert's playground was made of forest and creek, wildlife and sunshine, ruins of Revolutionary-era mills, swamps, hidden meadows, and fresh springs that he could drink from. An extensive trolley system also connected Kensington to DC in the 1940s. It was quicker and easier to get to Dupont Circle from Kensington via public transport than it is today.

But young Robert didn't have much time to enjoy this suburban paradise. He was relentlessly policed by Mary Frances, who wanted him to focus only on his studies. After parochial school, he moved on to Landon, a prestigious private high school in upper Bethesda, and when not at school, every aspect of his life was regimented. At dinner, he was not allowed to drink until he had finished eating—a rule that he followed religiously until his dying day. If he were to take a drink before he cleared his plate, he'd be beaten and locked in the basement. Mary Frances pulled the fuses so that the basement plunged into darkness and became a personal hell for this boy who dared take a sip of water at mealtime. In the dark, he would scream and pound on the door. The help were told to ignore him.

There's not much else in the way of a factual record of this child's life. Because of his mother's strict oversight, Robert had little chance to make neighborhood friends. Leroy Jr., roughly the same age, remembers playing with Dad before the feud between their fathers ripped the family apart. A high school friend said that he and Dad enjoyed the occasional Saturday out, maybe once a month. They'd study, or maybe ride their bikes around the neighborhood. Dad never brought any friends home. These few friends, kept at arm's length, paint a picture of a lonely boy, and an even lonelier teenager, living in abject fear of his parents.

Dad's time at Harvard seems a continuation of this loneliness. Few of the classmates I spoke with could recall him in any detail, even when I showed them Dad's yearbook picture. He graduated in 1960 with a master's degree in business and accounting. Twenty-two years old, he vanished for the first time. There's no trace of an income, taxes, credit, or property. There's no sign of him until 1966, when he volunteered for Vietnam.

But even his service records are spotty. Dad was assigned to Cold War Berlin as a member of an artillery unit that my research says didn't yet exist in 1966. Attempts to locate fellow veterans who served with him all failed, and there are no details of his actions or other postings. When pushed for details, an Army archivist told me to "stop asking questions."

The archivist's warning is bizarre and might suggest that Dad was involved in intelligence. If true, his obsession with cloak-and-dagger nonsense starts to make sense. Dad never spoke of his time in the Army. Friends, family, and workers at Gifford's had no idea that he served. Yet, when he died, the Army paid for his stone and put him in a national cemetery.

This mysterious military service is the only physical record of his existence in the 1960s. Before and after Vietnam, he lived in an apartment in upper Silver Spring, but I found no record of rent payments or even a signed lease. Perhaps this wasn't uncommon then, but his IRS records show something that was: though he worked at Gifford's, he didn't collect a paycheck.

He next appears in the official record in October 1973, when he marries Mom. His name also appears on my birth certificate. But then the paper trail thins out once again. The credit cards were in Mom's name, as was the lease at a new apartment. And there's still no sign of income or tax returns.

The only other appearance of my father in the public record before 1980 is when Mary Frances signed over the deed to the house in 1977. So it's striking, in 1980, when he's thrust into the spotlight following the death of Mary Frances. This man who had so successfully hidden from the world and officialdom for most of his forty-two years was now front and center on the DC business stage.

So was he always a bad guy? Perhaps. Mary Frances certainly didn't trust him. From her incapacitating stroke in 1977 until her death in 1980, George Milroy nominally ran Gifford's. But George didn't carry through on any of the plans he and John had developed in the first half of the 1970s. Instead, he simply maintained the status quo. A reliable million-bucks-a-year status quo.

It's hard to find evidence of bad blood between Dad and Milroy, though. Dad was a constant presence in the Silver Spring store and functioned as de facto manager. He had enough power over Milroy to bring in my maternal grandparents. My grandmother started working with the candy ladies and by 1979 was running the candy counter. Dad had also farmed out his less desirable weekend and evening managerial duties to Allen. When Mom and Dad and I went to Deep Creek Lake for weeks at a time during ice cream season's high holy summer months, Allen would step in as full-time manager.

Dad assumed the presidency of the company on January 29, 1980, a week after Mary Frances died. He was the last Gifford to hold the job, and, if there were any sort of deathbed shenanigans involving me (or more likely Milroy), there's no record of them. Dad's assumption of the throne was clean and easy. In fact, I heard many people say that Dad had actually been running the company since 1976 and Milroy only held the title of president, never bothering to show up.

On the same day Dad officially became president, Milroy happily retired—taking a twenty-five-percent stake in the company with him. According to some people I spoke with, Milroy got out with a lump-sum payment of several million and an annual retirement distribution of around $250,000. These were enormous sums in 1980, but Gifford's was still an enormously successful company.

The sea change that John had envisioned—shrinking Gifford's stores to expand its distribution nationwide—was the first thing Dad killed. Food trucks? Distribution centers? That sounded like work, I bet, and a lot of it. More to the point, it required a love for the company and for ice cream that he didn't share. Robert Gifford was not in the business to preserve any of his father's dreams. Instead, Dad had another master plan. He was going to take Gifford's for everything it was worth.

Much as the 1940s and 1950s saw ice cream parlors proliferate with the spread of modern refrigeration, the 1970s took the industry into a second revolution. Baskin Robbins, once family owned, had been bought in the late 1960s by United Fruit after the original owners died. United Fruit cut the product's quality, streamlined the process, and went global. Soon, lower-priced, lower-quality products began to appear from other new conglomerate ice cream franchises. Cheap ice cream means lower butterfat content. Government regulation allows for as little as ten percent butterfat before the product can no longer be called ice cream. Considering the budget prices this allowed, many palates quickly got used to the low quality.

The cheap stuff was a cash cow. Reducing the butterfat content also reduces the volume of the ice cream mix. To maintain a consistency like traditional ice cream, the mix is simply whipped—that is, the lost volume is replaced with air. Tillotson's method for measuring this volume also points out a simple truth: bulk low-quality ice cream producers were basically selling air. Nothing really shocking here, though. By the mid-1980s, even gourmet brands were lowering their butterfat content. Dad—the supposedly terrible businessman—saw which way the wind was blowing right away. He stepped Gifford's down to sixteen percent butterfat in 1980 and fourteen percent from 1981 on, but continued to raise the cost per scoop. The result: a spike in profits. Profits going right into his pockets.

The destruction of Gifford's didn't involve a frontal assault. Dad was working slowly, with a level head, quietly digging away to undermine the business. On the surface, it looked like he was doing everything right. His savvy didn't just shine through with the butterfat reduction. He also embarked on a new marketing campaign. Suddenly, Gifford's became "premium ice cream," with a revamped menu and plans for expansion into a network of new ice cream parlors, rather than in supermarkets.

Ignoring John's plans to adapt Gifford's to the changing world of ice cream production and sales, Dad went backwards. He was going to revive the old-style parlor-front ice cream stores. This ran completely counter to what other ice-cream firms were thinking at the time. But Gifford's parlor-based business was booming in 1980. Like his father before him, Dad was doing what seemed impossible. He made it look good. And everyone bought it.

Dad had quite a bit to work with, even if he was ignoring John's plans. If John had had his way, Gifford's would have marched right beside other big brands on the cutting edge of the ice cream revolution, sold on shelves in every supermarket in the nation. In 1974, the cheap stuff would go for around seventy-nine cents to a dollar for a half-gallon tub. Haagen-Dazs was charging two dollars a pint. Around the same time, though, John planned to charge as much as four dollars for a pint of Gifford's. This was an extraordinary sum for the time—roughly the same price paid today for a pint of Ben & Jerry's, over four decades later.

In the DC area, John probably would have won his gamble. He produced a quality product that had earned its customers' loyalty. A trip to Gifford's was a shared experience that people treasured for its place in their lives. A pint of Gifford's ice cream would have probably found its way to a lot of DC home freezers. Thirty years of attempted resurrections have proven that. A Gifford's reboot today could charge as high as six dollars a cone. Who cares about the quality as long as it's called Gifford's? And, even if it can't be called Gifford's, the barest whisper of association with the name is worth something. Because of John's early work to lend it a perception of quality, Gifford's has ever since been about the name—a name that justifies a premium price.

Dad knew that. As he announced his plans to save the company he'd already quietly set out to destroy, he was also going to profit off its name.

Dad's plan was simple. He was going to sell franchises—the opportunity for John Q. Public to buy his very own Gifford's outlet, modeled on the one-hundred-seat parlor of the Silver Spring store. George Milroy came out of his brief retirement to sign on to this new endeavor. It was purely a get rich quick scheme. Neither Dad nor Milroy intended to make these franchises happen—they were just going to cut and run as soon as the money came in.

The best evidence of this intent is the way Dad got rid of everyone who might catch on to him. He cleaned out the administrative staff, leaving the second floor of the Silver Spring store eerily depopulated. And then the games could really begin.

By the winter of 1981, Gifford's was still producing sales, still earning profits. Lines were still forming at the door. But my dad was also kiting checks to vendors and suppliers, sending payments made out to the wrong company, apologizing profusely, then repeating the "mistake." Bills went unpaid for months. Some for years. As a result, profits appeared to soar on the cash-flow reports he showed to potential franchisees.

Worse, the staff wasn't always getting paid, causing quite a bit of anger. One former waitress told me she had to take her paycheck to the bank in the company of whoever made the firm's daily deposit if she hoped to have any chance to successfully cash her check.

"Employees who didn't do that weren't always able to cash their checks," she added. "There wasn't enough money in the account."

By the end of 1982, Dad was paying many employees in cash. Every liability he could pay in cash, he did, to keep it off the books. As it turns out, the cash wasn't coming from earnings—it was coming from the trust fund that Mary Frances had set up for me. Meanwhile, the company's artificially-inflated cash flow was diverted to buy non-existent equipment and pay employees who were not on the books. A former manager told me that, one weekend, Dad purchased a fleet of trucks, only to return or resell them all within forty-eight hours. The behavior appears so erratic that the money trail is impossible to follow. Which, of course, was the point. Otherwise, Dad wouldn't have died a free man.

In mid-1980, Southern Maryland Refrigeration sued Gifford's. Dad had not been paying his bills for regular freezer maintenance. The suit dragged on, as my dad avoided multiple subpoenas, until 1982, when it was finally settled in full with a cash payment. Dad conducted ploys to avoid the various court summons. At work, he would use the service entrance, slipping up the steps to the offices unnoticed. Employees have told me they rarely knew when he was in the building.

In May 1981, the chocolate supplier sued for unpaid invoices. My dad was, once again, tough to track down. When he finally was served, in September 1982, he paid off the bill—another cash payment of $7,134.72.

In December 1981, Southern Maryland Refrigeration's replacement, Arctic Refrigeration, sued Dad for $11,636.06 in unpaid invoices and repair bills. They got their money, again as a cash payment, in April 1982.

This cycle is repeated again and again between 1981 and 1983. Dad had stopped paying company taxes in February 1980, and, even while under fire in the courts, he continued that same policy right up until he vanished. The bills he did pay he always paid in cash, and some of the vendors would even return to working with Gifford's and end up caught in the same trap multiple times.

Away from the store, the ruses grew more elaborate. So much bizarre behavior seen in my childhood began to make sense as I sat and researched this strange man.

Bexhill Drive was about seven miles from the Silver Spring store, yet on several occasions when I was with him, Dad would switch cars two or three times on his commute. We'd leave our garage and go down Beach Drive and then up Seminary Road through Forest Glen, Maryland—a reasonable route back then to get to Silver Spring. Forest Glen, at that time, featured a large collection of buildings that had been abandoned by the Army's Walter Reed complex. Many of the buildings had fallen into disrepair, so the area was like a strange dead zone. Dad kept at least two other cars stashed around the complex—one sat in a rubble- and weed-choked parking lot, hidden by trees and shrubs, the other in a tractor trailer graveyard behind the abandoned buildings. He would switch cars before completing the short trip to the Silver Spring store, explaining that we were avoiding the vengeful New Jersey farmer's son. Once, after glancing in the rearview mirror, he cursed under his breath and we drove right past the Silver Spring store, looping through DC and eventually back to Kensington. Mom seemed unfazed to see Dad arrive home in a car different than the one he'd left in.

In August 1983, thirty-eight months after Dad took over, Gifford's filed for bankruptcy protection. Ostensibly this was an attempt to reorganize and save the company, and Dad seemed happy to let everyone believe this. It was the ultimate distraction: poor Bob was in trouble. The bankruptcy was the perfect smokescreen for his endgame.

II

Since the opening day in December 1938, the Gifford family has presided over an ice cream empire that, on the surface, has never changed.... But, in the paneled corporate offices upstairs, strategies for the coming decade are being planned and refined.... The Gifford's Ice Cream Company is about to go national.

—*Regardie's*

The May/June 1981 issue of the Washington business magazine *Regardie's* lovingly highlights the announcement of Dad's franchise plan. Written by *Washington Post* reporter Scott Chase, the article also serves inadvertently as a fascinating outline, when reviewed so many years after the fact, of my father's grand con game.

"My father was always resistant to any type of expansion," Dad says of John Gifford in the *Regardie's* article. "He feared loss of control, and he never really believed anyone else outside the family would care as much as he did about his product."

The article also opines that Gifford's, having never expanded beyond four stores, could have been something greater—"the Marriott of ice cream"—and lays blame at John's feet for refusing to develop the business. The article seems based more in the fake history my dad was creating at the time than actual events—it even gets the date John Gifford died wrong and states that Dad took over the company immediately after that death, though it goes on to contradict that timeline a few pages later. After one last condemnation of John's backward thinking, the article mentions that "active planning for the franchises began less than a year ago." The declared goal was to put a Gifford's into every state of the union by 1989.

Chase's article weighs in on the state of the ice cream economy, and says that Americans "are returning to the corner ice cream parlor in ever greater numbers," a contention with which most of those in the know at the time would have strongly disagreed. John himself had predicted that the days of large parlors were nearing an end, soon to be replaced by packaged ice cream and the newer, more modern parlor with few seats and no table service. The article happily implies, though, that a one-hundred-seat parlor and waitresses in faux-pilgrim outfits were the wave of the future.

Dad blames the late-1970s stagnation of Gifford's on John's poor health in his final days, and then goes off on a wild tangent to fault the struggles of Gifford's on everything from Richard Nixon to the fuel crises of that decade. It's a tirade that might seem ridiculous if it didn't do such a brilliant job of deflecting attention from the very contradictions the rest of the interview so faithfully records. Chase's article continues: "But with a steady hand on the throttle, the company quickly bounced back. Gifford was soon able to begin his corporate experiments with expansion."

The article notes that, in September 1980, the Arlington store was closed down and a new store was opened in Burke, Virginia. Dad explains his reasons for the shift—the Arlington store was in bad shape physically, new road construction had resulted in limited access, and customers were moving farther out into the suburbs. And in fact, the Arlington store was about to be condemned. Black mold spread rampant in the walls, and rats had attacked several employees.

Dad is quoted as saying that the store in Burke was an "independent franchise," a "copy of the existing stores" run by an entrepreneur named Larry Tracy, with my dad acting as his "consultant." "Independent" seems to be used loosely, as the Burke store could buy ice cream only from the Silver Spring plant. By making Tracy reliant on this inventory, my father was able to punish him at will. These punishments were a delight to Mom, who hated Tracy. At home, she would scream "Larry is an asshole," and demand that Dad "strangle Larry's involvement." He replied with his usual: "Yes, Barb . . ."

Though Chase touted the Burke franchise, the truth was that Dad was refusing to deliver product to Larry Tracy. He was playing a cruel cat-and-mouse game, waiting for Tracy to lose his mind in desperation. An ex-employee and Allen both told me that Dad would oversee the loading of the delivery truck bound for Burke but insist that some of the ice cream be held back. The Burke store would only get a fraction of whatever it asked for. Allen said that Dad would return the rest to the Silver Spring freezer without comment or explanation, then avoid Tracy's increasingly frantic calls.

Then, in 1981, Dad started a new company. He founded Gifford's of Gaithersburg, Inc., a company that would create a new model franchise store in Gaithersburg, Maryland to illustrate the look and feel of the franchise plan. Since the model franchise in Burke was failing, Gifford's of Gaithersburg would now represent the franchise scheme, in the form of a glittering, million-dollar store.

Dad invited a "group of investor friends" who bought seventy percent of Gifford's of Gaithersburg. But this was just a shell corporation. His "investor friends" were actually in the line of fire. *Regardie's* details how Dad then partnered with Bill Mann, a local lawyer, businessman, and entrepreneur. Dad says that Mann "would bring critical skills into the organization" and encouraged his "group of investor friends" to transfer their seventy percent stake to Mann. And here's where it really gets shady. It looks like Dad sold this seventy percent twice, to two different groups. And in each case, he retained the controlling vote.

In 2009, one of the original group of investors called me and ranted about Dad for thirty minutes, calling him a "sex addict" who struggled with drugs and alcohol, a "monster" who swindled him and his friends out of their investment when Gifford's of Gaithersburg was transferred to Mann. He spelled out the initial deal for me: Dad's group of investors had contributed $100,000 apiece. But if this investor who called me is to be believed, his group didn't know its ownership share was then sold again to Mann. Neither he nor his co-investors were reimbursed. He claimed they filed suits against Dad, though I could find no evidence of that. By the time everything was going to court, he said, Dad had vanished.

Mann, now deceased, appears to have been a shyster through and through. He admitted to Scott Chase, on the record, that he knew very little about marketing, and Chase breaks from his adulation of Gifford's to mention that "the key to franchising is marketing, and that seems to be the skill most lacking in the Gifford/Mann operation."

In *Regardie's* and in other interviews, Mann comes across as a clueless blowhard. He granted Dad—who had a thirty percent share—full veto power in all Gifford's of Gaithersburg decisions and actions. Dad would use this power to destroy the effort before it even got off the ground. Mann, the lawyer who should have known better, didn't seem to imagine that Dad would screw him. Another victim who thought he had poor Bob wrapped around his finger. He even blusters about the meal ticket he found in Gifford's: "I'm a hunting dog . . . I've been one all my life!"

He goes on to talk about the "Giffording of the country." But Mann then presages his own sad demise. He says he's going to be the front man, but: "Everything else is Bob and, of course, that everything else that is Bob is very important. Without it, we're nothing."

The *Regardie's* article also features the only existing interview that I could find with George Milroy. He's credited as John's equal partner and co-founder, and Milroy toes Dad's line, calling his deceased partner John Gifford a backward thinker who didn't want to expand.

George Milroy remains something of a mystery. I haven't been able to figure out if he was always in league with Dad or not. Milroy died a childless widower some years after Gifford's closed and Dad vanished. I tracked down his brother's family in Ohio, and they told me that Milroy had cut them off around the same time John cut off his brother, Leroy, and Leroy's family. Milroy's tactics and approach mirrored John's—no one in his family would see or hear from him again. His handsome fortune, it appears, went to the boy who mowed his lawn.

Dad's final playing piece makes a debut in the *Regardie's* article. For the first time in the history of the company, "secret family recipes" are mentioned. It's that reference, in this article, that has acted as the jumping off point for the greatest red herring in the Gifford's saga.

Researching any mention of the recipes prior to the *Regardie's* article comes up with no results. The "secret recipes" didn't exist during John's time, or even during Milroy's interim presidency. They aren't ever mentioned in corporate documents or news articles until Dad takes over.

In fact, it turns out that the Gifford's "base formula" wasn't even made at Gifford's. It was produced and delivered by local dairy farm Shenandoah's Pride. Nor was this base mix exclusive to Gifford's—it was shared freely with other vendors. This had been the case since the early 1950s. But still *Regardie's* says: "Bob Gifford promises to scrupulously guard the recipes that made his father's product a legend in its own time."

The first mention of the "secret family recipes" sounds so convincing, so well-rehearsed, that it's hard to believe they hadn't really been a family secret for decades. Dad is quoted as saying: "Gifford's Ice Cream is based on a secret recipe derived from comments my father collected from old time ice cream makers. . . . There are actually two secrets: how the ingredients are combined and how much of each flavoring is used. These are secrets that will never leave the plant."

But even if there had been a proprietary formula to Gifford's ice cream, it's clear the franchise plan was never designed to work. There's going to be a Gifford's in every state of the union, but all inventory will come solely from the Silver Spring store? Even if that store was in good shape, this is patently impossible. The interview was conducted at the decaying Silver Spring store, which was falling down around everyone's ears. The Plant didn't have the means to supply the stores that were currently in operation, let alone fifty states' worth. But no mention is made of updating or upgrading the Silver Spring store. The article says "Gifford's is poised on going national" and suggests that it'll happen immediately—simply because those bogus franchises had already been sold.

The "model store" in Gaithersburg was a beautiful building. I remember it well. I loved to play on the construction site, running unchecked around rebar and power tools. When the store was completed in early 1982, it was a modern, glass-encased version of the Silver Spring parlor, celebrated with a ribbon-cutting ceremony full of pomp and circumstance. Mann told *Regardie's*: "We have many people asking for Gifford's franchises already."

For the article, Mann counted off three committed franchises: one in Morgantown, West Virginia, one in Charleston, West Virginia, and one in Annapolis, Maryland. The buy-in for a Gifford's franchise was $20,000. When I brought this research to Allen, he burst out laughing.

"Woah, boy," he said, "we really got that weasel Mann."

Allen said that, unbeknownst to Mann, he and Dad sold "at least fifteen franchises," collecting the money and promising first-in-line status once the Gaithersburg store was up and running. These investors eagerly forked over the cash with little more than a handshake.

When I was a child in the early 1980s, Allen portrayed himself as "the man on the ground," the one who, as Milroy had done with each new expansion in the 1940s and 1950s, would help start up each of these franchises. The perfect job to satisfy his wanderlust. He would travel the country to erect huge, fifty- to seventy-five-seat ice cream parlors. Allen went on and on about opening up franchises in San Diego (he loved the zoo there), Hawaii, and New Orleans. He said he'd have to spend six months at each location getting them open. He promised me I could tag along. But just before he died, Allen admitted that they'd never intended to open any new stores at all and that he'd been in on the ruse from the beginning.

So Mann funded the Gaithersburg store. A grand opening date was announced and staff was hired, but it would never sell a single scoop of ice cream. Dad refused to send inventory. The store sat empty until the bank foreclosed on the property. Shortly after that, Dad filed the August 1983 "suggestion of bankruptcy," a legal maneuver which forestalled Mann and the other investors from filing their own actions against Dad. In the end, Mann and the others lost their shirts. The original investors—those whose shares Dad resold to Mann's group—also lost their money.

Meanwhile, the franchisees Dad and Allen conned were also out of luck. I've spoken with two—one who was to open a store in Hawaii and another in Florida. They'd handed over their investment on the basis of a verbal agreement. And just like the others, by the time they realized they owned nothing more than a piece of Dad's worthless shell corporation, it was too late.

By the end of 1983, Dad was living at the Silver Spring store, hiding in the sad, dark warren of rotting offices. At home, the authorities would call, come knocking, and park outside our house day after day. People approached me at the bus stop, men lurked in our backyard, one man with a summons for Dad slipped into the garage as Mom was closing the door and as good as assaulted her. But we didn't see Dad, nor did anyone successfully pin him down.

A former employee told me that part of her job was to warn Dad whenever someone arrived looking for him. Even when it came to the point that lawyers and police were barging up to the second floor of the building, they'd never find Dad. He had eyes at the front of the store and at the back. According to the people who watched the front of the store, the code was to call Dad's office, let the phone ring three times, then hang up. Once Dad heard that, he'd slip out or find a hiding place.

I'm not convinced, though, that he was still in the area, even by mid-1984. As I look back on those childhood memories of delivering mercury and glass to the Silver Spring store late at night, I never once saw Dad. One time, as I looked up at the windows to the main office, I did see the glow of a single cigarette. Was that just Mom, up there all alone, staring back down at me?

The walls came crashing down in April 1985, when Gifford's met its ignoble, dramatic end. As the authorities sifted through the corporate rubble, they found that the franchise money was gone, the bank accounts had been cleaned out, and millions of dollars were unaccounted for. They searched high and low, but Bob Gifford had vanished without a trace.

III

There are scores of Washington area natives who have had a lifelong craving for Swiss Sauce. They fondly remember piling into the family station wagon and heading to Bethesda or Arlington, simply for the pleasure of pouring this rich milk chocolate syrup, served in individual metal pitchers, over glistening scoops of high-fat ice cream. These folks were happily "I scream, you scream" Gifford's bound.

—*Washington Post*

Find someone who remembers the classic era of Gifford's and they'll probably talk your ear off about the Swiss chocolate sauce.

They may even decree that, since Gifford's went under in 1985, they have never tasted a Swiss chocolate sauce that could compare. I've spoken to fans who told me that they took time off from their lives and their jobs to seek out sauces, candy, and ice cream that were on par with the original Gifford's Ice Cream, traveling the country and, in one case, the world. The cult of Gifford's devotees is obsessive.

It's natural to think that the key behind that incomparable Gifford's taste is a recipe. After all, as Gifford's entered a death spiral in the mid-1980s, that's all anyone talked about: the "secret family recipes" that Dad mentioned in *Regardie's* had infected fans and the media alike. From 1987 to 2010, the multiple attempts to reboot Gifford's lived and breathed the myth of the recipes. Even today they are a topic of conversation, still considered a commodity, still something people want to possess.

The most recent person to attempt a Gifford's reboot is DC chocolate maker Mark Schutz, who, in 2016, partnered with Dolly Hunt, the original rebooter in 1989. Schutz is just another in a long line of rebooters—and surely there will be more in the future—but his research into my family came at a time when I was asking my own probing questions about my family and wondering if I should write this memoir and clear the air. His discoveries led me down a fascinating path. For the first time in the turbulent history of Gifford's, the idea of "secret recipes" was challenged. The article announcing the 2016 effort in *Bethesda Magazine* says: "Hunt said making each batch of ice cream is a little different; it's not dependent on some 'secret' recipe."

Moving in what I consider to be the right direction, Hunt shifted the focus from recipes to the maker of the ice cream.

"You have to tweak it a little bit," Hunt said. "Some people just follow a recipe, but sometimes you have to do a little more for every batch. You have to taste it, then you know if it needs a little bit of something."

In fact, almost everybody in the reboot era has admitted, at one time or another, that it's not about the recipes. But for much of my life, I believed what Mom and Allen told me: that our set of recipes, which they had dramatically rescued in the final days of the company, were the real deal. I believed that the power behind the Gifford's brand was bound up in the recipes. I followed this thinking until just a few years ago, when the research piled up, when I demystified my family and the company and I saw that Dad had created the myth of secret recipes out of whole cloth. I took what I discovered and I talked to diary experts, professors, and former Gifford's employees who made the ice cream. I even extracted some truth from Allen before he died.

Everyone said the same thing: the true secret is that there is no secret. The recipe myth was dreamed up by my father and Allen and, perhaps, Mom. Their motivation was simple: to create the illusion of a proprietary process that could be franchised. The franchise scheme would make everyone very rich. Selling this lie was worth a million dollars—and maybe a lot more.

It didn't take exhausting research to uncover the truth about the recipes. Ice cream is easy. It doesn't require apprenticeship at the hip of a famous chef. It's not something that takes decades of struggle and experience. There's no culinary magic involved—no dash of this or alchemical pinch of that. Claiming to have a "secret family recipe" for ice cream is almost as absurd as claiming to have a secret family recipe for lemonade.

The so-called recipe cards—chocolate stained index cards that occasionally reference a mysterious "Gifford's Mix"—were on public display during John's era. And the mix itself was commonly available from the local dairy that sold it to John.

Ice cream is all about butterfat. That's the taste everyone remembers— that's what makes the ice cream so smooth, that's what we all crave, that's what we all scream for. The Gifford's base mix was usually somewhere between fourteen and nineteen percent butterfat, depending on the era and the whims of the manufacturer. Now defunct, the Shenandoah's Pride dairy farm delivered the mix weekly in a huge tanker truck. The mix was used for more than ice cream—it went into all the sauces and most of the candies, which is why Gifford's country caramels were so unique. Pouring so much butterfat into caramel sauce is somewhat unusual, and probably something the Surgeon General would frown on, but it lent the caramels that extra texture and flavor people loved. In terms of this being a "secret," well, many other companies did and currently do the same sort of thing. Gifford's sticks out because Gifford's was everywhere in an era with few other options.

It was Mark Schutz, the latest Gifford's rebooter, who discovered the truth about Shenandoah's Pride. After he told me, I went on a quest to find former employees from the dairy company, which had changed hands half a dozen times and has long since vanished. As I trawled through online forums and talked to ice cream professionals, I found the ingredients used to make one quart of Gifford's mix:

2 large eggs
3/4 cup sugar
2 cups heavy whipping cream
1 cup whole milk

There's nothing special about that list. In fact, it's the same mix that Ben & Jerry's originally used. It's currently in their recipe book, and they certainly didn't steal it from Gifford's. The recipe is, in fact, one of the most common versions of a base ice cream mix. For anyone looking to re-create the taste of Häagen-Dazs ice cream as remembered from their youth, or looking to copy that heavenly roadside ice cream bought from a dairy farm on a road trip, that's the mix.

That's not to say that the mix was unalterable. In the 1950s, when John turned the manufacturing of the mix over to Shenandoah's Pride, the massive scale on which it was produced required industrial additives. These included guar gum, a thickener that maintains an even texture, and an emulsifier called carrageenan.

In the late 1960s, John contracted a chemical flavoring company for the more common flavors. Vanilla ice cream at Gifford's, for example, used a flavor additive, not real vanilla. With several stores to supply, John's goal was to do with Gifford's what fast food outlets like McDonalds were doing—create a recognizable brand that always tasted the same. He did this in preparation for his aborted reorganization of Gifford's Ice Cream and its entry into supermarkets.

The second part of the "secret family recipe," according to Dad, in the *Regardie's* article, is how and when to add the flavors during the process. But anyone who's ever cooked at even a novice level knows the same is true of any culinary project. It's not that hard to pick up.

When people try to tell the story of Gifford's Ice Cream, or simply want to cash in on the legacy, it's really easy to get lost on the trail of secret recipes. I've watched newspaper reporters, filmmakers, authors, and historians laboriously try to follow Dad's false leads. No one wants to hear that Gifford's, that beloved icon, trucked in an utterly common, mass-produced mix.

IV

When Gifford's left the news in late 1986, I naively hoped that the company would fade away forever. But the efforts to reboot Gifford's were already underway.

Benny Fischer was the "sucker" my grandfather Allen once mentioned. He was the one who snapped up the Gifford's name and trademark from the bankruptcy auction. He took out a classified ad in the newspaper offering the recipes, trademarks, and rights to the name to anyone willing to pay for them. That's how Dolly Hunt got started, rebooting Gifford's when I was in high school.

Fischer is a DC entrepreneur, a man who has earned quite a name for himself in the last forty years. When it was announced in 1985 that the Silver Spring store had been seized by the sheriff and that everything was going to be auctioned off, Fischer, who was friends with the owner of the building, talked his way into the back offices. In an e-mail to me, he was surprisingly cavalier about his somewhat questionable acquisition of the recipes. He said that the recipes were "the real deal" in John Gifford's "own handwriting"—though I don't believe that Fischer ever knew John.

Fischer told me that no one else showed up to the auction, so he was able to purchase a quitclaim deed for the intellectual property.

When Fischer talks about his tour of the upstairs offices, prior to the auction, his story becomes a bit fantastic. The contents of the Gifford's main offices had all been placed in body bags by the building's owner, who also ran a funeral home. Fischer found this eerie sea of black body bags creepy. But he knelt down and slowly unzipped one of the bags, revealing the usual assortment of office materials. And there, among the books and memos and staplers and paperclips, he found a binder. Inside the binder, he discovered the ice cream recipes inserted in plastic covers, along with dozens of handwritten papers that he told me were "clearly your grandfather's."

"I read in the *Washington Post* that you believed the recipes were not real," he said, adding that this was "totally incorrect."

And, yet, Hunt was pretty clear that for her Gifford's reboot, in 1989, she'd really just bought the trademark and name. She had to learn how to make the ice cream, reverse engineering whatever Fischer found. She worked with the University of Maryland dairy sciences department, she said.

The dairy sciences department at Maryland came up again when Hunt partnered with Mark Schutz in 2016 to launch her second reboot of Gifford's. This time, though, there was a new spin. Schutz claims that a professor at the dairy sciences department "mentored" both my father and grandfather—implying that he and Hunt learned from the true master of Gifford's Ice Cream.

However, I can find no evidence of this mentorship. The man who allegedly mentored my family is now deceased, so, as is sadly typical with this story, I guess I'll never know the truth. But to mentor John, he must have lived in Ohio in the early 1920s, since John worked with Franklin Ice Cream for nearly two decades prior to opening Gifford's. What's more, considering that the real maker of Gifford's Ice Cream base mix was the Shenandoah's Pride company, the idea of a pivotal mentorship seems highly improbable.

I also have a hard time imagining my dad taking time to study under a professorial ice cream master. During Dad's thirty-eight months in charge of Gifford's, the true ice cream masters were the lifers in the Plant. After Milroy left, the person who made Gifford's Ice Cream was probably more likely to be Cal Headley. And certainly Cal's current ice cream business, York Castle in Rockville, Maryland, seems to come as close as anyone can possibly get to re-creating old-style Gifford's Ice Cream.

For all his talk about their authenticity, even Benny Fischer has dismissed the value of the recipes. They were, he said, "outdated, simple to produce, and wouldn't hold a candle to the modern expectations from ice cream companies like Ben & Jerry's."

Fischer is absolutely correct about this. High-quality, high-fat, delicious gourmet ice cream is now found everywhere. It's on supermarket shelves, it's on the roadside at dairy farms, it's in farmer's markets. Dolly Hunt made it in 1989. Cal Headley makes it today. But no one will ever be able to re-create the circumstances, the equipment, and the political climate that allowed for something like Gifford's Ice Cream to exist. And the people who try to reboot Gifford's are usually the first ones to admit that.

Hunt's first reboot rode pretty high for some time. Then, in 1999, she sold the company to two of her employees, Sergio and Marcelo Ramagem. Around 2002, Sergio sold his share to a man named Neil Lieberman. Under Lieberman, Gifford's enjoyed a second heyday. By 2006, a large factory was opened as the company split into two parts—retail storefronts and a wholesale distribution center. Everything seemed poised to finally realize the long-ago plan for "Giffording the country."

Lieberman, who managed the distribution side of things, teamed up with Luke Cooper, who was to run the retail outlets. But it soon turned out that these two sides were not working together, and, in fact, the ice cream being served at the retail outlets was unlabeled Hood's Ice Cream—a lower-quality, generic ice cream used at institutions and schools.

Cooper wasn't new to the ice cream business—in 2008, he purchased a "significant chunk" of a local Boston ice cream chain.

Citing the *Boston Globe*, the *Washington Post* reported that Cooper's outlets were in trouble soon after he took control: "Before the outlets Cooper controlled collapsed, he was allegedly paying employees in cash and had stopped paying rent."

Lieberman's firm was aware of the trouble in Boston, according to the *Post*, yet they still entered into a partnership with Cooper. Then: "On July 4, [2010], at 9:58 a.m., according to court filings, Lieberman sent Cooper a blistering e-mail telling him he was in default of the purchase agreement and taking him to task for selling Hood's Ice Cream in Gifford's shops."

Cooper, however, told a very different story to the *Post*, saying that Lieberman's group had failed to file the proper paperwork to keep the stores open, had "misrepresented" how he would buy the ice cream from the wholesale outlet, and had "set up obstacles that made it impossible for him to expand." Cooper said of Lieberman's group: "They were not honest about their business or the quality of the ice cream. We were forced to field multiple customer complaints about the vacillating quality of their ice cream."

There are so many parallels here to the way Bob Gifford treated Larry Tracy and then Bill Mann that it might almost be funny. Almost. Cooper's downfall happened at the same time Lieberman's firm was at war with Gifford's of Maine, embroiled in a bitter trademark lawsuit. Seemingly beset on all sides, Lieberman issued a statement: "It's horrible what has happened. It's horrible for the people who love Gifford's."

One version of the story says that in late 2010, during the legal battle between Neil Lieberman's firm and Luke Cooper, into the fray came Gifford's of Maine—now a much larger and stronger company—with the goal of defending the Gifford name. In another version of the story, it's Lieberman who struck the first blow against Gifford's of Maine, attempting to take it over. However, a carefully worded press release from Gifford's of Maine in 2011 implies a friendly merger with Gifford's of DC. Lieberman also listed an affiliation with Gifford's of Maine on his LinkedIn account through 2013. Both Lieberman and Gifford's of Maine, when asked about the fallout of the trademark case, strictly offered no comment.

So what is the truth? What really happened in 2010? I don't know and, in the end, I don't care. I find the second downfall of Gifford's despicable and disheartening, no matter the truth. All that matters is that the legal battle was tough and bitter, and the end result was this: All rights to Gifford's Ice Cream passed to faraway strangers in Maine. No longer would Gifford's be a DC-based institution.

But even after all of this, Lieberman was still flying the secret recipe flag—though he seems torn about their authenticity. He told the *Washington Post* in 2010: "[We] have changed some ingredients to try to make the ice cream all natural. For example, the Peppermint Stick flavor no longer uses Starlight mints."

Starlight mints? That's classic Barbara Gifford. That's what we wrote on the recipe cards she and I forged way back in 1984.

V

Cal Headley, of York Castle Ice Cream in Rockville, Maryland, was once the manager of the Gifford's Silver Spring plant. He was second in charge, and, when Dad vanished, Cal was left "holding the bag," as he told an NBC reporter. The courts ordered him to sell the last of the product and exhaust the inventory, using the money to cover the payroll and other debts.

Cal's a man who knows secrets, yet when asked about the recipes, Cal says there were no such things. And I believe him. He talks about the oral tradition kept by the technicians on the floor of the Plant, and other people who made the ice cream say the same thing. They knew what to make because they had been making it for decades. On top of that, there was no strictly regimented production process. Ingredients were added almost randomly. Under John, at least, experimentation was highly encouraged. And from the 1960s on, the equipment was antique and unreliable. Most importantly, there were few governmental health or safety standards.

So if the taste of Gifford's Ice Cream seems hard to re-create today, it's because the way it was made is no longer legally allowed. It's a dash of rust, a pinch of rat poison, a mistake made during a hangover Monday. Mark Schutz agrees, adding the important fact that there have been changes in pasteurization rules. No one could replicate the taste and style of the original Gifford's, even if they wanted to.

To understand this, it's important to understand the actual process for making the mix. I compiled the instructions below from Allen and a few other sources who worked for Gifford's and Shenandoah's Pride, where this process actually happened:

- Mix the whipping cream and milk together over medium-low heat.
- Beat the eggs in a separate bowl, until they turn light.
- Add sugar while whisking the eggs. Mix until well blended.
- When the cream mix reaches 142 degrees (Allen and others have said that it must be at exactly this temperature), place it on a cool burner. Continue to whisk the eggs and slowly add small amounts of the cream. You want to avoid cooking the eggs, so this can be a delicate step.
- Blend well.
- Put it all back on medium-low heat and stir constantly. If doing it the old-school Gifford's way, you're aiming again for 142 degrees, where you'll hold it for 30-60 seconds. (To kill all possible contagions, the modern cook's rule, from the FDA, is 175 degrees for half a minute. But that will probably ruin this recipe, so contagions it is.)
- Strain, and quickly chill to room temperature. (Allen said that it needs to be flash-chilled to exactly 35 degrees.)
- Add your flavoring. (These are the supposed secrets contained on the recipe cards.)
- Churn.

The biggest difference between a home kitchen and a professional one lies in the freezing process. The ice cream mix must be flash-chilled to a slushy consistency before churning—brought from 142 degrees to thirty-five degrees Fahrenheit in a few minutes. If this chilling method is too slow—as it would be in a normal household freezer—ice crystals will form and that's that. The recipe is ruined.

Once the freezing problem has been tackled, the now thirty-five-degree mix must be churned for thirty minutes or until the ice cream has a fast-food-style soft-serve consistency. To get it exactly right, it must be flash-frozen again. At the Silver Spring store, the churned ice cream was poured into containers and put on a conveyor belt that slowly ran about four feet into the main freezer. During this ride, the ice cream would be flash-frozen to a sub-zero temperature, a process impossible to replicate at home.

And there it is.

No big secrets or stunning revelations here. Except that Gifford's ice cream was never made entirely on the premises. It contained no secret ingredient that cannot be re-created. The recipes were a myth designed to fleece investors—and, later, the public. And anyone who claims to sell "Authentic Gifford's Ice Cream" is selling a fantasy.

CHAPTER EIGHT

ARMY OF GHOSTS

I

In the end, I got the chance to do something few abandoned children ever get to do: confront my father. Face to face. I got the chance to demand answers.

About two years after I beat him in a legal battle for my mother's estate, in late 2002, Dad began e-mailing me and writing letters. The best word to describe his correspondence is delusional. Now that we were re-united, he said, I should join him in Atlanta. I could live with him, in a second bedroom he'd already prepared for me in his house. He said that I could find a good job and support him in his declining years. He was even searching for a girlfriend to complete this creepy portrait of a rebooted family.

In late 2002 I was in the throes of my trigeminal nightmare. Otherwise, I suspect that these ridiculous notes would have made me even angrier than they did. Every letter ended with the same theme—he had emphysema, he didn't have long to live, he needed me to help him. He was asking me to not only be his live-in nurse but also help pay his bills. In what world did that make sense? After all, didn't he still have the millions he'd stolen from Gifford's?

When I finally responded, I asked him about the money, about Gifford's. I expected the letters to stop, but he replied right away. He avoided my question and instead made a demand that I send my mother's collection of vinyl records down to him. He told me those records were the real reason he was interested in Barbara's estate. My parents' cloak-and-dagger proclivities inspired me to carefully search through the record albums for clues.

But mostly, Dad was obsessed with death. In late 2004, when I was still three years away from a trigeminal cure, he entered the terminal stages of emphysema and required oxygen 24/7. He begged me to visit. With his delusional reply to my written challenges in hand, I decided to go down to Atlanta and face him. It's possible to lie in an e-mail, to revise and edit a posted letter, but how could he avoid my challenges if I stood there and pointed a finger at him?

Anger drove me to Atlanta. Anger and also greed. If Dad was sitting on a mountain of money, I felt entitled to it after all those long, hard years.

Most of all, I needed answers. Even in a haze of pain, I needed to know why he'd left. Still reeling from Mom's death and the extensive probate litigation, my heart sank as I thought about Dad's illness. Here I was, next of kin again, and this stranger, my father, would be another sticky death to deal with. I had come to realize that I couldn't run away from these people anymore, so, at the least, maybe I could figure out their motivations.

My dad had vanished from my life without a trace for fifteen years. Apparently, he had maintained contact with my mother until she died. But no word to me. We had never been close before, but it was hard to look at those facts and not feel singled out for rejection. I was past the stage of wanting an apology, though. I simply wanted a reason.

I flew down to Atlanta in January 2005. I left a cold, harsh, wintry DC behind and arrived in a big, warm, southern city. My father picked me up at the end of the MARTA line. When I stepped off the rail platform, he greeted me with a smile. In 1985, he had told me he was going away for the weekend. Now that Monday had finally arrived. I didn't know how to greet him. When he hugged me, I realized that I had been living that same weekend, over and over, for twenty years.

He lived in a quiet rancher with a large wooded backyard. A creek ran through the property. It was peaceful, calm, and very lonely. The house was spartan—a kitchen table, two chairs, and a few knick-knacks on the windowsills greeted me as we entered a side door from the carport. Only a drip coffee maker and two large jars sat on the countertops. The living room held a couch and an easy chair. A fake ficus stood in a corner. There was a cheap record player, two speakers, and a few records. A few pictures hung from the walls, but all of them were generic—the sort that come with the frame. The couch could have been recovered from the side of the road. Everything looked second-hand, but the house didn't have any smell. It didn't have any lived-in feeling at all.

One bedroom was his office. In it sat a computer on a piece of plywood stretched over two metal filing cabinets and a cheap rolling office chair. His bedroom had a dresser and a bed. A third bedroom was completely empty. He said he never used it.

After the tour, he sat down at the kitchen table and suggested that I make eggs for him. In the kitchen cabinets, I found just a few utensils and dishes. One of each item—spoon, fork, plate. The bottom of the dishwasher was full of black, filthy water. When I opened it, he laughed and said he always hand-washed his dishes.

I opened the fridge and found a container of Egg Beaters, a packet of string cheese, orange juice, one can of RC Cola, and two plates of leftovers in mystery-food mode. The freezer, though, was packed with frozen dinners. On the stove were a tea kettle and a skillet, the latter of which I used for the Egg Beaters. There was no butter or oil.

I cooked in silence, unnerved by the surroundings. It felt like a poorly stocked safe house. Yet Dad was not safe—he was weak and broken. Afflicted with late-stage emphysema, he meandered around this dark, empty house, dragging a long tube that linked to an oxygen tank in his bedroom. The tank wheezed and groaned like it had emphysema as well.

Dad spoke in gasping breaths, unable to complete a sentence without getting winded. His appearance shocked me. In my head, it was still 1985. I remembered the tall, seemingly healthy man bending down to speak to me. But that imposing younger man who had fled with all of the money, hopes, and dreams of two families and dozens of employees was not here anymore. This man was thin, frail, pale, old.

I watched him eat his eggs and drink some juice. I was afraid to eat or drink anything in his house, a voice in my mind screaming about poison and disease. Or perhaps my soul simply refused to let my body break bread with this man. As he ate, he breathlessly told me his master plan. I would come to Atlanta. I would take care of him.

"I'm going to get sicker . . ." he whispered. "I will need someone to tend to me."

I didn't know how to react or what to say. He'd abandoned me, yet he thought I owed him this? I blinked, my jaw set against the pain, and thought of my mother, papering the country with money that should have been mine, or my grandfather Allen and his exorbitant rent. Why did it seem that everyone in my family was so eager to take me for a ride? Finally, I blurted: "You know people still talk about Gifford's, right?"

He barked a sharp laugh, shaking his head, painfully sucking in shuddering breaths.

"Impossible," he rasped. "No one could remember the store after so many years," he said. "No one cares about Gifford's."

"People still go on and on about the ice cream, and their memories of the stores," I insisted.

He shook his head. "You're lost in your childhood memory. No one even came into the store after 1981. Empty all the time."

Every word seemed to be a breathless challenge for him, but I could see that he believed what he was saying. He'd rewritten his own history.

"They're still doing business under the name," I said. "It was all auctioned off. It's been transferred a few times, but it's still in business now."

He shook his head again. "No, no. We had an agreement to buy it back . . . when the dust settled."

I tried to keep calm. "An agreement? Who had an agreement?"

"Your mother," he gasped. "She knew what to do. She owned the company."

I shook my head. "She didn't own it. It was auctioned off by the courts in the eighties. A guy named Benny Fischer bought it and sold the rights to a lady named Dolly Hunt."

He laughed. "I knew Benny Fischer. He was a scam artist."

I told him that Allen had to mortgage his house to make ends meet for us. This seemed to stun Dad. He shook his head and muttered a barely audible "no."

"There was money," he said. "You shouldn't have had to worry. I sent all the money."

"You sent all the money?" I demanded. "To Mom? She never had anything. We were desperate. I'm still working multiple jobs to pay off my loans! If there was money, then why did we both suffer so much?"

Who was getting this money? What was he talking about? He nodded and said: "Barb had the money. That's why I tried to intervene when she died."

"To get the money?"

"For us. For you."

"How much did she have?"

"All of it. Everything."

"Like, millions?"

He nodded. "Hidden away."

A sickly feeling rose in me. I figured he was insane, or bullshitting me. As trigeminal pain shrilled through me and my drugs made the room tilt left and right, I could no longer concentrate enough to hold onto my anger. So I gave up. I sat there and looked at just another physically broken man. I asked the question I had flown down to ask: "Why'd you leave?"

He shrugged, smiled, and stared hard into my eyes. "It was the best thing to do for you."

"How was it good for me? How can you say that?"

"I had to stop the fighting. You needed peace. I gave you peace. And Barb had plenty of money for you. Everything was good."

"No. It wasn't."

I talked at length then about Mom's madness and her abuse. I tried to make him understand what he'd walked away from. We weren't just a family who needed his financial support. We needed an emotional rudder. But even as I spoke I realized he'd never been able to provide that, even before he left a monstrous mother with a defenseless child. Whatever delusions he had indulged for the past two decades—or more, perhaps—were not likely to be undone. He only shrugged dismissively and said: "Not true."

He looked at me like I was the liar, the delusional madman.

I left Atlanta the next day. I had found no peace. Dad's banal e-mails continued the same as before, with no hint that our conversation had ever happened. In fact, his messages implied that I had agreed to move to Atlanta and nurse him.

Over a decade later, in early 2016, I finally had the chance to read his e-mail correspondence with Leroy Jr., from around the same time as my visit. In those letters, he said that his married life had been so unspeakably horrible that he never really got over it. He was fearful of falling asleep in the same room as Mom "lest she stab me with a kitchen knife," he wrote. But with me, that day in his kitchen, he refused to believe anything I said about Mom's madness.

I don't know what to think about any of this. Was he attempting to scam me into supporting and nursing him? Was he simply insane? Had he convinced himself of a different history? Or was he, after all, the "poor dumb Bob" some people painted him to be? Did he honestly believe that meting out the Gifford's fortune to Mom would heal all wounds?

About two years after my visit, on January 4, 2007, a doctor called from Atlanta to say that my father would be dead in twenty-four hours. I had to come down right away if I wanted to see him one last time.

I went. I still entertained the idea that he was lying about the money. Despite the weirdly unfurnished house and even weirder lifestyle, I was convinced that the stolen millions were squirreled away somewhere. I had visions of treasure under the floorboards or buried in the backyard.

The dream of escaping my regular workaday life motivated these suspicions. This was just before surgical options had emerged for my trigeminal neuralgia, at a time when my neurologist wanted to switch drug treatments—a slow tapering off of my current drug cocktail and a build-up with a new one. Unmedicated, I knew the pain would be unbearable. It was unbearable while medicated! How could I keep a job if I was about to spend months even worse off than usual? Every word spoken, every smile, every sip of water that passed my lips, felt like someone was cutting behind my face with a blowtorch. If Dad had jars of money hidden away somewhere, then one of my problems would be solved. I could stop working and while away my pain-ridden life.

At great expense, I booked a last-minute ticket and I flew down to Atlanta to watch Robert Gifford die.

II

When I've talked about this trip with friends, I've often said that I went to Atlanta because I felt like it was a son's duty to do so. That lie came easily—I knew it was the right thing to say. I didn't want to explain that my father was a stranger. I didn't want to talk about his bizarre, sad life. I didn't want to say that I went down there to celebrate his painful demise and then hunt for stolen money. I didn't want them to know that, if I found that money, my plan was to run. Just like Dad. I'd pay cash for a car and then vanish.

Allen was typically unmoved. I said I was flying down to Atlanta because Dad was dying, and I barely got a response. Once again, I was left utterly alone to deal with the business of death.

From the Atlanta airport, I took a MARTA train to the station near Dad's house, where a neighbor of his waited for me. Dazed from making a flight in so much pain, I didn't register the neighbor's name. I can't remember it now. He told me that we had to get to the hospital right away. Dad could die any minute. As we raced through the suburban streets, I tried to bring myself back into focus and talk with the neighbor.

Perhaps in his early sixties, he was a stout, balding man. Someone who would look comfortable in a tool belt or wielding power equipment. He spoke with a flat mid-Atlantic accent as he told me he was a military veteran and a longtime resident of the area. His son was on the local police force. When my dad moved in next door to him, the neighbor had helped with the heavy lifting. I asked if they were friends. The neighbor shrugged.

"We barely spoke," he replied. "I was just watching after a sickly man. It is my duty in Christ."

I gaped at him, unsure how to respond. He took this as an opening.

"Your father and I went to the same church. Well, your father never actually went. He was too sick to leave the house. But he gave me very generous checks each week to donate to the church. They recorded the Sunday service especially for him, and mailed it to him each week."

I remained silent. After a few minutes the neighbor said: "You're going to get a lot of money. Your dad was very well off."

I remembered that Allen had said almost the exact same thing after Mom died. I wondered if this man's prognostication would fly just as far from the mark.

By the time I got to the hospital in Atlanta, Dad was drugged up and slowly choking to death. The doctor was brusque. He said that Dad was brain dead and that they had unplugged him from life support. I was too late to say goodbye, he said. Now we had to wait for him to stop breathing, which could happen at any moment. The doctor said it would be best if I stuck around with Dad and "made my peace" and that I should then call the nurse when Dad stopped breathing so they could "record the time he passed." From the way he spoke, I decided medical professionals in Georgia must have trained during the Civil War.

"So just wait?" I muttered.

"Yep." The doctor shrugged and walked out.

I sat vigil in the hospital room as Dad fought the fluid in his lungs, his face a mask of agony that made me wonder how brain dead he really was. Once, his eyes opened, glassy and unfocused, before they fluttered shut and he went a full minute before sucking in a desperate breath. The neighbor, who had also stood silent vigil on the other side of the room, shouted out: "Guide him, Lord!"

Dad went still again as the neighbor fell to his knees with a hard crack against the linoleum floor that made me wince. Muttering fervent prayers, he turned his face to the ceiling and stretched out his hands, palms up. After a little over a minute, Dad's body shuddered and he sucked in another breath. I exhaled, not realizing that I'd been holding my own breath, as the neighbor shouted out in exultation: "He's returned!"

We both watched as Dad went another full minute without breathing. Then he took another rattling, shuddering breath. I called for the doctor, who cast a withering glance in my direction, and then sat and watched Dad with a bored expression. Dad went nearly two minutes this time before sucking in another hopeless breath and the doctor nodded.

"Just pure reflex now," he said with a shrug. "The body refuses to give up." He glanced over at me. "Look, son, this is how people die. It's not pretty. But this is the reality of it."

"What now?" I asked.

The doctor shrugged again. "Once the breaths are fifteen minutes apart, give me a call."

"Is he in pain?"

The doctor sighed and said: "Look, son, he's brain dead. He's gone. He doesn't know what's happening."

"Can you give him something? Morphine?"

The doctor shook his head again and said, in all seriousness: "That could kill him."

It took five hours before I counted fifteen minutes between breaths. The neighbor had left the room. Exhausted by the spectacle, high on pain pills, not having eaten for nearly a day, I called the doctor. It was the late afternoon of January 5, 2007. When the doctor came, he brought a grief counselor with him. Dad's neighbor trailed behind. The doctor looked at Dad, listened for a heartbeat, and then said: "He's gone."

I had thought I would be immediately relieved of the pain of my childhood, the legacy of the name, but that wasn't so. Dad's horrible death was so lonely, so pointless. For such a major character in the story of a family, a company, and a legacy, his death seemed so small, so stupid.

The grief counselor put a hand on my shoulder and asked me if I needed to talk. I shook my head, turned to the three of them, and then started barking orders.

"Find a funeral home to take the body. Do whatever needs to be done to check out. I'll be at his house getting everything in order."

I stomped out, the neighbor trailing me, and headed straight for the parking garage without signing for anything. Once in the car, the first thing the neighbor said was: "Let's go get his money."

We drove to a bank, where he parked and leaned over to me to whisper: "Don't say a word. Follow my lead."

What followed was a farce in which the neighbor bullied his way through to a bank manager and demanded that Dad's account be signed over. When the manager refused, the neighbor became irate, pounding his fist and demanding the money. It was an exaggerated reenactment of that long-ago trip with my grandfather to open my first account at a credit union, except that the neighbor was nowhere near as convincing or intimidating as Allen.

We were escorted out. The neighbor drove me to Dad's house, fuming about how well-known he was in town, how he had "served his country" and "deserved more respect." I let my mind wander, tuning out his rant. My dad was dead, but thanks to my drugs, his death was shrouded in the same mental fog that blanketed most of my emotions. I was just anxious to tear the house apart. No way would Dad have put money in a bank.

In the kitchen of my father's house, the neighbor mumbled about finding a funeral home to handle the body. He wrote down a lawyer's name, leaning in to slide the slip of paper across the kitchen table towards me. I stayed motionless, quiet, staring at a pile of mail, and the neighbor finally said: "Do you want me to stay?"

I shook my head and looked around. The house appeared unchanged since my last visit two years earlier, still terribly sad. But I wasn't sad. I wasn't angry, either. I felt calm, centered. It was finally time, I thought, to close the book on the Gifford legacy.

"Are you sure?" the neighbor asked.

I nodded, and didn't look back or say another word as the neighbor let himself out. I stood in my father's kitchen and let the silence wrap around me.

III

I called Allen to share the news. He was silent for a few seconds, then he said: "Well, good riddance, I guess."

There are so many unknowns when it comes to my dad's story. When the Silver Spring store was auctioned in 1985, the sheriff told Allen that investigators figured Dad had $2 million in cash. Mom said that he had been siphoning off money every month since 1979, which added up to far more than that. He fled with as much as $10 million depending on who you believe. Then there's the lawyer who guided Gifford's through bankruptcy after Dad vanished. He told an interviewer in 2014 that he didn't even want to guess if there was missing money or not.

In 2014, when I finally confronted Allen with my questions, he confessed what he had discovered through his own lawyers and private investigators: that at least a portion of the Gifford's money was deposited in banks across the country, from Baltimore to Cincinnati, Omaha, and Atlanta. He claimed to have evidence of this. Of course, in keeping with my family's story, those allegations may simply be a bit of fanciful reckoning. But Allen told me that he knew Mom had lots of money, and that she had promised him monthly payments. He had even considered starting his own ice cream company with the potential income from Mom.

There are others who claim that Dad didn't have any money. That he ran, tail between his legs, with only the change in his pocket. These are people who have researched this story and concluded that Dad was just some poor schmoe. That Gifford's was in the red, so there was nothing to steal anyway.

No one—including me—has proof of anything. The fact that Dad had enough resources to live entirely off the grid from 1985 to 2002 is certainly telling, though.

Mom had evidence. It no longer exists, but when I was fourteen she had dragged me to the dreaded basement of the Bexhill Drive house, where she had set up a tape recorder with headphones. Next to the tape recorder were stacks and stacks of cassette tapes.

"Put on the headphones," she'd ordered, pointing with her cigarette.

I obeyed, slipping the giant headphones on my head. She pulled a cassette from the top of the pile and slammed it into the machine.

My father's voice drifted into my ears. His stumbling, mealy-mouthed stammer was the opposite of the cocksure, high-pitched voice of the man he was talking to. The two were discussing the dissolution of Gifford's Ice Cream. I looked at the tape case—the numbers "1983" written on it in black marker—and looked up at Mom. She stared hard at the tape recorder, smoking and avoiding my gaze.

The conversation was a phone call. My dad and this other man said their goodbyes, and a click ended the exchange. Another picked up with the sound of a phone ringing. Dad and somebody else I didn't know then talked about how to skim a $50,000 surplus from the month's earnings. My dad threw out ideas—"Can we take it all out at once? How about we say it's for upgrades and we're buying them off-market, used?"

Hours and hours of recorded phone calls played out, Mom switching tapes when they ended, moving through 1983 and 1984. Always Dad talked to one of these two men. The amounts under discussion were sometimes as large as $100,000 and sometimes as small as $1,000. There was a long exchange about how to "disappear," during which my dad enthralled his listener with a rant about what he'd learned from the Loompanics books, speaking with an energy I had never heard from him. But then Dad would talk about Mom, and his voice filled with a hatred that was just as alien.

"Of course the bitch knows," he said. "How could she not fucking know? She's part of this. But not for long."

When and how Mom had tapped the phones in the Silver Spring store, I don't know. After his death, I recalled those recordings. Back when Mom played them for me, I didn't really process their importance. And by the time she died, I was trying to forget her story and this saga. But now I thought about them. I didn't know what the Gifford's fortune would amount to—hell, I'd be happy with almost anything—but I knew it existed. I knew Dad had something.

I started in Dad's kitchen, tearing through the cabinets, up-ending the jars of sugar and flour, searching through the empty fridge and the freezer full of Stouffers meals. I worked my way through every room of the house, every closet, every crawlspace, and even found myself, late into the night, tapping floorboards and examining the walls.

There was nothing. The house was creepy, but empty. The man didn't have a TV. His stereo looked like it had stepped out of the late 1980s. The computer and the files in his makeshift desk revealed nothing. I found no money. Not even loose change between the cushions of the couch. Rifling through his office, I found no personal records dated before 2002, when he'd bought the house. His tax returns only went back to 2003, his reported earnings a pittance.

There were no letters, no Christmas cards, no diaries. His e-mail archives were empty except for those to Leroy Jr. and me, as well as a few sad back-and-forths with Match.com women. His address book contained only my address, his neighbor's, and his lawyer's. A note from the realtor who sold him the house, tucked in the top drawer of one of the filing cabinets, wished him well, but that was the only piece of posted correspondence I found. His bookshelf contained a few pulp novels from the likes of Lee Child, Stephen Hunter, and James Patterson. He was halfway through J.A. Jance's *Left for Dead*. In the closet of his office I found the tapes from the neighbor's church—years' worth of recorded Sunday sermons, sitting unopened in their mailers. He hadn't touched them.

I sat on the floor, surrounded by papers from the boxes I'd up-turned, and tried to understand. My father didn't have any credit or debit cards when he died. He kept almost no receipts. The few he did have—for his computer and his oxygen tanks—indicated cash payments. The unfinished basement was filled—floor to ceiling—with five years' worth of empty oxygen tanks. The tanks came from several different industrial companies, changing each year. I called a few and found that in exchange for Dad's work on their accounting, they had floated him industrial oxygen fit for his little emphysema machine.

I opened his hall closet—as empty as the rest of the house, except for Dad's briefcase. He had carried that briefcase to Gifford's every single day. I popped it open and found mundane documents—junk mail, inventory counts, all of the regular day-to-day Gifford's reports. These were from the final days of 1985, as if Dad had just come home and put the case down. What had this man been doing since? Had he ritually placed the briefcase—contents untouched—in every hall closet where he'd lived since 1985?

It was two in the morning when I gave up. Exhaustion had begun to overwhelm me. In a daze, I stumbled into Dad's bedroom, changed the sheets on his bed, and collapsed, fully clothed. I was asleep as soon as I closed my eyes.

The neuralgia woke me when I rolled over and rubbed my cheek against the coarse blanket. I lay there, staring into the darkness, waiting for the agony to subside. The silence was suddenly pierced by the house security alarm. I leapt to my feet in a panic, pawing wildly for my glasses. I glanced at the bedside clock—three in the morning—and, my heart in my throat, I charged into the hallway.

Dad's bedroom lay at the very end of a long, narrow hallway from the living room and kitchen. A motion detector at the opposite end of the hallway stared back at me, the alarm still blaring. I ran into the kitchen, where I had seen the alarm panel. The panel was dark, so I punched random buttons until the alarm stopped. For a few, tense moments, I stood in the dark kitchen, my ears ringing in the silent house. Cautiously, I called out a soft "hello?". Had the neighbor come to check on me?

I walked around the house, flicking on lights as I went, checking all the doors and windows. Maybe Dad had a pet I didn't know about? I went down into the basement with a flashlight, a screwdriver thrust out as a weapon, but all seemed normal. With all of the oxygen tanks, there was barely room to walk around. I returned to the kitchen and peered at the alarm's control panel, which remained dark. I tapped it a few times to see if the display would come on, but it didn't seem to have any power.

Too exhausted to be spooked for long, I shrugged off the incident and went back to bed. I was drifting off to sleep when the alarm started blaring again. This time, I came out of the bedroom at a run, shouting, ready for imaginary attackers. There was nobody. I rushed to the panel and again punched at the buttons until the alarm quit, the display still dark. Then I sat in the kitchen, the unfamiliar surroundings sinking in. Exhaustion gave way to a creeping fear. I searched the house once again, room by room. All sorts of scenarios played through my head.

Did my father have another family?

I checked every latch, opening and closing doors and windows. I turned on every single light. I found nothing, no sign of occupation outside of my dad's spartan existence. I tapped the walls, concocting images of hidden passageways and secret rooms. The lack of furniture and strange emptiness of the house was hardly calming. The place felt cold, unwelcoming, diseased. I stood in the living room and spoke loudly to the house, an old habit I'd practiced in the big, scary, creaking mansion at my weekend job: "Look, I'm just here tonight. I'll leave in the morning. I don't want any trouble. My father has just died!"

Gradually, I eased back into the bedroom, closing the door. Sitting on the edge of my father's bed, I tried to calm myself. My heart was roaring, my hands shaking. It took another ten minutes to finally collect myself. Then the alarm went off again.

This time my fear turned to anger. I slammed open the bedroom door, shouting incoherently, and stalked into the kitchen. I yanked the control panel from the wall, ready to sever all of the wires, and stumbled backwards when the faceplate easily came away. There was nothing but an empty hole behind it with one wire that had been capped and stuffed back into the wall. I stared at the dummy faceplate as the alarm continued to scream all around me. I don't know how much time passed, but I was jarred out of my fugue state when the alarm suddenly cut off on its own.

Still gripping the faceplate, I collapsed awkwardly into one of the chairs at the kitchen table. Numbly, I called my dad's neighbor. When the answering machine picked up, I hung up and redialed. It took four tries before he finally answered, his voice groggy.

"What?" he slurred.

"It's Andrew. I'm having a problem with Dad's house alarm."

The neighbor cleared his throat, hacked a bit, then wearily said: "He doesn't have a house alarm."

"It's gone off three times."

"I didn't hear anything. There is no alarm."

"Are you sure?"

"I've been watching his house the whole time he was in the hospital. I've been in there a hundred times. There's no alarm. Go to bed!" The neighbor hung up.

My next call was to information, asking to be connected to a taxi company. At 3:45 a.m., I sat out on the curb with my overnight bag. The cabbie took me to the nearest hotel. I returned to my dad's house only once more, to collect a handful of knick-knacks and belongings.

IV

Calling from the hotel, I secured a lawyer to set up Dad's estate, and I spent the day watching HBO and feeding myself from the vending machine, unwilling to wander far from the room. It took three days for the lawyer to get the wheels moving, and when he called, he sounded agitated.

"We need to talk," he said. "Where are you?"

We met the next morning in the hotel cafe, the lawyer spreading papers out across the table. I sat and sipped coffee, waiting for my dose of pain medication to take hold. He began: "I've never seen anything like this . . ."

I shrugged and rolled my eyes and thought: *Welcome to my life, buddy.*

Between 1985 and 1995, he said, there were no leases, no mortgages, no rental payments. There were no tax records, no employment records, and no bank accounts. There were no credit cards, no sign that Dad had registered to vote, no bills or official communication of any sort.

"It's a blank trail," the lawyer said.

He had found a few people—owners of small, independently-owned companies—who had been using Dad to balance their books and handle their taxes from 1986 on. They all said that they paid Dad in cash. When he resurfaced on the official record, in 1995, it was to receive the money from the sale of the Bexhill Drive house. Except it wasn't received by Robert Gifford. A special account was created and managed by a friend (to whom I must refer as "Peter," for the sake of his privacy.) This friend helped support and hide Dad during his absence.

Dad appeared in the public record once more in 2000, to sue me for control of my mother's estate. At this time, he had an apartment in Atlanta, paying the rent in cash. His landlord refused to comment, and my lawyer said it wasn't worth pursuing.

In late 2000, Dad was diagnosed with emphysema. He paid out of pocket to a local physician, whom he visited once a year. The physician had had no comment either, except to say that he'd monitored Dad's condition, suggested treatments, but otherwise "didn't get involved."

By 2001, Dad had gone on oxygen.

In 2002, he'd walked into a bank and got a sub-prime mortgage for a house, putting $10,000 down in cash. They really were giving mortgages to anybody then—including a man without credit or records, dragging an oxygen tank around with him.

At this point Dad started filing tax returns, but he reported so little income that he kept off the IRS radar. He got a library card. It almost hinted at a normal life. The lawyer concluded:

"If you sell the house, it'll just pay for the mortgage. You may see a couple thousand, but I doubt it. $1,500 in his bank account is all there is."

Given the fees and time involved to probate the estate, I would end up in the red. But I wasn't quite ready to accept that. A few days later, the lawyer met with me again. This time, he was more direct: "This is the most insolvent estate I've seen. You need to walk away."

The following week we learned that filing to probate the estate had finally woken the great IRS beast. The Gifford's debt was called up. The old crimes were still active. Lien holders poured out of the woodwork. Dad's estate was besieged.

But my case was as strong for escaping Dad's estate in 2007 as it had been for winning Mom's, eight years before. My lawyer used my estrangement, and Dad's abandonment, to get me off the hook. The court agreed that no debt would carry over to me as long as I walked away from the estate and claimed nothing.

During this process, the larger picture of Dad's life began to emerge. We discovered that he had stopped paying taxes—or recording any income at all—around 1970. The only official job he'd ever had was his time in the Army. My father didn't just vanish from the grid—he was never really on the grid to begin with. I asked my lawyer how all of that could be possible. He grinned. Gifford's was a business conducted largely in cash. And cash is what it takes to hide. That Dad had managed to hide himself in plain sight so completely, the lawyer added, took "talent." It also took a larger network.

"Accomplices, if you will," he said. "Enablers."

It took me fifteen minutes to abandon Dad's estate. I was free and clear. My lawyer waived his fee, out of pity, I suppose. I took the first plane back to DC. The Army buried my father. His neighbor, the veteran, may have helped arrange it, but I don't know. I don't even know where Dad was buried. It would be easy enough to locate the grave, of course. But I don't need to know. Our business is finished.

V

Of course, I still had questions. Dad was dead and in the ground and I was still alive and wondering why all of this happened. In so many ways, this story reads like a simple and straightforward tale of greed. But then, neither Mom nor Dad seemed to care about the money. I've always thought that Dad simply wanted to destroy Gifford's Ice Cream as an act of vengeance against abusive parents. But the amount of work involved in fleecing the company, investors, and potential franchisees seems too exhausting. If Gifford's was a temple to the rape and horror visited upon him, he could have torn it down a whole lot sooner than he did, and with less effort. For every seemingly obvious motivation, there's a twist.

After Dad's death in 2007, a man came forward claiming to be an old family friend—the one whose anonymity I protect by calling him "Peter." He had worked for John and then for my dad while Gifford's was booming. After Dad vanished, if Peter is to be believed, he handled Dad's finances and acted as his eyes and ears in the DC area. Peter's primary job was to deliver money to Mom through a series of dead drops and to check in on my progress.

Once a week, he phoned Allen to ask for an update on me. This started in 1986 and continued through 1999, shortly before Mom died. Allen would report that I was doing very well and was very happy with Dad out of the picture. For Peter, Allen painted a picture of wealth and joy. Allen never mentioned these calls until shortly before he died, when he admitted that he'd been receiving them.

"Yes," he said. "Peter never missed a week in all that time. You could set a clock by his calls."

Peter also told me that Dad never failed to send a card for my birthday, each with a one-hundred-dollar bill inside. Peter said he personally delivered all fifteen of these cards to Allen. When I confronted him with this, Allen blew a raspberry and said: "Lies!"

Maybe once a year, between 2007 and 2013, I talked to Peter

on the phone. Sometimes he called me; sometimes, as I struggled through the early stages of this memoir, I called him. At first, he had very little to say outside of patronizing comments like "your parents loved you very much." I didn't know how to react to that. The more I researched, though, the more questions I had. With each passing year, my questions became more and more pressing— I demanded an accounting of the missing money, of Mom's involvement in its theft. He began to feed me tidbits of information about my father and about the downfall of Gifford's. Finally, in 2013, I told him I was going to go ahead and publish this memoir. He was in his early nineties, and his voice was gruff and cracked over the phone.

"What do you think you know?"

"I don't know what I know," I replied. "I've deconstructed the recipes, I've looked over all the court records, I've talked to friends and employees. I'm going to draw my own conclusions."

Silence returned from the other end of the phone line.

"Unless you want to paint the bigger picture for me," I added.

He sighed and agreed to meet me because it would be irresponsible for me to publish the story of my family without first hearing "all of the truth." He described how to get to a particular spot in DC's Glover Park and told me to come there alone, without any recording equipment. Disconcertingly, he told me to make sure I wasn't followed. But I laughed.

"Should I call you Deep Throat? Or maybe Deep Dish, in honor of Gifford's?"

"These are my rules. If I suspect you've broken them, then I'm gone."

I laughed again, but was met only with stony silence. So I agreed.

I think everyone in the Washington area has, at one time or another, imagined being part of some clandestine political activity. This is a town of spooks, so I felt unfazed by Peter's demands. The meeting was so DC. The paranoia that gripped my parents had prepared me well for it. As when I was a child, I found myself aware of my surroundings. I watched the rearview mirror as I drove into town. Was I being followed? When I parked and entered Glover Park, I took a roundabout route to the lonely bench that would be our meeting place. A part of me enjoyed it. A boyhood cloak-and-dagger game. Another part of me dreaded the meeting. To me, Peter was a stranger. I was meeting him in a secluded corner of a large park. A voice in my head kept chattering as I sat at the bench, anxiously checking my watch. Would my quest to decode and understand my family end with my murder?

The meeting took place in the late summer. By then, most of the facts of this memoir had come to light. I had charted the downfall of Gifford's, and I had demystified the recipes and my grandparents. I had studied Dad's strange life and analyzed the implication that Mom and Allen were part of the mad family game early on. I'd spoken to people who painted wild and disturbing pictures of my family. I'd come to grips with my own part in the saga. Had I learned too much? Was I stumbling into something better left alone? The paranoia of my family was infectious.

Nor was I alone in such foolish, fearful thoughts. Some people I spoke with, for example, believed that Mom had faked her death, going so far as to pull out her teeth—which was the only way her body was finally identified. When a friend of hers first presented that theory to me, I laughed. And then I thought about it, and I realized I wouldn't be in the least bit shocked if the death of Barbara Gifford turned out to be the ultimate prank on all of us.

I arrived early for the meeting with Peter, sitting nervously on a bench set back from a mulched path. The sounds of sirens and cars and people on the streets faded away, the cool Appalachian-style woods taking the August bite out of the city. I heard children laughing and playing not far away and the sounds of the forest, amplified and newly frightening. There was little traffic on the footpath—an occasional jogger huffing past, a young woman and her dog, her face buried in her cellphone, a couple walking hand in hand. Finally, I saw an old man in a cap, making his way toward me. He favored his right side, a black and silver cane digging into the mulch as he walked.

"Andrew," he said. A voice I knew well from the phone.

"Deep Dish." I nodded back to him, trying to smile.

He harrumphed and sat down heavily beside me. "What are you planning to say in this book of yours?"

Right to business. I cleared my throat and gave him a rough outline of the memoir. He stopped me.

"Forget the kiddie crap. What are your conclusions?"

"Oh, well . . ."

I stalled. I wanted him to tell me what he knew before I blathered on about what I thought. But he had me on the back foot already. I was scared of the locale, intimidated by his age, and exhausted by this story. He listened to my tale and, when I was done, warned me to be careful. Jilted investors were still out there. The people involved in the reboots were dangerous: Lieberman "wanted my blood," he said, Cooper "was a criminal," and the well-organized public relations folks at Gifford's of Maine were "dangerous." If I started parading my history around in front of them, Peter warned me what to expect: "These people will cut at you."

"I don't think they'll give a damn about me," I replied, "but, okay, let's just talk about the dead. Where'd the money go? Dad left with millions, you've said, but then he died penniless."

Peter had prepared for my questions. He answered as if by rote. He spoke with little emotion, his eyes wandering along the tree line and up and down the path as if, at any moment, he expected cloaked figures to come lunging out at us.

He started to detail the trust fund that Mary Frances had set up—saying it had had about $7 million in it. This, he said, is what Dad used to keep Gifford's afloat in the 1980s. It covered payroll and corporate expenses. At the same time, Dad was bleeding the real Gifford's accounts dry. By keeping expenses off the books, he covered up the revenue he pocketed and made the cash flow look good for potential franchisees. I listened as Peter talked. Eventually he stopped, his story thus far unsurprising.

"So what happened to the money? How much did Dad have?" I asked.

"Both your father and mother had access to a fund which I held."

"So it's true that Mom knew where Dad was all along? And had hold of the money?"

He nodded and told me that Mom had received about $5,000 a month. Somewhat at odds with the idea that she had easy access, though, he ran off on a tangent about leaving the money for Mom at dead-drops—stuffed under trashcans or taped under benches, as in the movies. Seemingly ludicrous and impossible, but then I had found letters from Dad to Mom that alluded to such a scenario. Dates and figures and obscure clues about locations. In one letter to Mom from Dad in 1989, he wrote "4/15—$3200—at the usual place in Silver Spring."

I shifted course and asked about the Gifford's of Gaithersburg franchise scheme—how many people did Dad con? Peter seemed uncomfortable. The cane bounced atop his leg as he stared up into the trees and replied: "I won't talk about that."

"Mann is dead—" I began, referring to the dupe who bought the same shares my father had already sold to someone else.

"The other investors are not." He pounded his cane, hard, against his knee.

I asked about George Milroy—what had happened during the interregnum between Mary Frances' incapacitation in 1977 and her death in 1980? What role did Milroy play? Knowing that Milroy was also involved in the franchise scheme, though I wasn't sure how, I figured this might be a good chance to find a back door into the conversation I wanted to have. The picture Peter painted of George Milroy was a strange one, though.

Milroy ran the company for Mary Frances while she, unable to speak or otherwise properly communicate, lay dying in a nursing home. Other facts lined up with what I had already discovered—Milroy steered the course, but did nothing more, presumably because he was simply Mary Frances' hatchetman. Her will left the company to Dad so, when she died, Dad was in charge. Fair and square.

Except that Milroy hated my father and attempted to wrest

the company away from him. Peter suggested that there had been a long-standing feud, though no one else I've spoken to can corroborate it. In the end, Milroy agreed to step down as long as he kept a twenty-five-percent share in the company and received a retirement package upwards of $2.5 million. Reconciling this bad blood with what I read in the *Regardie's* article is something I've not been able to do, nor would Peter enlighten me, no doubt sensing it would return our conversation to the franchise scheme.

Our discussion turned to Mom. Peter told me that she'd had a steady income thanks to the fund from "at least 1988 onwards." She also maintained steady contact with Dad. All of that was happening while I was in high school, living in fear of Mom's rage and madness day after day and under the impression that we were struggling from paycheck to paycheck.

Her mysterious cross-country trip in 1995 remained mysterious, though. Peter had no idea what she had been up to. He told me that she'd received roughly $555,000 in cash from the sale of the Bexhill Drive house. This was close to the figure that my lawyer guessed at while probating her estate in 2000, but it doesn't appear to be accurate, according to the realtor who handled the sale and the official records.

As for her cross-country trip, had she been spreading this money around to her friends as I suspected?

"Maybe," Peter replied. He nodded. "Maybe."

"So she gave it all away?"

Peter smiled sadly. "If that's what you found out. You'd know better than I."

This was not easy stuff, I said. Normal people can't do these things and get away with them. It takes planning, forethought. The patience involved was mind-boggling to me. The long slow dissolution of Gifford's, the years and years of hiding. If all this were true, then Mom spent fifteen years hiding the truth as well. The whole time she was borrowing money from Allen, was she stockpiling a small fortune? Where was it going? Drugs? Friends?

But Dad suggested much the same thing when I confronted him in 2005, two years before he died, and Allen insisted multiple times that he knew Mom had money all along. On her impromptu visit with my uncle in Albuquerque in 1995, she was throwing money around and behaving oddly, and a string of people from Ohio to California all tell a similar story of money coming their way after unannounced visits from Mom during that summer.

"Why didn't she try to help me?" I asked, flabbergasted. "Why'd she hide the money? Why'd she borrow from Allen? Why all of this?"

Peter sighed and frowned. "Barb was . . . troubled."

"You mean crazy, right?" I said.

"Both of your parents were very sick, Andrew. You understand that, don't you?"

Our conversation wound down after that. Other questions were avoided, ignored. Peter talked, instead, about the mental state of my parents. He painted a deeply personal and troubling picture of Dad in the 1990s. A recluse with no friends, Dad spent his days chatting up strange women online, listening to records, and watching old sitcoms. Peter would talk with Dad at least once a month, dealing with the finer points of their stolen-money fund. What Peter encountered disturbed him. As the decade wore on, Dad seemed to be losing his grip on reality. Sometimes Peter would pick up a phone call only to discover Dad in mid-sentence, rambling away about something inconsequential as if he'd been talking to Peter for hours. Any attempt on Peter's part to take command of the conversation was useless. There'd be nothing to do but listen. Occasionally, Peter just hung up.

Sometimes, Dad would talk as if he were still married to and living with Mom, and as if I were living with him. In Dad's ramblings, Peter noted, my age never seemed to advance past six or so. More and more, according to Peter, it seemed like Dad was living in the year before he took over Gifford's. He would ask for details on computers and cellphones, but when Peter replied, Dad would react "like someone from the 1940s." I asked Peter if he was concerned, if he considered finding Dad help. Peter just shrugged and replied: "What could I do? I'm not family."

By 2002, Dad seemed to think that Gifford's was gone and forgotten. He called the company a "cancer," and he said that the cancer had been cut out. Peter repeated what Dad had told me at his sad little house in Atlanta.

"Bob said that no one could possibly remember Gifford's after so many years. No one cared about it."

To Dad, we were the crazy ones. To obsess about Gifford's Ice Cream three decades after it vanished from the face of the Earth? Madness. Who could possibly do such a thing? Why? Perhaps it was just the quiet hope of a broken child who wanted the past to be buried. Or perhaps he had a point. Since the first revival of the company, back in 1989, I have been asking the same questions.

CHAPTER NINE

ICE CREAM DREAMS

What's in a name?

I understand the power of a brand. The shopper's hand passes over the cheaper item, even though the ingredients might be identical and it might have been made in the same factory, and, instead, he selects the brand name item that costs twenty percent more.

But Gifford's isn't General Mills. It's not even Ben & Jerry's. It's a little family business from Washington, DC, that went bust in 1985 because the people who ran it were bonkers. But long before that, John and Robert Gifford broke many rules—ignoring health concerns, using already antique machines that don't exist anymore, promoting a tradition without any fixed recipe—and lied through their teeth about the authenticity of the product's basic source. Gifford's was dreamed up in a wilder culinary era by even wilder men. Because of this—and because of their mental state—the company cannot be re-created.

So when people tell me that I should revive Gifford's, I tell them that it's impossible. Yet the response is always: So what? What they mean is that I don't need to re-create the circumstances exactly. If I do anything with ice cream, they say, I'll make a fortune simply because I'm a Gifford. I've even had people offer me startup funds of a quarter million dollars. "A quarter million is nothing!" they say, convinced they'll make it back quickly and easily.

But I do say no, and people get mad. They don't understand. To them, my name means money. People will pay extra for a little nostalgia to go with their sweet treats and decadent desserts. And they've spent over thirty years frustrated as they watched unrelated people try to cash in on my name. They point to the parade of characters in the Reboot Era and say, look at them. They made money. Just imagine if an actual Gifford stepped up to the plate.

They're right. I know. Those thirty years' worth of people who have tried to reboot Gifford's have all made money. They simply needed to whisper "Gifford's" and the public flocked to them, no matter how tenuous or absurd their connection to the name.

Dolly Hunt was the first to bring Gifford's back to DC, and she was also the last, in my opinion, who actually cared about the product and worked hard to create something that would (and did) match the original Gifford's Ice Cream. Hunt loved the institution of Gifford's, and, in hindsight, I see that her reboot, steeped in nostalgia, was humble, honest, and joyous. I regret the twisted, adolescent anger that I directed at her. Being angry at Dolly Hunt was foolish. If she hadn't bought the intellectual property from Benny Fischer, someone else would have done so.

Dolly Hunt's retirement in 1999 was the beginning of the end of Gifford's of DC. By 2010, it was all over, and Gifford's of Maine owned the name and the trademark. So a Gifford's Ice Cream is back in DC now, but under the banner of another family far away, unrelated to my family and its long-closed parlors.

That's fine. In fact, I think it's a great thing. The Giffords of Maine share the same last name. They're entitled to the defunct, mismanaged, and too often criminal history that goes along with the name in DC, if they want it. In their hands, at least, my family name can't be further tarnished by opportunists and scoundrels. When they won their trademark case in 2010, I felt much as I did when my family's company passed out of the news in 1986. I thought, with Maine at the helm, that my family legacy would finally vanish. Even if Gifford's ice cream shops opened in DC again, the back of the menus would tell an unfamiliar history about people in Maine. My father and my grandfather would finally fade into their afterlife.

But that wasn't the case. John and Robert Gifford will never die.

A friend of mine once joked that the entire Washington area was still in a diabetic coma from Gifford's ice cream. The mere mention of the name sends remember-when groupies into conniptions. She said that all these nostalgia-addled people hear the name "Gifford" and they stop listening to anything else. She's experienced it herself simply by saying she's friends with me. Conversations stop and "the fucking Gifford's story" starts. She's come to feel that she could say almost anything about Gifford's— "Gifford's is running a terrorist training camp dedicated to destroying the United States!"—and people would still line up at the door with bibs on, waving money in the air.

Sadly, her cynical joke is true. After the 1999 hand-off, Gifford's entered the twenty-first century with a new purpose. Embracing its legendary name, the rebooted version of the company set out to expand wildly, with outlets at stadiums, a giant factory, and an attempt to corner every angle of the local ice cream market. No longer was the product important—hence the fiasco with unlabeled Hood's Ice Cream. Gifford's became nothing more than a name. But that seemed acceptable to the public. One of the potential proprietors once told me, as he set out to reboot Gifford's: "It doesn't matter what's in the cup, people will pay me anything if I say it's original Gifford's Swiss chocolate sauce."

And he's right. They will. I've received messages from people living thousands of miles away who've told me that if Gifford's Swiss chocolate sauce came back, they'd fly out for a spoonful.

But even after Gifford's of Maine rode in to scoop up and save the name, it didn't stop other people from trying to cash in on association with Gifford's of DC. It just forced them to try different tactics. Though he dismissed the importance of his set of recipes to the *Washington Post*, Neil Lieberman still reminded everyone he held them. He still tried to make a buck off of them. More disturbingly, as the most recent reboot got underway in 2016, with Mark Schutz and Hunt together at the helm, the story of the conveniently-deceased University of Maryland mentor re-emerged with a new "revelation": this mentor not only had helped Dolly Hunt reverse-engineer her recipe for Gifford's ice cream, but he had helped my father and grandfather polish their product.

Once again, I can find no evidence of the latter claim, which seems like an attempt to create an association with the Gifford's legacy out of whole cloth. Gifford's of Maine apparently agreed, and took a hard line on any unauthorized uses of the name. But Mark Schutz went forward anyway with his plan to sell Gifford's-That-Cannot-Be-Named for top dollar out of his DC chocolate store, his association with Gifford's becoming increasingly complicated with every step. In reality, the only connection he has with my family is that he's partnered with someone who bought the name from someone else who bought the name at an auction.

Both Schutz and Hunt have insisted in various news outlets, including WTOP Radio and *Bethesda Magazine*, that they are not setting out to make authentic Gifford's ice cream, that they're doing their own thing. And yet the *Bethesda Magazine* headline screams "Comeback!" and the article cites multiple connections to Gifford's, from Schutz's partnership with Dolly Hunt to a deal with Emery Thompson—"the same company that produced Gifford's equipment." This "comeback" narrative can make it seem very much like Schutz and Hunt are cashing in on the Gifford's name—which, ironically, they're not allowed to speak lest the lawyers come parachuting in.

I find all of this frustratingly unnecessary. I know Hunt can make a product that is superior to the old Gifford's mix in every way. She's a proven ice cream master. In fact, people have gone wild for her ice cream in the past. So why try to connect with Gifford's at all? Why even allude to a long-dead company name that has lived out all its potential incarnations? Why not capitalize on the native talent of an expert ice cream maker? The product should speak for itself. The ice cream is the thing that should be celebrated. It doesn't need to borrow a brand name—especially one so fractious and tarnished. After all, isn't that what all the nostalgia is really for—the taste of a superior product? It could have had any name, really—it just happened to be called Gifford's for a few decades.

Maybe I'm wrong. Maybe it's not about the product. Maybe it is purely about nostalgia. It's not hard to find ice cream of the same quality, or better. But repackaging institutional bulk ice cream—as happened during the Cooper and Lieberman era—and getting a premium price for calling it Gifford's proves the point, right? Plenty of customers care about the quality of the product—but plenty don't. What they want—what they'll pay more for—is a memory of something they lost in a decaying ice cream parlor over thirty years ago.

And that's the more important point: Gifford's Ice Cream closed down in 1985. It ended. It never really came back, and it never will come back. It's not possible to find a scoop of ice cream that will re-create that sticky table, that long-lost smell of sugar and old milk, that demolished ice cream parlor, that almost-forgotten childhood boyfriend or girlfriend, that moment, frozen forever in sight of the candy counter, when everything seemed perfect.

And all the while, through that service entrance, and up those rickety stairs, a family clawed itself to pieces and spent decades tearing down this perfect memory. For me, the name is not so sweet. I've spent my whole life trying to escape it.

I didn't write this book just because I have a story to tell. This isn't just therapy. In fact, I don't want to revive these memories. In my ideal world, Gifford's would be relegated to old pictures in history books and maybe the occasional retrospective on PBS. I would be able to have a drink in the city where I was born without the waiter looking at my credit card and asking: "Gifford of Gifford's Ice Cream?"

In that other world, maybe everything at home would have been different for me. The family wound would have scabbed over. We would have found our paths, as best we could. At the very least, maybe there would have been a more robust support network that could have brought me to Ben Carson before I lost a decade of my life to trigeminal neuralgia. I don't know.

For many, my name summons visions of sundaes and banana splits, but in my mind, I see Mom sitting on my bed in the early morning, ominously talking to me about the troubled ghost of Everett Earl. I see the scratches in the laundry chute. I hear all the horror stories I've been told while researching this book, and I see that dam at Deep Creek Lake getting closer and closer.

When people try to build an artificial link to my family and profit off of it, I struggle to describe the war within me. Supporting the rebooters feels like we're all just keeping the wickedness of my family alive. How can they embrace this legacy again and again, year after year, decade after decade? What gives them the right?

I know it's probably naïve of me, but I just want this saga to end. I've buried everyone who crafted this tale, and yet I still hear their names. In early 2016, Mark Schutz told me that his motivation was "to honor your grandfather's legacy."

Well, now we know John Gifford's true legacy. His brother's family lived in his dreadful shadow, and so has mine. We don't need to live in that shadow anymore. Let him die. Let them all rest in peace.

We were ice cream people.

But not anymore.

DISCLAIMER

I don't know the truth.

Everyone loves to talk about Gifford's and give me their impressions of my family, of the company, of me as a child. The lawyers try to remember thirty-year-old cases; old men sit on park benches and reveal the darkest of secrets; and friends, employees, and neighbors all have stories to tell. But did all these things really happen as they say? So much of this memoir relies on memory and hearsay. But . . . every family is like that.

People would tell me their stories and I would weave them into the missing pieces of this impossible jigsaw. Sometimes things added up, sometimes there were real "ah-ha!" moments, and sometimes a story would come so far from left field that I believed it simply because it was stranger than fiction. Many of the bizarre stories of my mother's cross-country odyssey in the summer of 1995 have been omitted, but they are plentiful, and outrageous, and quite a few people who knew her well believe them without question. And so do I.

I've drawn from court records, corporate records, news articles, and broadcasts. I pieced the downfall of Gifford's together thanks to all the talking heads out there who watched it happen and reported on it. I've read between the lines and attempted to make rational, informed guesses on the nature of the more obvious criminal acts. The genealogy painted a little bit of the family background, obituaries told me what some characters in this saga did right. But, in the end, this is a story told by the bystanders. It's a story told through the eyes of a child, and through the eyes of employees tiptoeing through the hallways. It's a story told by policemen and lawyers—the people who pick up the pieces, but don't always understand the facts.

It's a story told by the losers—jilted investors, fired waitresses, abandoned children, former friends, ostracized family members. People with axes to grind. Those of us who were left behind.

For some, nostalgia clouds their memories. There's not much you can glean from people who are mesmerized by the Wonkavision image of Gifford's. Or from those who covet and wish to profit from an association with the name. Or from those who have convinced themselves that Mom or Dad were merely innocent, kind-hearted, clueless victims of some larger conspiracy. (Surprisingly, there are quite a few of those people.)

The greatest mistake I made, for years, was trying to apply some sort of rational explanation to my family's actions. Why in the world did these people do what they did when there was no real endgame? Dad and Mom didn't seem to care about the money, so what motivated them? The more I researched, the more I realized that this is a story about deranged people who were obsessed with gaming life, with playing other people. Mom and Dad wanted to see what they could get away with. They wanted to see if they could convince, control, and con the people in their lives. Allen showed some of those same traits, or perhaps had become twisted by whatever spring went loose in his head way back when. John and Mary were probably just crazy for years and years before they finally kicked the bucket. Maybe what happened to brother Leroy was just the beginning of my grandfather's descent into madness.

Of course, that madness was clear long ago. My earliest childhood memories are steeped in it. The family house bears scars of abuse and insanity that date from around the time Leroy's family was disowned. During my young adulthood, Allen kept me forever in check and under his control. The game was always being played, and I was always the pawn, even after most of the bigger pieces had exited the board. Yet there was never any point, there was no way to win this game, nor does it seem there was ever a desire to win it. A game played simply for the sake of the game.

I never framed this story with mental illness in mind because I wanted answers. I needed answers. Just saying "Well, they were crazy" wasn't good enough. I needed to know why all this happened.

But there is no why. There never was. And now everyone is dead, so we'll never be able to grab them and shake them and ask: My God, what have you done?

ACKNOWLEDGMENTS

Every book takes a village. Especially this one, which has had a long and crazy journey.

There are lots of people who set me and kept me on this path. Among the most influential have been Pagan Kennedy, Laura Wexler, Lonnie Martin, Matt Maloy, John Casper, Colin Gibson, Jamy Bond, K.E. Semmel, Alan Cheuse, Genie Oliver, Tara Laskowski, and Paul Robertson (who kept reminding me that everything seems so much bigger when you're a little boy). But there were many others who have been valuable and extraordinary friends at times when it was hard to be my friend (you know who you are, so I'll avoid the long list of names).

I have to talk about my family . . . one last time. One of my editors feels that Allen comes off as a villain in these pages, but that wasn't my intent. He was a man who wanted a way out of the drudgery of life. He just didn't quite know how to do it. But the fact is that he tried to be there for all of us. He tried to care for us. He rarely talked about his childhood, but the scant clues that I pieced together show only tragedy, fear, loss, and abandonment. Allen was running away, like I was. Except that he never really stopped running. Allen was scared, deep down. Disappointed in what life had to offer. It was this trait of his that fueled Mom's madness and cast a troubled shadow over all his children. My maternal grandmother—a saintly, tolerant woman who loved us all as we will never be loved again—is the one who kept us all together.

My aunt and uncle are runners as well. We are all running away from the Gifford and the Currey families for a variety of reasons. And, yet, we are all, in the end, always coming home to sit and stare at the pieces and ask the most pointless of questions: Why? What happened? What if?

As I complete the final revisions on the memoir and get ready to consign it to the gods of copyediting, I realize that I've stopped asking those questions. I realize that I'm tired of running. I think the only real answer to what haunts my family is that there is no answer. We should probably all just move to Santa Fe, open up a bar or something, and try to relax.

SOURCES

in chronological order

"The Good Old Days of Bethesda." *Bethesda Gazette*, date unknown.

Myers Kelly, Virginia. "Local's Line up For The Gifford's Flavor." *Bethesda Gazette*, date unknown.

Martin, Lonnie. *The Lost Crown of the Ice Cream Prince*, Ningan Manga Productions. Transcript.

Chase, Scott. "Gifford's Grows Up: Washington's Hometown Ice Cream Maker Plans to go National. Immediately." *Regardie's* (Washington, DC), May/June 1981.

Mayer, Caroline E. ."Gifford's Asks Bankruptcy Protection." *Washington Post*. May 10, 1984.

"Gifford Liquidation Is Ordered by Judge; Ice Cream Chain Reorganization Fails." *Washington Post*, Apr. 26, 1985.

Py, Ray. "Gifford's Ice Cream Recipes Return to Bethesda." *Montgomery County Sentinel*, Jun. 22, 1989.

McAllister, Elisabeth. "Here's a Sweet Scoop: Gifford's Is Back in." *Washington Post*, Jun. 29, 1989.

Aun, Leslie. "Gifford's: Too Good to be Real?." *Montgomery Journal* (Rockville, Maryland), Aug. 11, 1989.

"Bitter Aftertaste Engulfs Family of Robert Gifford." *Montgomery Journal* (Rockville, Maryland), Aug. 11, 1989.

Greeley, Alexandra. "Ice Cream Dream," *Montgomery Journal* (Rockville, Maryland), Aug. 11, 1989.

Goldman, Lisa. "Gifford's Tradition Returns." *The B-CC Tattler* (Bethesda, Maryland), Nov. 22, 1989.

"Postcards From The Past." *Washington Business Journal*, May/June, 1990.

Gentry, Curt. *J Edgar Hoover: The Man and his Secrets*. New York: W. W. Norton, 1991.

"Couple Finds Fortune in Ice Cream Chain." *Washington Post*, August 2, 1995.

Nicholls, Walter. "For the Scoop on Gifford's." *Washington Post*, Aug. 9, 2006.

Sackett, Bethany. "Gifford's Frozen in Time, Not Ideas." *Washington Times*, Oct. 29, 2007.

Clabaugh, Jeff. "Gifford's Ice Cream Gets Nats Stadium Deal." *Washington Business Journal*, Jan. 23, 2008.

"Washington Nationals Announce Partnerships with Local Vendors." *All American Patriots*, Feb. 27, 2008.

Wexler, Laura. "Heir to a Scandal." *Washington Post Magazine*, Aug. 17, 2008.

Mui, Ylan Q. "Gifford's 'Scoop Shops' Sold to Investor; Ice Cream Chain to Seek Expansion Apart from Wholesale Business." *Washington Post*, Mar. 2, 2010.

Griffiths, Cindy Cotte. "The Trouble With Gifford's Ice Cream Shops." *Rockville Central Blog*. Oct. 6, 2010.

Rosenwald, Michael. "For Beloved Ice Cream Chain Gifford's, A Rocky Road." *Washington Post*, Oct. 23, 2010.

Youngentob, Dana. "Gifford's Chain Closes After Serving Imposter Ice Cream." *The Churchill Observer*, Nov. 23, 2010.

Wickenheiser, Matt. "Gifford's Ice Cream Buys Gifford's Ice Cream and Candy. Really." *Bangor Daily News*, Oct. 24, 2011.

Schott, Chris. "Gifford's Ice Cream Sold! Now to Become ...
Gifford's Ice Cream," *Washington City Paper*, Oct. 25, 2011

Basch, Michelle. "Local Shop to Bring Back Gifford's Ice Cream."
WTOP Radio, Feb. 16, 2016.

Metcalf, Andrew. "Gifford's Ice Cream to Make Local Comeback
Under New Name." *Bethesda Magazine*, Jan. 8, 2016, accessed May
19, 2016, http://www.bethesdamagazine.com/Bethesda-Beat/Web-
2016/Giffords-Ice-Cream-to-Make-Local-Comeback-Just-Dont-Call-
it-Giffords/

Photo: John Casper Photography

Born and raised in Washington, D.C., Andrew Gifford is the founder and director of the Santa Fe Writers Project (sfwp.com). Recipes and more about Andrew can be found at andrewgifford.com.